EDUCATION LIBRARY
UNIVERSITY OF KENTUCKY

BLAIR'S EDUCATIONAL LEGACY

MARXISM AND EDUCATION

This series assumes the ongoing relevance of Marx's contributions to critical social analysis and aims to encourage continuation of the development of the legacy of Marxist traditions in and for education. The remit for the substantive focus of scholarship and analysis appearing in the series extends from the global to the local in relation to dynamics of capitalism and encompasses historical and contemporary developments in political economy of education as well as forms of critique and resistances to capitalist social relations. The series announces a new beginning and proceeds in a spirit of openness and dialogue within and between Marxism and education, and between Marxism and its various critics. The essential feature of the work of the series is that Marxism and Marxist frameworks are to be taken seriously, not as formulaic knowledge and unassailable methodology but critically as inspirational resources for renewal of research and understanding, and as support for action in and upon structures and processes of education and their relations to society. The series is dedicated to the realization of positive human potentialities as education and thus, with Marx, to our education as educators.

Series Editor:
Anthony Green

Renewing Dialogues in Marxism and Education: Openings
Edited by Anthony Green, Glenn Rikowski, and Helen Raduntz

Critical Race Theory and Education: A Marxist Response
Mike Cole

Revolutionizing Pedagogy: Education for Social Justice Within and Beyond Global Neo-Liberalism
Edited by Sheila Macrine, Peter McLaren, and Dave Hill

Marxism and Education beyond Identity: Sexuality and Schooling
Faith Agostinone-Wilson

Blair's Educational Legacy: Thirteen Years of New Labour
Edited by Anthony Green

Blair's Educational Legacy

Thirteen Years of New Labour

Edited by

Anthony Green

Educ.

LC
93
.G7
B53
2010

BLAIR'S EDUCATIONAL LEGACY
Copyright © Anthony Green, 2010.

All rights reserved.

First published in 2010 by
PALGRAVE MACMILLAN®
in the United States—a division of St. Martin's Press LLC,
175 Fifth Avenue, New York, NY 10010.

Where this book is distributed in the UK, Europe and the rest of the world,
this is by Palgrave Macmillan, a division of Macmillan Publishers Limited,
registered in England, company number 785998, of Houndmills,
Basingstoke, Hampshire RG21 6XS.

Palgrave Macmillan is the global academic imprint of the above companies
and has companies and representatives throughout the world.

Palgrave® and Macmillan® are registered trademarks in the United States,
the United Kingdom, Europe and other countries.

ISBN: 978–0–230–62176–3

Library of Congress Cataloging-in-Publication Data

Blair's educational legacy : thirteen years of New Labour / edited by
Anthony Green.
p. cm.—(Marxism and education)
ISBN 978–0–230–62176–3 (hardback)
1. Education and state—Great Britain—History. 2. Education—
Political aspects—Great Britain. 3. Critical pedagogy—Great Britain.
4. Labour Party (Great Britain)—History. 5. Labour Party (Great
Britain)—Platforms. 6. Blair, Tony, 1953– I. Green, Anthony G.
LC93.G7.B53 2010
379.41'09051—dc22   2010021454

A catalogue record of the book is available from the British Library.

Design by Newgen Imaging Systems (P) Ltd., Chennai, India.

First edition: December 2010

10 9 8 7 6 5 4 3 2 1

Printed in the United States of America.

Contents

Chapter 1

Blair and New Labour: Contexts, Legacies, and Prospects for Educating the Educators

Anthony Green

> *I am a Socialist not through reading a textbook that has caught my intellectual fancy, nor through unthinking tradition, but because I believe that, at its best, Socialism corresponds most closely to an existence that is both rational and moral. It stands for co-operation, not confrontation; for fellowship, not fear. It stands for equality, not because it wants people to be the same but because only through equality in our economic circumstances can our individuality develop properly.*
>
> Tony Blair: *Maiden speech in House of Commons as MP for Sedgefield, July 6 1983*

Well said, Tony Blair! The rhetoric of a consummate politician who manages to sound progressive without attending to the sources of ongoing structures of inequality; the stuff of textbook *intellectual fancy*, no doubt.

This volume was generated at one of those paradoxical historical conjunctures when, while all that is solid seems to be melting into new cultural and political forms, nevertheless, all remains much the same, while crisis deepens around the questions of *equality in our economic circumstances* and the proper development of *our individuality*. It identifies and discusses important dimensions of a complex historical "moment," and maintains an open dialogue over the specifics of the mode of analysis and methodology, and on progressive political strategies namely Open Marxism (see Neary and Taylor, 1998; Rikowski, 1996). Now, as we enter 2010, what is happening in British education and society seems to be a world away from the time when New Labour came to power in May 1997, yet the situation is little different in many vital respects. Some of the superficial valences are reversed, no doubt. Euphoria becomes gloom for progressive parliamentary politics, and the prospects for the conventional form of popular expression of "centre-leftism" the Labour Party. So, "New" now becomes tired, old New Labour. But then, when did social radicalism ever take off through progressive parliamentary politics alone, to *realise equality in our economic circumstances* and the *properly developed individuality* that Blair might have had in mind at the inception of New Labour? Its prime constituency, middle Britain, will hardly be shifted without extra-parliamentary movement and backbone struggling in the social, cultural, and political structures of economic production, mobilising to glimpse wider and realise higher horizons of social and democratic possibility. The prospects are obviously not encouraging for socialism. The market TINA (there is no alternative) hegemony has morphed into its lubricant alter-others—money and credit—with the fatalist message that the structures of finance capital are too big to be allowed to fail, and, as things stand, no doubt it is so. Thus, the British state under New Labour continued to operate as the executive committee of the whole "national" bourgeoisie, and as a working subcommittee of the global neoliberal, geopolitical corporate bourgeoisie. And we're all in it together, as the "real" capitalist economy is struggling to realise and expand "value," while the prospects of a deepening recession continue, largely unaffected by slightly revamped neo-Keynesian measures. Financial reforms and talk of regulation will do little to shift the main structures of class power, and the longer term prospects for "recovery"—through state-led class selective austerity—will impact most detrimentally on those who are least well placed across Britain and the world, in their efforts to form solidarities, to resist and transform the dominant social relations of local, national, and global capitalist production. There exists state-led *socialism for the economically and financially rich and powerful,* and *capitalism for the rest,* who are reliant upon their market positions for their own commodification, while repressive pedagogy of foreshortening "humanitarian" individuality remains hegemonic.

Simultaneously, David Cameron, Conservative Prime Minister in waiting, morphs into Tony Blair—on education policy, "responsibility" and "participative community," and more—as the leader of the caring capitalist party of Great Britain, and the spinning images highlight the ambiguities of the politics of *representation* for what they are, *repressive,* so far as democracy, let alone democratic socialism and increasing equality, are concerned. Cross-iconographic fancy dressing with Margaret Thatcher remains the prime media political pantomime game of now-you-see-me-now-you don't. Above all, *Workers of the world unite! Global capitalism is good for you! It's good for everyone with labour power to sell...or financial political leverage to apply, for profit and expanded power, to the noncapitalist preconditions for capitalism, while the beast, faltering slightly, is restructuring in and through its multilayered state forms in order to regain its stride!* Thus, within this capitalist hegemony, class differentiation embeds yet deeper into ever-more effectively disguised, complex cultural and institutional forms, and the dominant mode of production remains intact, penetrating and colonising in all directions; capitalism is victorious in its relentless war of position (Gramsci, 1934/1971). Proliferating structural complexities, articulating cultural forms, and politics of identities continue to disable oppositional working-class formation *for itself* in concerted action, thereby disorganising critique and dialogues that are challenging that dominant mode of production, too.

This chapter provides an introduction and overview to the themes addressed in the contributions to this book, and health warnings are in order to make clear that this volume cannot do full justice, in historical materialist idiom, to the critique of New Labour, Blair, and Blairism, even if limiting its remit for the purpose of focusing on "education." There is a sense in which, to call on Tzou Enlai's realist assessment of the historical significance of the French Revolution, "it is too early to judge." That said, the issue is also more broadly methodological; our metatheoretical frameworks for historical materialist analysis, itself, is open, too. This chapter's aim, therefore, is to set a scene in which Marxist traditions of penetrating critical analyses are demonstrated to be alive and relevant at all levels of description and explanatory critique *of, as,* and *for* "education." The chapter will highlight areas of correspondence and relative consensus amongst contributors, as well as key points of controversy and continuing development, dilemma, and ambiguity, fitting for a discursive terrain which is, indeed, unbounded, save for the parameters immanent to the dominant mode of production. In educational and pedagogic terms, these themes concern aspirations for social and political possibilities in the face of multidimensional boundaries, and limitations that are emergent and imposed in the increasingly capitalist and, therefore, commodified mode of production of social life. There is, however, realistic consensus amongst these contributions, and a sense of crisis regarding the short-term prospects for socialist democracy, equity, and emergent equality. Both the present and near future remain bleak in these terms, while the stakes rise ever higher, and threats deepen for the possibilities of convivial global sustainable development and survival. New Labour has contributed to this.

Before developing these themes, it is valuable to highlight that, at some levels of "appearances," New Labour seems to have done quite well in and around social and cultural issues such as education, welfare, and health. Certainly, Tony Blair proved to be a brilliant politician and model "communicator." On some accounts, state spending and outcomes can be seen to have been mildly redistributionist, and while the underlying structures were Thatcherite, they could well be depicted as *Thatcher lite*, perhaps; "society" was apparently reasserted, and the harder edges of neoliberalism eschewed ideologically, at least, in a comfortable illusory humanitarian formulation of *community* and *inclusiveness*. Few would dispute that New Labour is centre-*left*, and has been part of a shift to a more humanitarian political vocabulary of *respect* and *fairness*. In education, for instance, the principle of selection by tested "ability" for differential allocation to a hierarchy of school types is openly advocated only by those who are indifferent to charges of overt elitism by supporting unfair educational sponsorship. Social selection and sorting is less direct, though no less real, and is achieved by student identification by "aptitude," and by apparent desire of parents for their children to experience one of a number of schools' different forms of "specialisation" and ethos, including religious faith and backgrounds. In this context, however, the point here is to develop immanent critical analysis, along with ideology critique to draw attention to the mechanisms and educational processes and emergent structures that have been shaping the *systemic nature* of relations, inequalities, and patterns of injustice, despite formal freedoms and immense consumer affluence in Britain today.

Three broad themes—two substantive, one methodological— emerge and will be returned to and refocused in the concluding section of this chapter. They are: *New Labour and the Education Market State*; *New Labour, Education, and Ideology*; and thirdly, methodological focus on *Totality and Open Marxism*.

Patrick Ainley and Martin Allen's chapter, *Education and the Crunch: Gloom and Opportunities*, opens this collection by providing a wide-ranging descriptive overview that accompanies its concern for Marxist dialectical *totality*, while raising many of the themes and issues addressed and elaborated in other chapters. Drawing methodologically on Marx, Hegel, Lukacs, and Mao, they develop a substantive analysis in order to provide a broad framework for a distinctively Marxist approach. This enables them to assess the Blair period and its implications in the context of the deepening financial crisis and credit bubble, paralleled by an educational *credentials bubble*, with the structures of paperwork articulating social class, education, and occupational recruitment to economic production. Under New Labour, much of public-sector education has been pitched into a continuous round of containment and regulation, which is antithetical to the fulfilling discipline and expansiveness of educational ideals and aspirations for social and cultural well-being.

Ainley and Allen's framework calls attention to *totality* and the need to avoid an empiricist, abstracted focus upon different sectors (e.g., primary, secondary, Further Education [FE], Higher Education [HE], etc.), or, narrowly, on specific disciplinary perspectives (sociology, psychology, etc.) separately. In their conclusion, they engage substantive analysis, policy scrutiny, and the needs for activism and engagement at all levels, including those of education workers expressing their capacities to bring collective potential to bear on issues that have as much to do with the purposes and aims of educating as on their own conditions of production and pay. This approach contributes materially to active ideological and immanent dialectical critique of the contemporary "educational" dimensions of political economy by identifying irreconcilable oppositions and contradictions, and by outlining alternatives for achieving possibilities of progressive transformative totality, and the strategic political means to address these.

In this context, Ainley and Allen propose a robust but delicate and nuanced form of *class analysis*, recognising the changing relations of education to changing occupational patterns, labour markets, and social opportunities, articulated by a new wave of credentials inflation, partly associated with the increasing application of new technology. The top and bottom of the class and occupational structure remain clearly marked, and dominant echelons are as relatively closed as ever by elite economic, social, and cultural capital reproduction that is divergent from the rest, in large part by access to private education and their class networking. The descriptive and immanently critical analysis makes the case that, despite variety and complexity, and the proliferation of policy initiatives by New Labour, class and educational patterns are as tightly connected as ever, and social class consolidation and more intensive polarisation of class structures are emergent.

Closing, Ainley and Allen set out a series of suggested measures; perhaps controversially, *most reformers would agree on* the need for continued discussion and dialogue on many of the other themes they raise, while working for developing a strategic socialist movement that broadly aims to remove state education from the grip of the new market state. These activist themes are returned to at various points in other chapters, most notably in Ken Jones's concluding analysis of New Labour, viewed in the broader context of educational *contestation* in Europe and beyond, reinforcing the need for critical political formation with tactical thinking in the contexts of multilevel strategic analyses.

In his chapter, *Education, Education, Education or Business, Business, Business?*, Kevin Farnsworth focuses on New Labour's business ideology. He highlights, historically analyses, and develops substantive Marxist critical review, indicating that the Blair government's education *priorities [were] to embed capital—business priorities, business people—into the heart of the state education,* providing relatively seamless continuity with the main thrust of the preceding Conservative regimes. Indeed, reopening the issue for left progressives of the role of "centre left" governments that prove the most comfortable for capital accumulation was presaged, in recent historical perspective, by the broader shifts of the Harold Wilson and James Callaghan Labour governments during the 1960s and 1970s away from the welfare state capitalism of the post-1945 social democratic "statist" settlement. By the late 1970s, state schooling was to be connected more closely to human capital formation and local employer needs, while the 1980s saw Thatcherism and the emergence of reforms, whereby business practices began to penetrate deeply into state services, including formal education. *Managerialism* strengthened its educational hegemony, and democratic representative local state forms for delivery of education were weakened and undermined as part of an emergent *postdemocratic formation*, which continues into the present (Crouch, 2004).

Part of the novelty of the "new" Labour was in redesigning the "partnerships" between national state, local state, and the voluntary sectors...*Blairism in governance*. Farnsworth's evaluation of the role and achievements of Blairism draws on Marxist dialectical analysis to articulate the mutuality of state and capital, in which the state subordinates its role and policies to the overarching *needs*, in order to maintain the social, political, and cultural contexts *for* the contradictory contexts of capital accumulation. These developments are complex in historical reality, especially so in the face of globalisation and the deepening hegemony of neoliberalism, market forms, and privatisation at all levels of social relations, and their emergent products structuring and restructuring of those very social relations. These dynamics articulated the "natural order of things" from above, the TINA (there is no alternative) to structural and agency power of capital *globally* and *nationally*, plus their more open domains of state-capital relations *locally*. This became the ideological terrain for deploying the vocabulary of "inclusion," the Blairite alternative to redistributionist policy to undermine embedded class structures. It involved proliferation of institutional forms and complexities, attention to educational *structures* as distinct from *standards* (of measured educational attainment), and, in the process, blurring public- and private-sector boundaries, described in detail by Ball (2007). Egalitarian aspirations and deliberative democracy emerged fleetingly with New Labour, as seen most clearly in the ill-fated Education Action Zones (EAZ) initiatives (Gamarnikow and Green, 1999b).

The broad, superficially paradoxical theme central to Farnsworth's analysis is that Blairism both failed and succeeded as an ideological form, and as an ideological state apparatus (Althusser, 1971). In "educating the repressive educators," as it were, the main *success* of Blairism was in nurturing and deepening the conditions for private-sector corporate power. Farnsworth demonstrates how it *failed* to curb corporate power where it was inefficient and weak, for instance, in relation to some private-sector takeovers of local education services and outsourcing initiatives. However, it also *failed* in professional, managerial, and technicist terms in its commitment to evidence-based policy and planning; the latter demonstrated to be a largely rhetorical commitment to "what works," part of the illusory practices of supporting the corporate structures of domination with professional technicist backup. Much of this is detailed where Farnsworth reviews the Public-Private Finance Initiative (PPI), especially around *transparency, value for money,* and *efficiency*—all part of overweening faith in the corporate private sector as the obvious and natural locale for such professionality.

Farnsworth argues that the Blair government *failed* to understand the complex and contradictory nature of what motivates business interests in public policy, not least in its widespread apathy towards and ignorance of education policy and practices; this is not unlike the experience of previous Conservative regimes, especially when it came to providing monetary funding rather than in-kind services for supporting educational initiatives such as EAZs, and, subsequently, academies and trust schools, etc. In fact, it is highly doubtful, even in conventional terms, that public education services are more effectively delivered by private-sector interests, though these continue to claim a high profile. This is evidence of overconfidence in and

New Labour's partiality towards business, particularly in relation to the local state sector, for instance, concerning business influence on vocational training and Further Education, in relation to trade union and labour interests—themes echoed and developed by Gleeson (this volume). And, despite the in-built differential "needs" and tensions between forms of capital (industrial, business, finance, etc.), Blairism also forms part of the emergent hegemony of corporate financial powers that have dominated the Anglo-Saxon deregulated capitalist model from the 1990's until today. Not least, these subsequently provided the Blair/Brown legacy of financial New Labour's contributions to the "almost" collapse and "recovery" of global financial capitalism in the latter half of the first decade of the twenty-first century.

At the heart of this analysis is the Marxist critique of the *state and regulation,* demonstrating that private-sector interests will inevitably come into conflict with public-service ethos and interests in general, including education in particular, because these cannot properly be *determined by markets and profitable returns to providers* alone. This theme is the background to the chapter by Molly Bellamy, *Valorisation and the Role of the University under New Labour: Reclaiming the Commons in a Knowledge-based Economy,* in which she deploys a *post-Marxist* critique for an analysis of the *privatisation* of changing modes of organisation in Higher Education, including labour processes and their "products." Her case is that this amounts to the capitalist *enclosure* of the higher educational *commons.*

Bellamy draws, as do several of the other contributors, on Jessop's account (2002) of the knowledge-based economy and indirectly on longstanding Marxist humanist themes of *reification* and *alienation,* showing that the economic/noneconomic are dedifferentiated under capitalist *valorisation;* thus, commodification penetrates ever more deeply and extensively into all aspects of everyday life. She provides critical analyses of market forms and the emergence of what she calls the new HE *learning lexicon,* and argues that these attest to New Labour's consolidation of neoliberal capitalisation, indeed, more broadly to *accumulation by dispossession,* in Harvey's terms (Harvey, 2005). Working on the highly contested ground of the "immaterial labour" theory, she notes Marx's concern both to specify and historicise the tendencial nature of exchange value (Marx: 1867/1990) and the *immeasurability of immaterial labour.* Thus, Bellamy brings a note of what some may regard as Marxist *post-Marxist skepticism* in order to understand capitalisation of higher education under New Labour.

Bellamy's account builds on awareness of the complexity of managerial control, particularly at the point of measuring labour power and regulation through "responsibilisation." This account articulates with wider hegemonic thrusts of New Labour concerning networking and social capitalisation, (Fine, 2001; Portes, 1998; Gamarnikow and Green, 1999a, 1999b, 2009, etc.) as well as flexible and self-managed production. In a variety of contexts, these connect to neoliberal forms of governance working through culture (Rose: 1998), and the postmodernisation and poststructuralisation emergent prior to but consolidated with New Labour policy forms; in part, it might be suggested as political foils to neoconservatism. Bellamy thus profiles cultural ambiguities and paradoxes that are characteristic of contemporary models of educational governance, showing resignification of the work *ethic* in *immaterial* production. In her analysis, the university becomes something analogous to Marx's metaphor of the *spinning jenny*, and learning powers and products are separated from higher education worker/producers as objects potentially alienable, fetishisable, mystified, and reified into "something grotesque" (Marx, AG: 1867/1990), as commodities. The position of teachers and researchers becomes relatively more precarious as their own knowledge is made property of the university, as in-house structural capital of the organisation and their roles as worker/producer of knowledge are rendered vulnerable and dispensable. Furthermore, and articulating with Denis Gleeson's chapter, Bellamy explores ways in which these processes operate at the levels of lived identity, while serving to structure the commodified self of academic staff and students, defined by the specification of the *learning* lexicon as the pedagogic framework in forms of literacy functioning in a closed auditable system of production (Powers: 1994). Bellamy expresses this as a species of articulated regulation and *governmentality* (Foucault, 1991) with an interpretive framework that connects policy across several levels—local, national, and international (European Union, World Bank, International Monetary Fund, etc.)—whereby employer power is enhanced and market forms are institutionalised.

Bellamy's case is that these developments have been very significantly realised through the HEFCE (Higher Education Funding Council for England) under New Labour, which is part of the quango-state form, and is supportive of a neoliberal project that functions to reduce the emancipatory capacity of higher education. These state-sponsored institutional and ideological effects serve to disguise contours of real complexity in the educational social and cultural dynamics, which are articulated through an homogenising vocabulary in which the project of the self becomes the regulating new *opiate* of the masses; it might be suggested that the *hypohumanitarian* structures and process generated in U.S. higher education complement them (Ebert and Zavarzadeh, 2011) . In conclusion, Bellamy expresses the need for a wider social movement to reclaim the *intellectual commons* and resist accumulation by dispossession.

Denis Gleeson's *The Professional Imagination: Remaking Education Policy in a Neoliberal Context* examines Blairism and the New Labour project through the lens of shifts in *state forms* and pressures on public professionals' practices, identities, and powers in terms of the *Professional Imagination* in the specific context of English Further Education (hereafter FE). While the analysis takes a different form, it echoes, and in key respects complements for FE, the themes taken up by Ainley and Allen across the whole educational system, and with Bellamy for HE, though leaving aside the structuring of commodification that she highlights. Gleeson's approach specifically directs attention to dense and richly existential and phenomenological aspects of *lived identity* of educationists' *professionality*. These reported phenomena, with fragments of identity narratives, articulate cultural forms for and with neoliberalism. Thus, both Bellamy's and Gleeson's methodological forms are dialectical, active, and materialist, and vital to political and cultural practices of forming a social movement *for itself* in Marxist proletarian class terms.

Gleeson's focus is the complex and socially situated cultural production of professional workers' identities in the context of changing state structures and employer pressures, emergent from the restructuring of the public sector in the 1980s, and new models of accountability in the FE and vocational training sectors. His report assumes the long history of FE catering to vocational and professional skills against the background where British employers have relied upon a large section of nonskilled and and poor working practices, migration, and the importation of low-skilled workers, and where a significant proportion of employers and companies were unwilling to undertake funding of training because they have been able to recruit effectively for their needs on an ad hoc basis, or are simply not in a competitive position to systematically contribute to decision making and policy for planning human capital formation.

Thus, traditionally, in Marxist terms, such *labour power* in the British context has been relatively cheap and plentiful, adequate for a low-skills economy, and, of course, generally the first to be hit during recessionary downturns. Globalisation and the shifts in production and labour market demands—with relatively fewer low-skilled jobs becoming available, the emergence of the so called "knowledge economy," and the proliferation of the application of new technology—have moved the agendas of professional and vocational training. In addition, New Labour's noisome concern for social cohesion and inclusive remaking of civil society as contributory to economic regeneration has come into play, at least rhetorically. As *ideological state apparatuses* (Althusser, 1971) playing a key roles in *governmentality,* FE and HE are sites for interpolating professionals' identities and instantiating discourses of professionality, as structures and contexts for action, reproduction, and resistances in which specific modes of individuality and market accountability have become relatively hegemonic, and worker collectivist forms (in and beyond educational production) have become weakened and incorporated. Gleeson's analysis mirrors wider shifts in centralised deregulation and the subsequent reforming of public services that reflect the increasingly familiar emergent privatisation of governance of public institutions, the *dispersed state* (Clarke and Newman, 1997). He demonstrates the frustrations and alienation of knowledge workers; they continually expose themselves to exploitation, despite and because of their active resistance as mediating professionals working in volatile environments.

Gleeson's central methodological point is counter to naïvely foreshortening structuralist analysis. These nonmanual, professionalist workers must be understood to be *active*, engaged, and not simply blindly *expressing* a repressive system. Thus, his central theme is that the reconsideration of the *professional imagination* is in order, where critical professionalism is connected to *potentiality* in struggles with market and audit hegemony over democratic forms of accountability and governance, in both state forms and civil society. This materialist approach, which deploys phenomenological levels of descriptive analysis, leaves little room for romantic possibilitarian optimism, while asserting the place of professionalist commitments in conflicts and struggles over working conditions and practices beyond assumed baseline consensus and trust.

Effectively, little has been achieved for social justice, scarred as it is by deepening class inequalities in a low-skill low-wage economy. Herein, class struggles are emergent, in which professional knowledge workers are important players who are expressive of potentials for critical pedagogy and democratisation through active deliberative public scrutiny, opposed to the continuing pressures of prevailing narrow neoliberal reforms. Importantly, lived worlds, these phenomenological levels are vital as terrains and media of struggles *in* and *for* critical class identity and the formation in pedagogy of critiques, with key dialectical moments in testing the dominant political economy of exploitation immanent to capitalist value forms. In this context, the legacies of Durkheim on *moral education* and Wright-Mills's *sociological imagination* have parts to play. As such, the chapter reopens longstanding, and yet to be *finally* resolved, issues in left progressive (see O'Neill, 1972) materialist and Marxist critical methodology, to which we will return below.

Terry Wrigley's chapter, *Curriculum Change and the Blair Years*, spotlights New Labour curriculum policy and is critically inspired by Gramsci through Raymond Williams. He realistically notes the impossibility of doing full justice to his theme, especially so with the intense, complex, and tension-ridden policy busyness of New Labour and its delicate Machiavellianism of often pulling in different directions. The chapter provides an historical overview of the politics of the National Curriculum (Education Reform Act, 1988) under the Thatcher regime, preceding and framing New Labour. This is background to his theme of the parallels between the social sorting of pupil *filtering* of capitalist schooling and *knowledge filtering*, the ongoing struggles over selecting, organising, and delivering the school curriculum. Wrigley's analysis of the Blairite reforms of literacy teaching indicates no loosening of the central government's grip on the school curriculum, despite pre-1997 election positions, which emphasised professionality, teacher discretion, and flexibility. He reports his analysis of the literacy curriculum in primary education and the vocationalism in secondary education, indicating that the changes that emerged were marked by neoliberal interests, some of which were articulated with religious and faith schooling, and what he calls a "messianic sense of certainty." Such "certainty" characterised the style of the Blair administrations, with increasing standardisation in education, which even came under fire from conservative interests for it "narrow instrumentalism" and "cultural disempowerment." Previous Conservative governments' secondary education curriculum policies did not resolve the ongoing complexities and tensions between neoliberalism and cultural conservatism, despite an overall conservative disposition, and these continued as issues for New Labour education policy. Partly, this constituted remarking the contested boundary between education and production, which is symptomatic of class formation and cultural and institutional dimensions of indirect class struggles in contemporary British capitalism, not least around the fraught theme of "vocational" education, indicated by Gleeson in the previous chapter. Wrigley provides detailed reporting and policy analysis, indicative of tensions in the educational formation of "human capital" potential as preparation for labour power exploitation.

Finally, Wrigley's critique makes clear the need to appreciate empirical and material complexity and liberal progressive sounding policies, such as *Every Child Matters* (DfES, 2004) citizenship education policy, which have to be put into context and approached dialectically. Benign education policy vocabulary may veil repressive outcomes, particularly when viewed in the context of the regulation and "performativity" that frames teachers' work, especially for between-schools competitive pressures, which reinforce hierarchical institutional forms and class structuration in and through education. Socialisation and compliance abound, and basic skills for "the many" in relation to "the few," a favourite Blair trope (Fairclough, 2000) appear hegemonic, despite deep uncertainty about what exactly constitutes such "basics," or what their role is in preparation for contemporary work and participation in civil society.

Philip A. Woods's chapter, *Academies: Diversity, Economism, and Contending Forces for Change*, complements and continues several themes that it shares with other contributors, but focuses in critical detail on a keynote New Labour educational governance and institutional policy: the *academies* programme, part of the institutional restructuring of schooling and governance. His report and analysis aims to capture the realist dynamics and something of the potential terrain for activism for progressive educational change within the wider constraining economic and financial structures of contemporary British capitalism. He develops this by deploying two competing hypotheses: one, suggesting academies' *convergence* around an instrumentally driven, business oriented model of entrepreneurialism and educational priorities, and two, that there is real progressive political and educational potential in such variations in institutional meanings and educational practices. The analysis coordinates Marxist concern for realising human potentialities, both individual and collective, and "new openings theory" (Antonio, 1998) on the capacity for contemporary society for self-transformation by recognising that under capitalism, institutional and cultural hegemony is not absolute, but is always contestable. Both in principle and in practice, capitalist repressive forms are challengeable, and the fundamental Marxist philosophical tradition and aspirations for development of all human powers and creative potentialities are not absolutely extinguished, nor, arguably can ever be (see Rikowski, 1996). He identifies developing varieties of subpattern(s) of cultural spaces, within what are elsewhere identified as the "private market state" forms (see also Ainley and

Allen this volume), which may open spaces to work against the dominant view of capitalist state-sponsored instrumental and economistic rationalities.

The analysis leaves open as political, historical, and empirical concerns the balances of tendencies and material outcomes across the totality of a variety of forms of academies, their *clienteles* and sponsors, and their emergent roles in class formation. As with many areas of social, welfare, and education policy, empirical analysis, politics, and class struggles will in time determine if academies are unambiguously to be the sites of social and cultural reproduction, as locales of class *distinction* (Bourdieu, 1986) complemented by their symbolic roles in keeping progressive hopes alive, while in contradistinction, ambiguously burning bright in small protected pockets of *repressive tolerance* (Marcuse, 1965), and/or as constituting what might be termed *avant guarde positional advantage*. Or, are they unambiguously to be regarded as arenas for nurturing energies articulable with and for building critique and wider movements to undermine and transform instrumental and economistic rationalities, along with challenging the whole paraphernalia of capitalist property and value production relations, as such? Nothing less than full-scale human flourishing in *properly developing individuality* is at stake, much as Blair recognised—sincere or tongue in cheek (or *sincerely tongue in cheek*)—in the segment of the speech we opened with.

Alpesh Maisuria's chapter, *Ten Years of New Labour Education Policy and Racial Inequality: An Act of Whiteness or Neoliberal Practice?*, concentrates on the contradictory nature and outcomes of New Labour education policy, especially on social justice and *choice,* and he specifies these in relation to "racial inequality," picking up deep problems that he identifies with Critical Race Theory (CRT) and its central theme of "whiteness" and neoliberalism on race-class intersectionality. This provides a thematic policy backdrop on New Labour education: inclusivist *widening participation, educational choice and social stratification,* and *educational attainment.* The analysis then moves to firstly deploying CRT to address New Labour policy, and finally to assessing the efficacy of CRT in this context, developing critical issues to make the case that the hegemonic project of New Labour is best appreciated through a mode of Marxist analysis beyond CRT. Miasuria is concerned to transcend *economic essentialism* while focussing on *intersectionality,* and he draws inspiration for Marxist race-class analysis on the conceptual theme of *racialisation* that was developed by Robert Miles (Miles, 1987) and extended by himself and Mike Cole (2007, 2009). He demonstrates the foreshortening and superficially critical effects of CRT "whiteness" conceptual focus in strategic social and political terms. This analysis exemplifies sensitivity to the historical significance of key global and national events, not least the effects upon education policy of shifting politico-cultural forms, in this case "terrorism" and their impact generative of Islamaphobia, and diverting attention from minority group educational attainment to discussions about *radicalisation* and recruitment to *extremist organisations.*

Maisuria's chapter provides contextualisation and a snapshot analysis of New Labour's education policy, focussing on "racial" inequality by contrasting CRT and Marxist frameworks and their relative merits for a socially progressive critique. His approach asserts that Marxist analysis does not suggest that culture is unimportant, quite the opposite; it is the recognition that social class can (perhaps *must*) work through ambiguous and seemingly autonomous cultural forms. In essence, Marxist critique of education policy and practices aims to demonstrate how the latter is functional for and, in this respect, "needed" by capitalism, namely to produce the human capital conditions for capital accumulation, an issue that is obfuscated in CRT analyses. In these terms, CRT may be a part of the problem, and Maisuria's case is that advancing *white supremacy* cannot be specifically attributed to New Labour, as either policy aim or as distinctive outcome, as structural to the system of oppression, while capital nevertheless constantly "trades on" social and cultural differentiations in its markets for labour power.

Ken Jones's chapter, *Patterns of Conflict in Education: France, Italy, England,* comes full circle for this volume, connecting with Ainley and Allen's opening emphasis on struggles in *totality* accepting the needs to develop critical analysis beyond that of solely focussing on "policy or policy making." The broad issue for Jones is to address "educational contestation," and more robust attention to active engagement itself as intellectual political analysis working in the Marxist traditions inspired by Gramsci (1971) and Poulantzas (1978). Complex intermediations of state, unstable class conditions, and changes in relations of production become topics and resources in analysis and struggles, and instantiations of what has been termed elsewhere as *pedagogy of critique* (Green, 2007; Macrine, et al, 2009). His approach is internationalist and comparative, and it requires attention to particularity, in this case drawing out points of specific similarity and contrast in political cultures and practices in England, France, and Italy. He concludes by relocating the New Labour project in yet-to-be-resolved political tensions in the wider context of European capitalist *modernisation*. Jones's focus on politics aims to indicate something of the significance of geographical specificity of political struggles in relation to global neoliberalism, not least the *peculiarities of the English* in relation to the European economic zone. His theoretical aspiration is to integrate the analysis of education policy in relation to the role of *collective actors* and their impacts on the contestation of *education state* strategies.

The developing contemporary financial crisis underpins the broader topicality of this theme for alternative prospects of deepening political crises coalescing, with anticapitalist class formation emergent, and/or, for these crises being sites of reintensified reregulation of civil society, as well as renewed dispersal of critical energies for progressive changes and the reembedding of international state capitalist forms. Thus, cultural contexts and terrains of varieties of struggle in and against capitalism, locally, nationally, and internationally, in a regionally constituted international bloc such as the European Union need to be understood and acted upon and within.

Here, Jones deploys the concept of *precarity* and demonstrates the increasingly central role of educational dimensions to political conflict. Precarity captures cultural and discursive specificity in the senses of uncertainty of excluded working class youth, in ways more deeply cultural-political than, while resonating with New Labour's notion of *inclusion*. It also captures senses of uncertainty of advantaged youth's confidence in the dominant educational institutions', and their reliability for making their social and cultural security and futures. In this, we simultaneously see the security in the social meaning of (highly inegalitarian) elite credentials for advantaged youth seemingly dispersing. Thus, there is a *generational critical imaginary* with complex intersectional mixes of class-based resentment and demoralisation, along with traditional respect for stratification of educational institutions, disciplinary traditions, and qualifications. This is set in a context of pressures on the European social egalitarian model that is located in political turbulence in which the European tradition of corporatist, state-regulated capitalism is caught in struggles to redesign itself in European Union guise, while resisting full-scale Anglo-Saxon style neoliberalisation, modelled by Blairism. The Bologna Agreement and Lisbon Treaty processes are contexts for class struggles, and Jones provides a complex descriptive analysis that shows the contrasts between UK and French and Italian specificities respectively, thus demonstrating differentiating rates and forms of development both within the EU and between France and Italy and the UK. Such concerns are important for contextualising political struggles around the complexities and twists of dialectical insight into different European societies' modes of submission to capitalist disciplines of modernisation and, in their critical relation to New Labour, with ambiguous potential that is supportive of forces of both left and right as part of the Blairite legacy.

This analysis also indicates senses in which particular combinations of circumstance, histories of structures and cultures constitute the existential frameworks of *contestation* for both national policy making and politics of resistance and transformation. These are important when trying to understand and assess particular policies, governments, and political movements, for instance concerning feudal remnants in Italian universities where "baronial power [and] web of clientalism" and the deep contempt with which these are held by Italian protest movements, and in relation to which, by contrast, French and English universities were seen, ironically (perhaps) from within UK educational class analysis, as relatively "meritocratic."

Jones therefore draws attention to political cultures and traditions, not to displace a Marxist approach with liberal progressive sociology and cultural analysis, but to indicate the need for complex articulation in time and space, where specificities and ambivalences are strategically and tactically vital in anticapitalist contestation, not least because they are generally deployed rhetorically, in what we might term *progressive reaction*. In the Italian case, for instance, they play up and on modernist antifeudalism and the superiority of neoliberal alternatives of which Marx himself may well have approved. The state cannot act beyond its conditions of existence; it is variable and constituted in tensions, never finally settled, and its effectiveness is "always being shaped by capacities and forces that lie beyond it" (Jessop 2008: 126), not least in relation to its main "domestic" security problem, "the masses." Thus, the state continues to engage in passive revolution and develop new institutional forms to incorporate, regulate, and demobilise fundamental socialist opposition. Jones concludes with key points about the New Labour—Blair (and Brown) legacies for cultural cementation through institutional complexity—thus securing that it's passive cultural revolution will make reversals increasingly difficult to achieve. The educational managerial state, with ever more proliferating forms of institutional "diversity," thus seems assured for the foreseeable future, and is becoming ever more deeply embedded by social capitalising "network" mechanisms of distribution and social control. There is also the legacy of support by exemplification to neoliberal interests in France and Italy, along with international state formation, etc. This is nevertheless an open horizon and may not simply represent the goal for European societies, or the European international state must travel. The point of political contestation is to settle the question of "Will it"?

Concluding Focus: Thematic Legacies and Prospects

The broad Marxist assessment in these essays is that as a political party and coalition of interersts operating in our globalised world, New Labour has been concerned, primarily, with creating conditions for reproduction and the expansion of capital while retaining parliamentary power. In this context, educational *productivity*, as indicated in a variety of forms and contexts, is about creating conditions for production of labour power, the commodifiable capacity to labour in the performatively regulated system of globalising, neoliberal commodified production. These essays provide exemplification of Marxist analysis of education policy and practices, and the continuing significance of the "regulative" (Jessop, 2002; 2008) state and education in several substantive respects. They also raise one more general and broadly methodological context, concerning analytical *totality*, which comes into play across the specific contexts addressed.

New Labour and the Education Market State

Each analysis directly addresses the senses in which the New Labour context has been building on and reinforcing, more or less subtly, the neoliberalising project of the previous governments, after coming into being as "New" by dropping the iconic "common ownership" aspects (Clause IV) from the constitution of the Labour Party. This signalled developing and working within "modernised" neoliberal industrial relations frameworks that have delivered relative industrial quiescence, a low-strike economy in which in education, for instance, the transformation in production relations have been managerialist, performativity driven, and constituting the context for a new generation of workers becoming trained to these forms of regulation and restrictive ideology of public service (Jones, this volume), amounting to deprofessionalisation (Gleeson, this volume; Furlong, 2005). This is now occurring in a framework of educational governance articulating in complexity business interests and cultures of capitalisation (Bellamy; Farnsworth; Jones; Woods; Wrigley, this volume). Nevertheless, the capitalist state, while central, cannot be decisively hegemonic, as Jones points out, and never has total direct regulative power, but has always to "negotiate" forms of indirect regulation, through its revolutionary war of position (Gramsci) of complex cultural and institutional transformation for the capitalisation of civil society. In addition, New Labour's enthusiasm, along with the popular consensus, saw it supporting finance capitalisation hubris for the Anglo-Saxon model of deregulated and light touch role of the state from the 1990s until today. Not least, these subsequently provided the Blair/Brown legacy of amplified financialisation, New Labour's contributions to the "almost" collapse of global financial capitalism in the latter half of the first decade of the twenty-first century.

New Labour Education and Ideology

This overall theme articulates with the New Labour legacy of *Ideological Obfuscation of Commodification* of educational forms with critical progressive de-formation (Jones on comparative sociopolitical cultural contexts; Bellamy on universities; Maisuria on academic forms, CRT, this volume), or at least the redrawing of the terrains of struggles wherein progressive possibilities may be built with and upon (Woods on academies, this volume), despite, for instance, the generally deeply critical stance of left oppositions with regard to the academies programme seen as as socially regressive, likely to reinforce social and cultural differences, and embed unfair class advantages. These, in turn, connect to the wider themes of institutional diversification, networking, and social capitalisation, deepening the democratic deficit (Crouch, 2004) and the overall theme of the complexity of capitalisation cementing and obscuring its structures by embedding intersecting networks of commitment.

Totality and Open Marxism

Finally, the general methodological theme, *Marxist Open Totality*, runs through each of these essays. For Marxism, this involves attention to analytical and strategic political dialogues about both epistemological and ontological dimensions of analytical articulation, *knowing in relation to being*, for recognising specific mechanisms within the *totality* of multilayered realities of social, cultural, and economic relations. Totality is general while open, restlessly specified in myriad contexts. This approach is thus required, for instance, in understanding the necessary interconnected deployment of existential/phenomenological and critical cultural analysis, as well as, crucially, their articulation with the emergent structuralist explanatory critique of social reality (see Corrigan and Willis, 1980). In the cases considered in this volume, critical analysis is formed in relation to (education) policy and emergent patterns of understanding of and conditions of the possibility for resistance and class formation—the class politics of education under New Labour. This must develop by acknowledging degrees of *relative* autonomy of education and society, for instance, of historical culture specificities of and in the dominant mode of economic production, in which the key analytical and political issues are *to address and understand that relativity,* while working counterabstractively to understand and act *within* historically specific fields of capital-generated tensions and opportunities.

Thus, the point, so far as Marxian methods are concerned, is that, as for instance, exemplified with understanding racism in Maisuria's analysis, any "purely" i.e., abstracted cultural form (here "whiteness") cannot be taken to be socially critically *fundamental* under the totalising effects of capitalist conditions of production. In Marxist terms, such foundations lay in modes of property and exploitation that underpin the creation of "value" for and capitalisation. This is not to suggest, for instance (amongst literally millions of other possible examples), that the evolving "globalisation" of European mercantile capitalism from the sixteenth to the seventeenth centuries did not "trade on" and contribute to existing forms of xenophobia, or articulate with many varieties of othering. Nor is it to suggest that cultural and discursive formations are irrelevant to capitalist production. Far from it. They are essential to materialist analysis and active intervention and will always be, so far as the production of social life is concerned, not least in the commodification of cultural artifacts, including personal identification. Marxist analyses should therefore address the *articulation of labour power in intersectionality,* generally in very complex forms, through lives lived *in culture* as "simple common senses," objectified and reified as objects of struggles about and within, and structurally differentiating mechanisms for selection, exploitation, and injustice. That's to say, developing structural *relative* positioning entails the distribution of benefits, losses, advantages, and disadvantages that are *unearned* at the individual and collective levels in the context of the complex totality of the dominant mode of property and production, and, as such, abound for us all, relentlessly and globally in and for capitalism as *totality.*

Thus, while capitalism's lifeblood—labour power (exploitable human capital)—may, and generally does, take on culturally specified and politically hued and racialised (and gendered, etc.) forms, their *necessity for and as capital* is in relation to the exploitation of human beings' *capabilities,* of whatever colour or other empirical *sectionalities* and potential foci of identification and illusory *determinations* for dividing workers/producers against one another in competition for places in production and supporting capital's "self-realisation," in profit. It is these structures that are generative of emergent capitalisation and the realisation of *surplus* "value" as the fetishised *property identity* that is *capital*. This is the *mechanism* that makes it "work" as a system. This mechanism is immensely fluid, multiform, and becoming ubiquitous as capitalism increasingly gets into its stride in globalising conditions. As the basic mechanism, it empowers and necessarily disempowers in complex specifications, structuring injustices *othering while naturalising* them, in a wide variety of historical, cultural, and political forms, which in turn set the *cultural conditions of possibility* of all actions and of social formations in contemporary struggles to conserve, resist, and transform. These phenomena, as expressed in lives lived, are realised emergently, both structurally and experientially, in often deeply contradictory and ambiguous ways, thus (in part) inspiring materialist dialectical analyses. They always do so *intersectionally*, so far as historical aspirations for equity and social justice are concerned, not least in the creation and social distribution of knowledge, understanding, sensibilities, and skills—*education* and practices which are potentially generative of materialist *pedagogy of critique*. This is both terrain and inspiration for Marxist practices *of and for educating the educators in social contestation and reproduction*, and to exposing and acting against this system of capital domination so repressive of the full extension of human capacities, both individual and collective.

Misrecognising surface for the complex reality that is the condition of existence of such appearances *in illusion* is an example of the necessity *for*, but disempowering and reifying potential *violence of abstraction* (Sayer, 1987) and short circuiting the need to conduct multilayered dialectical analysis. In other words, it constitutes the methodological underpinning and a dialectical context for the pedagogy of critique instantiated in the work presented here. This "poverty" (of abstraction) is the general account of misreading and so realising empiricisms, in which an abstraction is taken to be the fundamental structure rather than recognised as the empowering/disempowering ideological reality of an *immediated* surface, illusory if mistaken as the total explanatory form, and often critical *to conservation in injustice in and through that very superficiality*, rather than *explanatory in critique* (Bhaskar, 1987, 1989; Callinicos, 2006; Frauley and Pearce, 2007; Hartwig, 2007; Sayer, 1983) for advancing realist historical materialist understanding and practices of contestation, along the lines inaugurated and practiced by Marx and Engels. The *ideological effect* is to give rise to potentially false antagonisms of identity politics, the ever-present potential for intersectional differentiation in lived cultural forms, rather than positive articulation in recognition of differences and the emergent dialogues for cooperative specification of *species being* required to coordinate anticapitalist class identity and formation *in itself in struggles*. This is the endlessly complex business of realising socialist transformation amid the moving "cultural" waves of the existential present...educating the educators, who are, of course, *ourselves* always already "educated" (Marx, 1845/1974). The general legacy of New Labour is to have done little to materially advance this emancipatory process in education, and much to repress it, but can never eradicate this energy altogether, as its source is an ever-present possibility in the very structures of repressive capitalisation on restless human ingenuity and creativity, the bases for emancipation the capitalist mode of production trades upon and generates, too.

References

Althusser, L. (1971) Ideology and Ideological State Apparatus, in *Lenin and Philosophy and Other Essays,* London: New Left Books.

Antonio, R. (1998) Mapping Postmodern Theory, in Sica, A. (ed) *What Is Social Theory? The Philosophical Debates,* Oxford: Blackwell.

Ball, S. J. (2007) *Education Plc: Private Sector Participation in Public Sector Education,* London: Routledge.

Bhaskar, R. (1987) *Scientific Realism and Human Emancipation,* London: Verso.

——— (1989) *The Possibilities of Naturalism: A Philosophical Critique of the Contemporary Human Sciences,* Second edition, Hemel Hempstead: Harvester Wheatsheaf.

Bourdieu, P. (1986) *Distinction: A Social Critique of the Judgement of Taste,* London: Routledge.

Callinicos, A. (2006) *Resources of Critique,* Cambridge: Polity.

Clarke, J. and Newman, J. (1997) *The Managerial State: Power, Politics and Ideology in the Remaking of Social Welfare,* London: Sage.

Cole, M. and Maisuria, A. (2007) The "Shut the F*** Up," "You Have No Rights Here:" Critical Race Theory and Racialisation in Post-7/7 Racist Britain, *Journal for Critical Education Policy Studies,* 5 (1).

——— (2009) Racism and Xenophobia in Post-7/7 Britain: Critical Race Theory, (Xeno-) Racialization, Empire and Education: A Market Analysis, in Kelsh, D., Hill, D. and Macrine, S. (eds), *Teaching Class: Knowledge, Pedagogy, Subjectivity,* London: Routledge.

Corrigan, P. and Willis, P. (1980) Cultural Forms and Class Mediations, *Media, Culture and Society,* 2 (3): 297–312.

Crouch, C. (2004) *Post-Democracy,* Cambridge: Polity Press.

DfES. (2004) *Every Child Matters,* London: Department for Education and Skills.

Ebert, T. and Zavarzadeh, M. (2011) *Marxism and the Task of the Humanities,* New York: Palgrave Macmillan.

Fairclough, N. (2000) *New Labour, New Language,* London: Routledge.

Fine, B. (2001) *Social Capital versus Social Theory: Political Economy and Social Science at the Turn of the Millennium,* London: Routledge.

Foucault, M. (1991) Governmentality, in Burchell, G., Gordon,C. and Miller, P. (eds), *The Foucault Effect: Studies in Governmentality,* Hemel Hempstead: Harvester Wheatsheaf.

Frauley, J. and Pearce, F. (eds) (2007) *Critical Realism and the Social Sciences: Heterodox Elaborations,* Toronto: University of Toronto Press.

Furlong, J. (2005) New Labour and Teacher Education: The End of an Era, *Oxford Review of Education,* 31 (1): 119–134.

Gamarnikow E. and Green, A. G. (1999a) Social Capital and the Educated Citizen. V, *The School Field,* X (3/4): 103–125.

——— (1999b) The Third Way and Social Capital: Education Action Zones and a New Agenda for Education, Parents and Community? *International Studies in Sociology of Education,* 9 (1).

——— (2009) Social Capitalism for Linking Professionalism and Social Justice in Education, in Allen, Ozga and Smyth (eds), *Social Capital, Professionalism and Diversity,* Rotterdam: Sense Publishers.

Gramsci, A. (1934/1971) *Selections from the Prison Notebooks,* edited and translated by Q. Hoare and G. Nowell-Smith, London: Lawrence and Wishart.

Green, A. G. (2007) Marxism, Education, and Dialogue, in Green, A. G., Rikowski, G. and Raduntz, H. (eds) *Renewing Dialogues in Marxism and Education: Openings,* New York: Palgrave Macmillan.

Hartwig, M. (ed) (2007) *Dictionary of Critical Realism,* Abingdon: Routledge.

Harvey, D. (2005) *The New Imperialism,* Oxford: University Press.

Jessop, B. (2002) *The Future of the Capitalist State,* Cambridge: Polity Press.

——— (2008) *State Power: A Strategic-Relational Approach,* Cambridge: Polity.

Macrine, S. (ed) (2009) *Critical Pedagogy in Uncertain Times: Hopes and Possibilities,* New York: Palgrave Macmillan.

Marcuse, H. (1965) Repressive Tolerance, in Wolff, R. P., Moore, B. and Marcuse, H. (eds) *A Critique of Pure Tolerance,* Boston: Beacon Press.

Marx, K. (1845/1974) Theses on Feuerbach, in Marx, K. and Engels, F. (1845) *The German Ideology,* London: Lawrence and Wishart.

——— (1867/1990) *Capital,* Second edition, Harmondsworth: Penguin.

Miles, R. (1987) *Capitalism and Unfree Labour: Anomaly or Necessity?* London: Tavistock.

Neary, M. and Taylor, G. (1998) *Money and the Human Condition,* London: Macmillan.

O' Neill, J. (1972) *Sociology as Skin Trade: Essays towards Reflexive Sociology,* London: Heinemenn.

Portes, A. (1998) Social Capital: Its Origins and Applications in Modern Sociology, *Annual Review of Sociology,* 24: 1–24.

Poulantzas, N. (1978) *State, Power, Socialism,* London: Verso.

Power, M. (1994) *The Audit Explosion,* London: Demos.

Rikowski, G. (1996) Left Alone: End Time for Marxist Educational Theory? *British Journal of Sociology of Education,* 17 (4): 415–451.

Rose, N. (1998) *Inventing Our Selves: Psychology, Power, and Personhood,* Cambridge: Cambridge University Press.

Rossi, U. (2006) The Struggles of Precarious Researchers and Demands for Social Change in (post-) Berlusconian Italy, *ACME—An International E-journal for Critical Geographies,* 4: 2: 277–286.

Sayer, D. (1983) *Marx's Method: Ideology, Science and Critique in Capital,* Brighton: Harvester Press.

——— (1987) *The Violence of Abstraction,* Oxford: Basil Blackwell.

Chapter 2

Education and the Crunch: Gloom and Opportunities

Patrick Ainley and Martin Allen

Introduction

Now that we are all, as Larry Elliott and Dan Atkinson put it in 2007, "Waking up to the incredible economic, political and social illusions of the Blair era", what would be distinctive about a Marxist assessment of the period for education and training in England? Possibly three things: firstly, an examination of the role of the state, seen as changing from one capitalist state form to another, as clearly exemplified in education and training. Second, particular attention is paid to social class, which we see as also in a process of transformation, a transformation to which schools, colleges, and universities have contributed. Lastly, there is an emphasis on the totality of the area under review—the whole of institutionalised education from infant to postgraduate schools, and including training on and off the job and in and out of employment. This contrasts with the typically empirical academic approach, which tends to subdivide and specialise so that different sectors of education (primary, secondary, etc.) and their particular "problems" are treated from different disciplinary perspectives (of psychology, sociology, etc.) separately from others.

This is not to say that these three aspects or perspectives on education and training are definitive of a Marxist approach. As Mao Tse-Tung once said, "Marxism contains thousands of truths," and other Marxist accounts in this collection point to the ultimate determination of educational developments by the economic, for instance, or to the role of education in reproducing labour power. Or they describe the effects of the now discredited neo-liberalism that the French always called Anglo-American hypercapitalism, or the "new public management" of educational institutions and the consequent alienation and fetishisation experienced by staff and students. All of these, and other perspectives that might inform a Marxist standpoint, are important and contribute to the overall totality: "the all-pervasive supremacy of the whole over the parts" that Lukacs (1923) argued was "the essence of the method which Marx took over from Hegel and transformed into the foundation of a new science." "Totality," "essence," and the lately derided "binaries" (or Marxists might say dialectical oppositions generating irreconcilable contradictions) are all terms that this collection and others can now reassert against the previously pervasive postmodern "discourse" associated with neo-liberalism.

The chapter grasps New Labour (NL) education policy as a whole, because it was New Labour governments that sought, much more systematically than had been attempted before, to integrate the reproduction of knowledge in education and training institutions with the economy. This was undertaken alongside social policies that contributed to what the OECD and the World Bank called "active labour market policies," as opposed to the provision of "passive" welfare benefits. As education for "employability" was thus substituted for employment, education at all levels came to play a larger part in social control, especially of young people (see Mizen 2004). Responding to globalisation by "raising standards" or, rather, raising the level of qualifications for the majority, has not affected the position of the privileged minority. As an extended education no longer guarantees what it used to, the reality has, as this chapter will emphasise, seen New Labour implementing a policy of "education and training without jobs" (compare Finn 1987).

The Changing State of Education

Of course, New Labour inherited and developed the new post-welfare state (Tomlinson 2006) from the Tories. It had been imposed by the Thatcher governments and was marked for education and training by the 1988 Education Act, together with the 1992 Further and Higher Education Act. So, in a sense, it did not matter which of the two main parliamentary parties won the 1997 election. Indeed, on election night, the Adam Smith Institute held a "Victory for the Free Market" celebration without radio or TV to report the results. Similarly, the last edition of the U.S. magazine *Newsweek* before the election (28/4/97) featured a cover picture of Baroness Thatcher with the title "The Real Winner."

What New Labour inherited and developed, rather than challenged and transformed, was the centralised "new market-state," identified by Bobbitt's (2002) argument that, contrary to much confused discussion at the time about globalisation and "the end of the nation state," change in the state "by no means presages the end of the state" (xxiii). Instead, Bobbitt saw Reagan and Thatcher pioneering the imposition of a new state form in the 1980s to replace the post-war welfare state compromise between public and private sectors. In English education and training, the consequences are perhaps clearer than in any other area of public policy. The 1988 Education Act replaced the national system of locally administered state education, which had existed since 1944, with a national system nationally administered (Ainley 2001). In this new state form of administration, power was concentrated in the centre, despite responsibility for delivery being devolved to local agents. Responsibility for consumption was also placed on individuals, who had only themselves to blame if they did not take advantage of the new learning opportunities "enabled" by the new state.

This process of substituting one state form for another began in education and training with the end of post-war full employment and the raising of the school leaving age in 1972. A series of make-work youth training schemes (YTSs) were introduced by the Manpower Services Commission (MSC) as one of many quasi-autonomous nongovernmental organisations, or "quangos" (now mutated into "non-departmental public bodies"). YTSs initiated the transition from "lifelong earning" (for men at least) to the "lifelong learning" that followed. To implement YTSs, democratically accountable local authorities were bypassed to give money on a per capita basis to local training agents, in return for enrolling unemployed school leavers. These schemes were intensely unpopular, provoking, in 1985, the largest ever school pupil strike in British history (Allen and Ainley 2007, 56). Nor did YTSs prevent the 1981 "riots" or "uprisings" that occurred in response to Thatcher's abandonment of the Keynesian welfare state commitment to full employment (ibid.).

Young people voted with their feet and stayed on in new school sixth forms or migrated to FE colleges. These latter were removed from local authority control and followed the polytechnics in competing for students funded per capita by centralised funding councils. Subsequently, the polytechnics joined the universities under the Higher Education Funding Council for England while, following a bipartisan agreement in 1997 to end free public-service Higher Education, students paid fees to top up their central unit cost.

Adapting to, rather than challenging, the main ideas of Thatcherism, New Labour government gave the "new market-state" its own identity, with the new form of centralised state administration setting quantifiable targets requiring armies of auditors and inspectors to check whether they were being met. Thus "Education plc" was to be run like a corporation, with thousands of outlets inspected and policed by the semi-privatised Office for Standards in Education. At school level, a "new managerialism" (Clarke and Newman 1997) predominated, in which old assumptions about "professional judgement" were subordinated to a business style "micromanagement" that ostensibly promoted "school improvement." As in business, failure to meet production targets could result in the merger or closure of the enterprise.

At the same time, and consistent with the new approach of the "new market-state," schools have continued to be promoted as being increasingly "autonomous" from their Local Education Authorities (LEAs)— the administrative bedrock of the post-war settlement. Indeed, autonomy and particularly "diversity" were seen as vital to raising standards. Even schools that have not become foundations, academies, or "trusts" and remain in the local authority aim to "outperform" their neighbours (Allen and Ainley op cit., 9). Funding schools, colleges, and now universities according to the number of students allows "popular" institutions to expand, and the competition may threaten others with closure. So, "setting schools free from local authority bureaucrats," as the *Daily Mail* put it, actually subjected them to an oppressive new bureaucracy.

This was nowhere clearer than in Further Education (FE) where, although funding for these community colleges has from 2010 been returned to local authorities on a formula basis, the content of many of their courses remains dictated by the employer-run Sector Skills Councils and delivered in competition with private providers. HE could soon go the same way, with mergers, if not yet closures, of universities and departments within them already happening, as is now common with colleges (reduced from 465 at incorporation in 1993 to 373 in January 2008). The New Labour government was integral to sustaining and developing this new mixed economy of education and training, as with other former-welfare state public services in which a state-subsidised private sector is indiscriminately intermingled with a semi-privatised state sector. This transformation of the form of the capitalist state from a welfare state to a "new market-state" accompanied an ongoing process of class reformation.

Education and the Recomposition of Social Class

Social classes are understood by Marxists and many other sociologists as "social facts" that consist of millions of people constituted by social divisions of labour and knowledge, with corresponding class cultures such those in the same class positions use as bases for their actions. Thus, compare Bourdieu (1984, 1): "the set of agents who are placed in homogeneous conditions of existence imposing homogeneous systems of dispositions capable of generating similar practices." Class may be experienced variously by individuals and defined differently by sociologists (see Crompton 2008 for the current options), but for Marxists, the struggle between classes is central to explaining and acting upon the contradictions in society that drive it forward. However, as Karl Polanyi said, "Given a definite structure of society, the class theory works; but," he asked, "what if the structure itself undergoes a change?" (1944, 154).

Fundamental to our arguments about the increased significance of education policy and its link to social control is that under New Labour governments, this has been linked to an ongoing transformation of the occupational class structure of Britain, as well as of other advanced capitalist economies (Allen and Ainley op cit., 15 *et seq.*). The upper-middle-working class "social pyramid," reflected in the private schools supplemented by grammar-technical-modern secondary state schools established by the 1944 Act has been pulled apart. This is not only because the gap between the richest and poorest has widened since 1976 (up to which time it had narrowed slightly but steadily in the 30 years before then—see Hills and Stewart 2005, 1). It is also because in the traditional model, the most significant division in the employed population was between manual and non-manual occupations. This was invariably a division between those with academic qualifications and those without, so that, in academic educational research, qualifications became proxies for social class (whereas today, free school meals are the proxy measure).

Although secondary education became universal after the 1944 Act, many working-class youth did not identify with it, and they left school as soon as they could. They turned their backs on the opportunities that state secondary education was supposed to provide for upward occupational mobility. Indeed, the raising of the school leaving age to 16 in 1972 was met with hostility by many working-class school students and their parents, who were anxious to exploit what was becoming an increasingly tight labour market for school leavers. However, the traditional working-class communities that supported types of father-son succession, which Wilmott and Young described in their classic 1958 study of working-class family and kinship in East London as a "recognised practice" and a sort of "informal labour exchange," were disappearing. The fact that traditional industries were invariably localised meant that many school leavers made what could be described as a "collective transition" to work with those they had been to school with (see, for example, Carter 1962 in Sheffield). In comparison with the period of full employment to 1973, the transition from education to employment not only takes much longer today, but it is also far more of a fragmented and individual process.

Likewise, the circumstances have changed which allowed Paul Willis in 1977 to follow a group of white working-class secondary modern boys through their last months of compulsory schooling in Birmingham and into local factory employment. They left school without qualifications but also with a deep resentment towards education, its expectations, and teachers, as well as a disdain for those pupils who tried to use it to achieve modest social mobility. "The lads," as Willis fondly referred to them, did not need school to help them with *Learning to Labour*. The same cannot now be said for the large numbers of the current generation of 16-year-olds who are faced with a new type of labour market in which less than 15 percent of the workforce are employed in manufacturing and where, at the beginning of the twenty-first century, more than 40 percent of occupations can be officially described as "administrative and managerial" or "professional and technical." Progression within the occupational order can thus be seen to have expanded from what used to be referred to as "white-collar" employment associated with a minority non-manual "middle class." Nowadays such progression increasingly depends on gaining worthwhile educational qualifications. Most individuals who seek to enter the labour market now rely on such qualifications to signal their "skill assets." These can be contrasted with the "organisational assets"—the advantages, skills, and knowledge enjoyed over outside applicants by employees who have been able to establish themselves in relatively secure positions in an organisation, compared with somebody just entering. These "organisational assets" have been undermined by rapid changes in technology and organisation, concomitant with economic globalisation (Allen and Ainley op cit., 15).

Yet, if acquiring educational qualifications has become a precondition for both gaining and maintaining secure employment, this does not mean that the occupational structure is necessarily any more open or that rates of social mobility (the extent to which individuals are able to move up or down the class structure) have increased. Indeed, even the last New Labour government acknowledged that opportunities to move up the occupational ladder have decreased since the 1970s (Cabinet Office 2009). Britain and the United States remain less open than other societies (Aronowitz 2008, 20). In fact, towards the top end of the class structure, educational credentials continue to have less significance than other forms of cultural and social capital that are transmitted via family connections and through the network of private schools that have their own longstanding links with elite universities and colleges within them (e.g., the current leadership of the Conservative Party nursed at Eton and Christchurch College, Oxford). Qualifications are therefore necessary "to get a foot in the door" but not to get through it. Ultimately, for those at the very top, who Marxists refer to as the upper or ruling class, this type of cultural capital is supported by levels of wealth, property, and financial capital that are unavailable to others lower down the occupational hierarchy.

Below the elite are what could previously have been defined as the "established middle class" that some sociologists call "the service class" of senior managers and higher professionals (the "governing caste," as Marx called the political establishment of his day). who can also be seen in traditional terms as an "upper-middle" class. They rely on being able to secure entry into the more academic state schools in premium suburban areas. Or they have the financial resources to ensure that in the absence of a "good" local school, private education secures their children's entry to one of the Russell Group of most selective universities (the equivalent of the U.S. Ivy League), or at least to one of the better mainly "teaching universities," not—save for exceptional and specific courses—to local increasingly "training universities," with their links to FE. In this respect, it is no accident that in inner London, for example, where a "gentrified" middle class lives next door to those still clinging to the remnants of social housing, approaching 15 percent of parents rely on private schooling, compared with nearly 8 percent nationally—10 percent across the South East as a whole, though 20 percent in Bristol compared with just 4 percent in the North East (*Education Guardian*, 29/1/08). Only the exorbitant cost of current private schools prevents their further expansion.

Meanwhile, the majority of the population make up a new but also an increasingly fragmented "working middle" of society in which there has been a slight rise in those occupations that can be considered white-collar and above. These were up from some 35 percent to 37 percent of the total of directly employed and self-employed occupations in the UK labour market since 1992, according to successive

Labour Force Surveys. The growth of Information Technology (IT) and services thus erodes the former manual-mental division of knowledge and labour between the postwar middle and working classes. These "knowledge workers" join the "Middle England" of "hardworking families," who are ideologically proclaimed as the norm by the popular press and politicians whose electoral bids are aimed at winning over this "centre ground." The working-middle class could also be said to include other areas of employment in which there has been real growth in services and sales, as well as in office work. Alongside this has been an expansion in support workers, especially in health and education services, with increased work for carers such as care assistants, welfare and community workers, and nursery nurses. These are often low-paid jobs, many of them carried out by women. Meanwhile, the same statistical sources indicate that manual workers still accounted (before the latest recession) for a relatively stable 10.5 million workers—approaching 40 percent of total employment. If clerical and secretarial work is added to this, then the traditional labour force stood, until recently, at some 15 million—approaching two in three jobs. This belies the notion of a substantial shift in the demand for labour to a supposed "high-skills economy."

However, many in this majority group find that they invariably need to acquire more and more educational credentials, both to obtain and keep (through perpetual training and retraining) stable/core employment and to be guaranteed "a proper job" with career prospects, paid holidays, and a pension. So, gaining relatively high levels of qualifications continues to be essential if they are to maintain their position and avoid relegation to the new so-called "underclass," which has also been ideologically and politically constructed beneath them and into which illness, unemployment, accident, or the lack of worthwhile qualifications can so easily cast them (see Mann 1992). This "rough" section of the traditionally manually working class could be seen as a new version of Marx's "lumpenproletariat." Semi-employed, casualised, and low paid, they are an increasingly denigrated section of society, ducking and diving in a peripheral "grey economy," and including economic migrants, legal and illegal, from the EU and elsewhere. For some social commentators, like Castells (1996), the expansion of these McJobs is as significant as the growth of the professional and managerial sector noted above, while both Toynbee (2003) in the UK and Ehrenreich (2002) in the United States have provided detailed accounts of life *On the margins of inclusion,* as Smith (2005) has it in a definitive account.

Children and young people who are identified—even before they are born—as belonging to this "Status Zero" group are policed, curfewed, given Anti-Social Behaviour Orders, tagged, and mentored by arbitrary and repressive state measures on the basis of their "risk of social exclusion." In schools, they find themselves medicated, statemented, and on correctional behavioural programmes in "sin bins" within schools, if not excluded to Pupil Referral Units and/or under the supervision of Youth Offending Teams out of them. As "persistent truants," whose absence from school is unofficially tolerated, many still fall through the Careers Service net and eventually disappear into the unregulated grey economy mentioned above. For too many of them in the country with the highest prison population in Europe, as for their counterparts in the United States, *Learning to Labour in New Times* (Nolan and Anyon 2004) is less a preparation for employment and independent living than for "Learning to do time" (ibid.). This permanent pool of un- and semi-employed people maintains downward pressure on the wages of those in the working middle who live in fear and loathing of this derided and criminalised "underclass" beneath them. Meanwhile, the pressure on companies to downsize and outsource work overseas has further reduced core employment, and this also increases insecurity and pressure on the majority of the population. Thus, as secure core employment contracts, and work is contracted out to a growing insecure periphery, those in the new working middle are caught, as has been said, "between the snobs and the yobs" (e.g., Ainley 1993, 67).

Jon Cruddas MP calls this an "hour-glass economy." In the top half of the hour glass there has been an increase in high-paid jobs, performed by those with significant discretion over their hours and patterns of work. However, in the UK, the growth at the bottom of the hourglass of low-paid, unskilled, and insecure, often part-time work has been more significant. So after "Twenty years of schooling," as Bob Dylan sang, "they [still] put you on the day shift"—if the day shift continues to exist, that is!

Looking at the Totality of Education and Training after Ten Years of New Labour

In his first major speech on education as Prime Minister (Greenwich University 1/11/07), Gordon Brown, like Blair before him, renewed the emphasis on raising standards and argued that the global technical and economic revolution provided unbounded opportunities for social mobility and individual advancement: "There is virtually unlimited global demand for new talent. Unskilled jobs are disappearing." In so far as this was true, it was primarily because, as employers ruthlessly applied new technology to automate, deskill, and outsource labour, those in employment had to train and retrain just to keep their jobs, while new entrants to the labour market face rising qualification hurdles to secure employment (Allen and Ainley *op cit* 33).

That rising qualifications do not reflect rising standards was shown by the independent review of primary schooling by Professor Robin Alexander, which has suggested that reading standards have not improved since the 1950s, pointing to the "persistence of a yawning gap between high and low attaining pupils—bigger than in most comparable countries" (*TES*, 2/11/07). OfSTED (2008) has also reported that 20 percent of children still leave primary school functionally illiterate. Additional resources spent since 1997 on increasing the "diversity" of secondary schools have also failed to significantly improve results. According to the OECD, Britain has fallen from seventh to seventeenth place in reading and from eighth to twenty-fourth in maths (reported in the *Independent*, 5/12/07).

The Children's Plan (DCFS 2007), which was published six months into Brown's leadership, set itself the task of making Britain the "best place in the world to grow up." After ten years of New Labour, it identified some of the problems blighting the lives of many children—relentless commercialism, screen-based entertainment instead of outside play, fast food and growing obesity—and the Plan promised more facilities in inner-city areas. Yet, its repeated reference to the need to improve the educational performance of the lowest achievers revealed that for Brown, as for Blair, "world class children" could only be those who did well in the SATs and GCSEs. The Plan addressed parenting and the early years, but with the costs of full-time nursery places around £8,000 a year, and those of out-of-school clubs increasing at more than six times the rate of inflation, its funding proposals were paltry. Moreover, the Plan lacked details, and without funding, it remained no more than a list of aspirations.

Nor was there then any let up in the creation of state-funded private academies (Beckett 2007), although the dumping of their champion in the government, Lord Adonis, indicated no further spending on them and a predictable turn to making all schools independent academic foundations competing for pupils, as foundation hospitals supposedly compete for patients. But even before his departure, Adonis had already been forced to rethink their sponsorship. As Beckett argued, the turn towards elite universities and the involvement of local authorities as junior partners in sponsoring academies was the result of the refusal of leading British businesses to volunteer to run a service that many of them considered should be provided by the state, while "second order" sponsors sought political influence and peerages. Worse, some of the initial academy sponsors were such a ragbag of second-hand car dealers, creationists, and other adherents of fringe religions, that they had alienated parents and aroused hostility from backbench MPs. New sponsors now include FE colleges and universities, along with the trades union AMICUS and the Steiner Foundation.

However, the reality remains far from the TUC's 2007 call for reintegration of academies into democratically accountable local authority frameworks for schools. The new academy prospectus prevents local authorities from sponsoring academies, and the intention seems to be for Children's Services Departments, as local education authorities have now become, to provide little more than a brokerage service in handing over schools to private investors. Academies were springing up anywhere sponsors could be found, though Education Minister Ed Ball's 10/6/08 threat to replace "failing schools" with academies (even though some of them were academies already!) would necessarily mean that many of them would be in deprived and inner-city areas, or secondary moderns in the remaining selective local authority areas. Academies therefore continued to represent an extension of the "new market-state," through the transfer of public assets away from local authorities in a process of state-subsidised privatisation. Defaults can now be expected from the various bankrupt contractors to public-private partnerships financing academies and other schools and colleges through the Building Schools/Colleges for the Future programme, so that a Brown or Cameron regime may just gift them to their private sponsors, while allowing them to recoup their costs by charging fees on top of vouchers.

As to curricular and qualifications reform, Ed Balls's announcement of three new "subject based," rather than just "vocational," Diplomas for 14- to 18-year-olds was not a return to the Tomlinson proposals for reform of A-levels that were rejected by Blair in 2005. Balls was merely attempting to shore up another ailing programme that had failed to convince parents, employers, or headteachers. The initial uptake for the first batch of diplomas in September 2008 did not meet government targets, for who amongst the thousands of existing A-level candidates will risk untried diplomas in subject areas that are already well provided for? Despite their rejection by schools—only 12,000 of the original 45,000 places in the first cohort were filled—the Ministerial statement can be seen as a signal of intent about the future developments in schools, where they replace the old 11-plus with a new 14-plus, but it also relates to what may happen to colleges and to the new tertiary tripartism in universities.

The diploma also remained fraught with logistical problems, particularly, as Allen (2007) has noted, in relation to the operation of local partnerships, in which, ironically, the employers who are supposed to benefit have played only a minor role in drawing up the syllabuses, which were rushed out by the Qualification and Curriculum Authority (QCA) to meet the 2008 pilot deadline. Meanwhile, the fast-food giant McDonalds got backing from Gordon Brown for their own "McDiplomas," which count as GCSE and A-level equivalents. In general though, there is little connection between the content of vocational qualifications and the demands of the "new" workplace, and so the role of vocational training in the social control of youth has to be recognised as its primary function. This applies also to the new apprenticeships that have been announced, along with the raising of the school leaving age to 17 in 2013 and then to 18 in 2015. This is aimed at the 10 percent of young people who are estimated by OfSTED (2008) to be "Not in Employment, Education or Training" (NEET). This is a group clearly identified with the so-called "underclass," most visible on inner-city estates, many of whom will be streetwise enough to avoid what is, in effect, a return to a form of national conscription.

Above these "non learners" and in place of the traditional educational divisions, "learners" have been divided into "pathways"—the vocational now being a "middle track" between the academic road above and the "work-based" route below. As a result, the diploma syllabuses have become less practically orientated and more academic, as was the case with the previous academic drift of General National Vocational Qualifications into "Applied A-levels" (Allen and Ainley op cit. 91). In the prolonged recession that is now anticipated, dips provided in FE could become the end-qualification for apprenticeships. In a return to the youth training of the 1980s (above), they would lead only exceptionally to employment, but this time more commonly to two-year foundation "degrees" in former-polytechnics.

The consequence of the persistent failure of vocationalism has been that young people continue to sign up for A-levels as the only show in town, resulting in a situation where a qualification designed in 1951 for a small postwar elite of less than 5 percent now attracts well over 800,000 individual entries. The increased recognition of the importance of qualifications for labour market placement has inevitably led to grade inflation—one in four A-level candidates now obtains an A grade. Private and "better" state schools have therefore lost confidence in A-levels as the "gold standard" qualification. For this group, despite the introduction of an additional A* grade from 2010 onwards, modularised A-levels have become "too easy." Their argument is that modules encourage a fragmented approach, with assessment concentrated on data handling instead of reflecting candidates' academic subject knowledge. Rather than Brown and Balls abandoning A-levels, it would appear that the private sector is doing it for them. Some private schools are signing up for the International Baccalaureate, but it is the new Cambridge Pre-U that is most favoured as an A-level substitute (Allen and Ainley 2008, 13 et seq).

The Pre-U is a return to a traditional linear approach, reemphasising the importance of literary presentation. The Headmaster of Eton told *The Times* (27/11/07) that Pre-U exams offered pupils more stimulation and tested creativity and lateral thinking, while the Head of Dulwich College said that the Pre-U represented a return to traditional A-levels as university entrance qualifications. The Pre-U lobby is disingenuous. According to the Headmaster of Harrow, reported in the same *Times* article, A-levels are flawed because too many pupils get top grades. In other words, the private sector can no longer ensure what the parents are paying for—that their pupils are first in the queue for top universities—despite the latest figures from the Independent Schools Council showing that pupils at its schools are five times more likely to gain a place at one of the Russell Group universities referred to above (*The Times*, 27/11/07). The Pre-U gives them a new gold standard. It is unlikely to feature in many state schools, being designed to restore the positional advantage of top private schools. Needless to say, the Pre-U quickly received backing from the Russell Group, and syllabuses in up to 19 subjects were expected to be available from September 2008, the same time that new A* A-levels began. This contrasts with the Russell Group's attitude to the new diplomas: according to the *Telegraph* (23/11/07), their admissions tutors are "not likely" or "not at all likely" to consider students with diplomas, despite Balls introducing an "extended" diploma worth four and a half A-levels in University and Colleges Admissions Service entry points.

For the really rich (the now semi-internationalised ruling class), as we said above qualifications have always been less important than other aspects of social capital in guaranteeing the future earning power of their inheritors. This is not to say they won't happily spend £25,000-plus annually to secure a place at a leading private school. This compares with the £9,000 average across the private sector as a whole, with its ubiquitous cut-price crammers, private tutors, and online courses of variable quality. In such a competitive market, the personal connections between the top private schools and their associated Oxbridge colleges are highly valued. If, as a result of the 2010 review of university fees, the 20-strong Russell Group of elite universities raise their fees closer in 2011 to the market levels already being obtained for overseas students, then, notwithstanding increasingly frequent references to bursaries for the poor, the ability to pay will be at least as important an entry qualification as A*s or Pre-Us.

Whether or not undergraduate fees rise after 2011 (by which time the numbers of young unemployed may be the decisive factor in keeping them low), HE is increasingly divided into three tiers, as we have already noted. The research universities, represented by the Russell Group, select students internationally, with many graduating to an international labour market. They want to raise their tuition fees up to and beyond the £20,000 per annum Oxford has been claiming for some time that it needs to cover its annual undergraduate teaching costs. Below them, the mainly teaching universities, represented by the campus-based 94Group, recruit nationally for a predominantly national labour market. Finally, local/subregional former-polytechnic training universities, represented by the Million+ Group (so-called because its members have the majority of undergraduates, full- and part-time, if least research funding), have desperate recourse to clearing for students who graduate, if they are lucky, to mainly local labour markets (Ainley and Weyers 2008). In many of this third group, it is an open secret that widening participation on a reduced unit of resource has turned large parts of "higher" into de facto Further Education. This tertiary tripartism reproduces exactly the postwar 11-plus secondary tripartism of private and grammar, technical, and secondary modern state schools, where a binary divide existed between the privates plus grammars and the rest, just as the binary line is today redrawn in Higher Education between former-polytechnics and the rest. Under pressure to "Go to College or Die!," as Aronowitz (2008) says of the strikingly similar situation in the United States, the mass of 18-plus students and trainees who are working their way through this certification system get less and less for more and more debt.

Education After the Crunch: Overschooling, Undereducating, and Unemployment

The return of "boom and bust" economics, where governments committed to the free market have been forced to respond to an imminent collapse of the banking system, will understandably put education reformers on the defensive. Some in New Labour's ranks seek to resurrect the ghost of Keynes, promising to spend their way out of recession and discard their own "golden rules" about public borrowing and national debt. Yet the October 2008 banking bailout was socialism only for the rich (Lanchester, 2008, 5), and it marked a further extension of the state subsidisation of the private sector by the semi-privatised "new market-state."

The lack of fit between New Labour's "skills agenda"—also referred to as the "standards agenda" in schools—and the more general developments in the UK economy have become only too apparent. Rather than confirming the benefits of globalisation as espoused previously by Blair and now by Gordon Brown, the steady expansion of GDP, which was a feature of New Labour's period of government, was propelled by a "housing/credit" bubble, the collapse of which has now sent the economy into a thumping recession. As Turner (2008) observes, this "growth," coming on the back of the record borrowing of the last decade, has sought to compensate for the transfer of production overseas and as a consequence, the declining share of the national income enjoyed by labour.

Rather than education providing the opportunities promised in Brown's Greenwich speech, education has presided over its own "credential bubble." There was an increase from 48 percent of students attaining five A-C GCSEs in 1999 to just under 66 percent in 2008, a 20 percent increase in A-level entries (and now a 97 percent pass rate) during the same period, and a huge expansion of universities, with 40 percent of students now moving on to some form of HE. Just as the credit bubble attempted to compensate for the lack of return on physical capital, a new generation of students, faced with having to work more to attain less, increasingly experience a fall in the returns on their human capital. The subordination of the national economy to the vagaries of the global economy, and in particular the transfer of what once constituted "core" employment to low-wage economies, has only intensified the process of class recomposition referred to above. The recession that resulted from the unravelling of the credit crunch will, as the labour market contracts and (for young people in particular) employment opportunities disappear, heighten the importance of education as a form of social control—a continuation of the policy of social regulation by what we, following Finn (above), call "education and training without jobs."

Many in the education service will be engulfed by feelings of fear and uncertainty. Continuing to be ideologically opposed to the

New Labour "public-private" partnerships at the heart of the "new market-state," they are faced with a scenario in which private providers will not be able to honour their contracts, or, for example, sponsors will withdraw from academies, where the current system of teacher pensions becomes "unaffordable," and—under the Coalition cuts—local authorities, being forced to make major budget cuts in service provision.

If the immediate response to the recession by teachers and lecturers will understandably be defensive, at the same time there is a growing and widespread recognition that some alternative has to be found that is more than an impossible return to the "good old days" of the national welfare state. In education, this critique is sustained by the contradiction between academic study at all levels to acquire commodified credentials for heightened selection and the irrelevance of these qualifications to the increasingly evident economic, social, political, and ecological crisis.

There are therefore some clear long-term goals that most reformers would agree on. The aim must be to reverse privatisation and instead move education and other (former) public services towards the democratic control of civil society. This requires an end to academies and free schools parents want good local schools, not competition between supposedly "specialist" schools. OfSTED needs to be reformed or abolished and exam boards brought under democratic control. Charitable status and other state subsidies for private schools have to go if the government is serious about promoting its recently rediscovered enthusiasm for social mobility. Student fees must be abolished so that free public-service Higher Education is restored, as in Scotland, where there are no fees for Scottish students (although most Scottish students borrow from the Student Loan Fund and, as in England, a high proportion have part-time jobs). Under- and postgraduates should no longer mortgage their futures in the often subprime markets of academic HE.

On other issues, however, we need more discussion. For example, without an alternative conception of "standards," how can we engage with the upsurge in opposition to testing, which has seen even the National Association of Headteachers support a boycott and a Parliamentary Select Committee call for the abolition of all SATs? The collapse of 14-plus SATs following the 2008 marking fiasco was a pyrrhic victory, achieved without popular pressure, the result of an overloaded system of assessment. It left primary SATs in place along with secondary and primary league tables. The predictable demise of diplomas will be the same and not the result of pedagogic rejection of an unsound idea.

If there is an urgent debate still to be had about what an alternative curriculum could look like, there is also a need for active forms of accountability and democracy within schools, colleges, and universities. We need to bring educational institutions together in new ways at local and (sub)regional levels, rather than just going back to the democratic control of local authorities, because these too have changed. A-levels and diplomas should be replaced with a multilevel general qualification at 18 that entitles students to a range of learning experiences. Beyond that, a continuous grading system, together with a report on undergraduate experience throughout the whole of their courses, should succeed Platonic divisions of first-, second-, and third-class degrees. First degrees should be lengthened to four years, in line with Scotland, followed by two years for Masters. Research should be undertaken both in dedicated national research centres and also in the activities of scholarship, scientific investigation, and artistic creation by all teachers and students, from primary to postgraduate schools.

To achieve such reforms, there is a need for new types of campaigning alliances between teachers, students, and local communities. While recognising the central importance of education, trade unions—particularly the NUT and UCU—should use their resources and organising power in new ways, transcending their narrow "professionalist" perspective on teaching and learning and turning outwards to become social movements, able to engage in real discussion about programmes for education. Organised teachers can challenge academic selectivity and competition across the board, along with particular inanities like diplomas and apprenticeships without jobs. This is as important as building workplace militancy over pay and conditions. To transform schools, colleges, and universities from credential mills—where the curriculum is dominated by standardised tests and exams—into sites of genuine education, we need a national conversation concerning the nature and purpose of education. This would be "a movement" for the political construction of "a national popular collective," such as Stanley Aronowitz (drawing upon Gramsci) has suggested in the United States. It is not, he says, a question of abandoning state educational institutions but rather of rendering them benign, by removing them as much as possible from the tightening grip of the "new market-state."

References

Ainley, P. (1993) *Class and Skill, Changing Divisions of Knowledge and Labour*, London: Cassell.

—— (2001) "From a National System Locally Administered to a National System Nationally Administered: The New Leviathan in Education and Training in England," *The Journal of Social Policy*, 30 (3): 457–476.

Ainley, P. and Allen, M. (2010) *Lost Generation? New strategies for youth and education*, London: Continuum.

Ainley, P. and Weyers, M. (2008) "The Variety of Student Experience," in J. Canaan and W. Shumar (eds), *Structure and Agency in the Neo-liberal University*, London: Routledge.

Allen, M. (2007) "Learning for Labour: Specialist Diplomas and 14–19 Education," *Forum* 49: 3.

Allen, M. and Ainley, P. (2007) *Education Make You Fick, Innit? What Has Gone Wrong in England's Schools, Colleges and Universities and How to Start Putting It Right*, London: Tufnell.

—— (2008) *A New 14+: Vocational Diplomas and the Future of Schools, Colleges and Universities, An Educational and Campaigning Pamphlet*, Ealing Teachers' Association and Greenwich University UCU.

Aronowitz, S. (2008) *Against Schooling, For an Education That Matters*, Paradigm: Boulder.

Beckett, F. (2007) *The Great City Academy Fraud*, London: Continuum.

Bobbitt, P. (2002) *The Shield of Achilles, War, Peace and the Course of History*, London: Allen Lane.

Bourdieu, P. (1984) *Reproduction*.

Cabinet Office (2008) *Getting On, Getting Ahead. A Discussion Paper: Analyzing the Trends and Drivers of Social Mobility*, London: Cabinet Office Strategy Unit.

Carter, M. (1962) *Home, School and Work, A Study of the Education and Employment of Young People in Britain*, London: Pergamon.

Castells, M. (1996) *The Rise of Network Society*, Oxford: Blackwell.

Clarke, J. and Newman, J. (1997) *The Managerial State: Power, Politics and Ideology in the Remaking of Social Welfare*, London: Sage.

Crompton, R. (2008) *Class and Stratification*, 3rd edition, Cambridge: Polity.

Department for Children, Families and Schools. (2007) *The Children's Plan*, London: DCFS.

Ehrenreich, B. (2002) *Nickel and Dimed: On Not Getting by in America*, New York: Henry Holt.

Elliott, L. and Atkinson, D. (2007) *Fantasy Island, Waking up to the Incredible Economic, Political and Social Illusions of the Blair Era*, London: Constable.

Finn, D. (1987) *Training without Jobs, New Deals and Broken Promises*, London: Macmillan.

Hills, J. and Stewart, K. (2005) *A More Equal Society? New Labour, Poverty, Inequality and Exclusion*, Bristol: Policy.

Lanchester, J. (2008) "Cityphobia," *London Review of Books*, p. 5.

Lukacs, G. (1923) *History and Class Consciousness*, http://www.marxists.org/archive/lukacs/works/history/ch02.htm/.

Mann, K. (1992) *The Making of an English "Underclass,"* Buckingham: Open University Press.

Mizen, P. (2004) *The Changing State of Youth*, Basingstoke: Palgrave Macmillan.

Nolan, K. and Anyon, J. (2004) "Learning to Do Time: Willis's Model of Cultural Reproduction in an Era of Postindustrialism, Globalization, and Mass Incarceration" in N. Dolby and G. Dimitriadis (eds) *Learning to Labour in New Times*, New York: Routledge-Falmer.

Office for Standards in Education. (2008) *Integration of the Inspections of Welfare and Education from September 2008, Consultation*, London: OfSTED.

Polanyi, K. (1944) *The Great Transformation, the Political and Economic Origins of Our Time*, Boston: Beacon Press.

Smith, D. (2005) *On the Margins of Inclusion, Changing Labour Markets and Social Exclusion in London*, Bristol: Policy.

Tomlinson, S. (2006) *Education in a Post-Welfare Society*, Maidenhead: Open University Press.

Toynbee, P. (2003) *Hard Work, Life on Low-Pay Britain*, London: Bloomsbury.

Turner, G. (2008) *The Credit Crunch*, London, Pluto.

TUC. (2007) *A New Direction—A Review of the School Academies Programme*, London: TUC.

Willis, P. (1977) *Learning to Labour, How Working Class Kids Get Working Class Jobs*, Aldershot: Saxon House.

Wilmott, P. and Young, M. (1958) *Family and Kinship in East London*, London: Routledge.

Chapter 3

Education, Education, Education or Business, Business, Business?

Kevin Farnsworth

What stands out most when we look back on Blair's education policies are his government's concerted efforts to embed capital—business priorities and business people—into the heart of state education. Although this strategy was pursued with vigour by Blair, it can actually be traced back, not just to the previous Conservative governments, but to the previous Labour administrations of the 1960s and 1970s. Wilson's governments, in the 1960s and early 1970s, experimented with corporatist intermediation: the integration of organised business, alongside organised labour, into decision-making and agreement structures covering a range of issues from pay to the establishment of local training strategies. In the 1970s, shortly after succeeding Wilson, James Callaghan argued that Britain's economic malaise was caused by the failure of education to fit with the needs of business. The answer lay, he argued, in the development of closer and more formal links between schools and local employers.

Although the post-1979 Conservative governments abandoned corporatism, they continued to look for new ways of utilising business interests to assist in state-service reforms. The Conservatives were more interested in how business might benefit state services than how welfare services might benefit businesses. A key priority for the Conservatives was to marketise public services in the hope of increasing efficiency, quality, and choice (Cutler and Waine, 1998). Because state monopolies are not subject to market disciplines, the public sector was considered to lack the ability and innovation to respond effectively to the challenges facing the welfare state. *Managerialism*—the imposition of market "values," such as entrepreneurialism, risk taking, and customer-oriented focus, into public services—constituted an important part of the Conservative's programmes (Clarke and Newman, 1997; Cutler and Waine, 1998). Towards the end, successive Conservative governments sought to remove locally elected representatives from the public services and replace them with business people (Peck, 1995). Senior business people were guaranteed a majority presence within various quango bodies, including the Training and Enterprise Councils (TECs), and key roles on the boards of local education authorities (LEAs), grant-maintained schools, city technology colleges (CTCs), Further Education colleges, and the post-1992 universities. By the time Labour returned to power in 1997, therefore, the perceived needs of business were already being prioritised in education policy, and a concerted effort had already been made to more closely integrate business people into various education services.

New Labour, Business, and Education Policy

The Conservative's education strategies fitted well with New Labour's Third Way approach, which sought to locate solutions to problems within state services that went beyond traditional statism. Where the left were perceived to have historically viewed the state as a superior mechanism for managing and delivering welfare services, compared with the private and voluntary provision, New Labour's Third Way project would draw upon the strengths of all three sectors "in a partnership for a new age" (Blair & Shroeder, 1999; Department of Social Security, 1998, p. 19).

The reality was much less evenhanded, however. Engagement with various institutionalised forms of capital—business representatives, business people, and firms—was afforded a far higher priority for government than with other stakeholders within the welfare mix. Although the Blair government promised to put into place policies and programmes based, not on ideology, but on evidence of "what works," private-sector solutions have been pursued, promoted, and fetishised in spite of evidence to the contrary. Where the evidence pointed to real problems relating to private-sector engagement in education, as reviewed in the sections below, this was largely ignored. Although the Third Way did shift the debate from purely free-market solutions, the end result was that private capital, business people, and business ideas were far more deeply embedded into education by Labour than was achieved by the previous Conservative government (Grimshaw, Vincent, & Willmott, 2002). As Falconer and McLaughlin (2000, p. 122) put it:

> A clear distinguishing feature of "New Labour," as opposed to "Old Labour," is the nature of its posture toward the private sector. A political party which once held firmly to the view that the State should play a leading role in the workings of the nation's economy now promotes the belief that very little can be achieved in government without the active support of business.

The rest of this chapter seeks to make sense of, and evaluate the effectiveness of, what we might term these corporate-centred education reforms (Farnsworth, 2004) under the following themes: structural imperatives and the needs of capital, attractiveness of private funding streams, perceived strength of the private sector, and concluding on increased corporate power.

Structural Imperatives and the Needs of Capital

The dialectical mutual dependence of business and state is a major theme in Marx's work. In the Communist Manifesto, he famously argued that the state manages the general affairs of the capitalist class or, to put it another way, states must operate to satisfy capital's systemic needs in relation to its viability in the face of in-build contradictions as a mode of production. The base-superstructure distinction in Marx's work also describes a structural-functional relationship in which the reproduction of the economic base is dependent on state intervention within the superstructure; and the state, in turn, is dependent on growth and subsequent revenues raised on the back of economic activity (Wetherly, 2005). At the most basic level, therefore, the capitalist state must deliver services that help to promote economic accumulation, and put in place measures to control challenges and threats to capital relations of production (Miliband, 1969; Gough 1979). To put it more simply, capitalist states, and labour for that matter, depend on corporate investment and profits in order to fulfil their own "needs": the state for tax revenues and labour for wages (Offe & Ronge, 1984).

By increasing the number of investment options open to firms, economic globalisation has effectively increased the relative dependence of the state and labour on footloose capital. At the same time, political globalisation—which shifts some aspects of governance to the international level—has tended to favour business interests and business priorities above others, and reinforce the position of national capitals (Farnsworth, 2004; Korten, 1995; Sklair, 2001). The effect of this has been to increase the hegemonic power of capital, creating political environments where business interests, preferences, and ideas became the natural order of things.

This elevation of business concerns higher and higher up the political hierarchy has strengthened both its agency power (which Marxists often refer to as instrumental power) and its structural power, which can be defined simply as systemic and emergent differential relational opportunities for power with, or without, action (Farnsworth & Gough, 2000). Organised capital, at both the international and national levels, also became more adept at defending and promoting their political and economic interests, making use of new lobbying arenas beyond nation states, and capitalising on the perception that, if governments did not meet with and placate business leaders, those business leaders would shift their investment anywhere (Farnsworth & Holden, 2006). Businesses not only became much more adept at shifting capital over the globe quickly in order to chase the most favourable production and investment environments, they managed to do so with such effect that it risked undermining governments and destabilising economies. But the most important factor in the steady rise of corporate power in the 1990s was the ability and willingness of large corporations to threaten governments with disinvestment if they did not meet the demands of those same corporations. As Blair put it in 1995 and 1999, respectively:

> The determining context of economic policy is the new global market. That imposes huge limitations of a practical nature…on macroeconomic policies. (*Financial Times*, 22 May 1995)

> If the markets don't like your policies, they will punish you. (Tony Blair, speech to the Economic Club, Chicago, 23 April 1999)

Business, for its part, has also wasted few opportunities to remind governments of the situation. The Director General of the Confederation of British Industry (CBI) used the occasion of the run-up to the 2001 general election to point out the dangers.

> Nobody can afford to ignore the shift towards a more globally competitive world in which investors and companies are extremely mobile. Any government must create an environment that not only attracts business but also encourages companies to stay…(Digby Jones, Business Manifesto, 2000)

The Blair government set about responding to such pressures by reframing British education policy so that it fitted better with competitive international markets and better accommodated the perceived needs of capital within the global economy. In other words, the Blair government responded directly to the increased structural and agency power of capital that was unleashed as a result of globalisation.

It is against this backdrop that we can more clearly understand the direction of Blair's education reforms. From the outset, Labour began to engineer a move towards more corporate-centred educational provision, which tried to meet both the generic and specific needs of employers (Hatcher & Hirtt, 1999) in order to strengthen UK businesses and attract new foreign investment to the UK. The government's approach was clearly laid out in 1998.

> The most productive investment will be linked to the best educated and best trained workforces, and the most effective way of getting and keeping a job will be to have the skills needed by employers. (DfEE, 1998, p. 10)

One of the early strategies employed to achieve this was to commission key business people to report on the needs of business and how they could be better met. Howard Davies, former Director General of the Confederation of British Industry (CBI) and subsequent head of the Financial Services Authority and the London School of Economics, was commissioned to investigate how business school linkages could be increased (Davies, 2002). The CBI had been campaigning since the 1970s for stronger direct links between schools and local employers (see Farnsworth, 1998). Richard Lambert, former editor of the Financial Times, recommended in his review of Higher Education in 2003 that universities and research bodies should devote a higher proportion of their research outputs and budgets to steering provision *towards the needs* of *business* and the economy (HMSO, 2003). In 2003 the government sought to address the needs of local employers (Adburgham, 1997) by promoting more vocational training in schools. It released its White Paper on skills which promised to "test new ways of engaging employers in the learning of 14–19 [year-olds]" in order to "deliver a comprehensive range of vocational and practical opportunities in ways that suit the needs of local employers" (DfES, 2003, p. 78), adding that "we must make colleges and training providers more responsive to employers' and learners' needs" (DfES, 2003: foreword). The role of the Higher Education Funding Council for England (HEFCE), meanwhile, was redefined in order to make it "more responsive to the needs of business and industry," and the government established the Higher Education Research Development Fund (HERDF) and the Higher Education Reach Out to Business and the Community (HEROBC) initiatives in 1998 and 1999, respectively, in order to channel over £100 million into those universities that promised to enhance the relevance of programmes of teaching and research to the needs of employers and the economy.

Economic structural imperatives were thus important from the outset of Blair's period in office: education priorities would help to boost the economy, and a reformed education sector would (eventually) help to pay for increased public expenditure elsewhere. This idea wasn't especially controversial, but what was more controversial and more problematic was the view that the education system could, and should, service the needs of business. Marxists have long since pointed out the contradictory and conflicting needs of specific capitals, and attempts to shift general education more closely towards the needs of business, even localised business, inevitably comes up against these problems (Ian Gough, 1979; Miliband, 1969; Offe, 1984).

How firms and organised business view education policy—indeed, whether they have any interest in education policy at all—varies over time and between business groups (Farnsworth, 2004). Concerning the specific needs of business, there are many different business needs and a myriad number of business preferences. Well-documented cleavages exist between small and large business interests and between financial and industrial interests (Dahl, 1961; Longstreth, 1979; Mann, 1993). One local factory may have very few educational requirements of its workforce and may value discipline and physical labour above all else; a local supermarket may value social skills as well as speed and dexterity; and a local bank may need a good level of numerical and interpersonal skills. The only common "need" here is that workers should be constituted as labour power and "exploitable." The fact that production methods and local economies can change rapidly highlights the dangers of trying to gear provision towards employers, and inviting local employers into policy making arenas is equally problematic. Business people, if allowed, will naturally make public policy in their own interests, which may directly harm the interests of competitor firms and which may conflict with long-term national interests. The danger to other parts of industry was spelt out by The Economist in 2003.

> The job of a chief executive is to make profits for his (sic) company and, no doubt, feather his own nest; it is not to make public

policy—especially in his own industry, for that is where his selfish interests will be greatest. Inviting him to help his industry is sure to divert public policy to private ends. This is not the fault of executives or their companies; it is the fault of government. (*The Economist*, 26 June 2003)

Business opinions, in short, are highly dependent on environmental factors. They are often short-termist, dominated by big business, and centre on particular sectoral or company interests at a given moment in time.

However, self-interest was only one problem that Blair's reforms had to deal with. A far greater one for the government was the opposite problem of apathy amongst the business community. Business people have, in practice, been reluctant to become involved in small-scale educational ventures, including school governance (Pike & Hillage, 1995). Such linkages, in market terms, bring few benefits but quite a few costs, especially in the form of free-rider problems (IiE, 1995). As a result, the government's attempts to generate voluntaristic engagement, as opposed to commercial engagement in evolving educational markets, have often met with disappointingly low levels of interest from the business community.

Labour's whole premise, that it is possible to know what business needs, was therefore flawed. It was not even possible to extract a clear perspective from the national representatives of business. The CBI, for instance, representing large, mainly industrial capital, called for increases in public expenditure for education and for the expansion of Higher Education during the mid-1980s, and was supportive of Labour's aspiration for a 50 percent university participation rate and of public expenditure increases in education. On the other hand, the CBI campaigned heavily during the 1980s and 1990s for lower taxation, especially business taxation, and lower levels of public expenditure, which inevitably led to underinvestment in education and other services. The Institute of Directors (IoD) lobbied even harder for reductions in state expenditure and taxation across the board throughout the 1980s and 1990s (Farnsworth, 2004), and campaigned against Labour's 50 percent participation rate. Instead, it argued for an expansion in vocational training which fits with the Blair government's subsequent 14–19 agenda (as already noted above) (Institute of Directors, 2002).

All of this raised serious questions over the wisdom of prioritising business needs, preferences, and agendas in education policy, although it did nothing to deter the direction of Blair's educational reforms.

The Attractiveness of Private Funding Streams

For the Blair administration, business engagement in education also held out the hope of new funding streams for its educational priorities. This was especially attractive given the administration's perception that globalisation and the prevailing political mood ruled out tax increases on income and profits. The government accordingly set about trying to attract private financing through sponsorship deals and match-funding for new city academies and specialist schools. The academies had to raise around £2 million from the private sector, and specialist schools initially had to raise £100,000 (although this was later reduced to £50,000), with the business community contributing at least £250,000 to each Education Action Zone (EAZ). The government also encouraged universities to establish stronger financial links with business in order to attract a greater level of funding from the private sector along U.S. lines, where top institutions attract as much as 20 percent of their income from the private sector, compared with 4–6 percent at Cambridge and Oxford (NEF, 2004; Wintour, 2003).

There was general reticence on the part of firms to become more closely involved in educational services in which there were no obvious and immediate returns. A similar story prevailed when the previous Conservative government tried to raise corporate sponsorship for city technology colleges (CTCs). Labour found that attracting even relatively modest financial contributions from business for its key initiatives has been similarly difficult. Although some EAZs did manage to attract interest and financing from large companies, including the likes of Shell (which chaired the Lambeth Zone), IBM, ICL, McDonalds, Tesco, and Barclays Bank, others struggled to generate any real business interest or finance. Newcastle's EAZ, to take one example, failed to raise the minimum private finance it needed, despite getting some support from Newcastle United Football club; it managed to raise just £71,000 (7 percent) of its total income of £955,000 between 2000 and 2001, and the majority of what it did raise was "in-kind" (OFSTED, 2002).

In-kind contributions became an important feature of other EAZs also. According to the government's own figures, the average cash donations from business to the various EAZs amounted to less than £110,000 in 2001, and just 12 of the 73 EAZs that were launched between 1999 and 2001 had successfully raised the expected £250,000 per year from business (DfES, 2001, p. 23).

Difficulties were also experienced in raising the necessary contributions from business for the development of city academies and specialist schools. In order to provide a boost for the flagging project, the government had to reduce the amount that specialist schools had to raise from the private sector, from £100,000 to £50,000, and it set up a Partnership Fund in September 2002 in order to assist those schools that were finding it difficult to reach even the reduced target. For similar reasons, Labour has subsequently abandoned its requirement that city academies raise £2 million in private sponsorship. By 2009 the government had reduced the requirement of £2 million private sponsorship for each academy to an undertaking on behalf of private businesses to demonstrate the "skills and leadership" to run an academy (DCSF, 2009).

The Blair government hoped that companies would want to get involved in educational services because of the opportunities such involvement presented to shape local provision or establish them as "responsible citizens." In reality, however, the number of companies that could afford to invest in public-private partnerships (PPPs) with few financial gains was limited to larger companies that might benefit from the "soft-marketing" opportunities that such involvement offered. Moreover, the extent to which those companies that did get involved were able to represent business views in general, as opposed to the idiosyncratic views of particular business people or firms, is questionable. Critics thus questioned the merits of exposing schools and their pupils to large corporations with self-interested motives and their governing bodies to narrow elite interests (CPS, 2003, p. 46).

By the beginning of Labour's second term in office, it was becoming clear that not even business interests appeared to be happy with the situation that was developing. Even amongst companies that had responded to calls for support in the past, there were growing signs of impatience at the level of financial support being sought, leading to "partnership-fatigue" for many businesses and business people (Davies, 2002, p. 175). There was also growing frustration within the business community that appeals for business representation and private-sector funding was not leading to greater business influence. Instead, local authorities and public services were simply trying to fulfil funding requirements laid down by central government. As one senior business person put it in an interview with me:

> business is constantly asked to fork out because that's what they (schools) want in the end; they want resources.... We've had five or six schools come to us because they need match funding to become specialist schools, and when you (say) we haven't got the money, but how

else can we help you...it starts off okay in theory but when you get
to the crunch point it's money they want. And that's just too much.
We do put a lot of money into the system but there's not a bottomless
bucket. (cited in Farnsworth, 2004, p. 144)

In addition to these relatively small funding deals, the government
also expanded the Private Finance Initiative (PFI). Under PFI, or
public-private partnerships (PPPs), private companies bid to build
and maintain schools, with the state agreeing to lease them for a
designated period, often exceeding 30 years. The PFI scheme offered
the opportunity to generate high levels of capital investment without necessitating high levels of public borrowing. Although it was
widely assumed that the government's use of PFI would diminish
as borrowing decreased and revenues increased (Ruane, 2002, p. 2),
the scheme has continued to expand, a fact that says a great deal
about the government's ideological preference for this form of funding and of its desire to place greater weight on the importance of
injecting private capital, and private-sector values and methods, into
state services.

The PFI and various initiatives to contract out services have been
criticised on a number of grounds. To begin with, the necessity for
projects to generate high returns for investors and its long lock-in
periods led to criticisms that PFI represents an inefficient, expensive,
and risky way to fund new investment. Questions were also raised
regarding one of the key justifications for PFI by the government
that it facilitated additional investment that would otherwise not have
been available. This claim was in fact undermined by the lowering
of public borrowing beginning in 1997, and by the introduction of
the new "Golden Rule" by the Treasury, which facilitated greater
borrowing for investment. As a result of these changes, the Treasury
Select Committee concluded in 2000 that:

When the aim was to reduce the Public Sector Borrowing Requirement,
particularly when there was a large deficit, PFI was an attractive means
of increasing investment. However, the new fiscal framework has made
it easier to provide publicly-funded investment, because such investment has no effect on the golden rule [where the government limits
borrowing to fund investment], and could be increased significantly
without breaching the 40 per cent limit on the debt ratio. In the new
framework, the case for PFI as a means of obtaining extra investment
is very much weaker. The main justification should now be the prospect of obtaining better value for money. (Treasury Select Committee,
2000 Paragraph 23)

Although the government endorsed the Treasury's findings at the time (see Treasury Select Committee 2000, it nonetheless continued to rely disproportionately on PFI for major investment projects, and it ignored mounting evidence, from various quarters, that questioned the extent to which PFI offered real value for money.

The debate on PFI was made all the more contentious and difficult by the complexities surrounding the measurement of efficiency and value for money. The Blair government expanded PFI extremely rapidly without properly evaluating its relative merits, according to its critics (Pollock, 2004; Pollock, Shaoul J., Rowland D., & Player S., 2001). The details of the major PFI deals were often shrouded in secrecy, with "market-sensitive" information commonly withheld from the public gaze, which prevented proper public scrutiny (Gosling, 2004). The financial accounting practices of the Treasury and the contractors involved in PFI projects were also criticised by research commissioned by the Association of Chartered Certified Accountants (ACCA, 2004) for lacking an adequate level of transparency "necessary to measure the financial performance of the contracts." Where detailed early analysis of PFI schemes was possible, the apparent gains of the scheme were seriously questioned. The IPPR concluded in 2001, for instance, in what was otherwise a generous report written by a think tank with close links to the Labour Party, that PFI hospitals offered no better value for money than public-sector builds. Criticism was also levelled by the government's auditors with regard to schools built under PFI. An Audit Commission report concluded in 2003, for example, that PFI schools were "statistically speaking, significantly worse than that of the traditionally funded sample on four of the five matrices" (Audit Commission, 2003, p. 13). The matrices against which they were assessed included scores for costs, upkeep, space, storage, and general "enjoyment" of the new builds. In terms of the overall costs of the new buildings, the study did not find any significant difference between PFI- and LEA-funded schools, nor did it find any real difference in overall satisfaction scores. However, there were significant differences on other measures. It found, for example, that the PFI schools would require higher levels of future investment for upkeep, and that the best examples of innovative measures to reduce running costs and improve fitness for purpose tended to be found in LEA-built schools (ibid, p. 14–20). In contrast to the key justification used by government to defend PFI, the report also found "no evidence that PFI schemes delivered schools more quickly than projects funded by more traditional ways" (ibid, p. 21). Finally, local authority schools scored higher against measures for architectural and aesthetic appeal (ibid.).

One further problem with relying on private-sector finance in key services such as education is that, unlike other markets, government cannot allow such services to collapse. Situations in which private companies pull out of agreements to provide support or services, government has to step in. This was illustrated by the withdrawal of WS Atkins from its contract to deliver educational services in Southwark (see below). Economic crises, which are endemic to capitalism, also risk undermining any deals made with the private sector. The economic crisis that began in September 2007 had, by November 2008, caused Amey to withdraw its backing of Union City Academy in Middlesbrough.

The Perceived Strength of the Private Sector

The Blair government wanted to utilise the perceived strengths of business actors in devising solutions to institutional problems within public services. The hope was that such engagement would bring innovation, entrepreneurialism, efficiency, and customer orientation to education. To this end, New Labour made a concerted effort to create new opportunities for business people to fill strategic decision-making positions from the highest levels of government down to individual services. As already noted above, a number of senior business people were charged with undertaking major reviews of education policy over the Blair period of office.

One of the first significant indications of the government's intention to draft business people directly into failing public services came in 1998 with the introduction of the Education Action Zones initiative. Under this proposal, local firms were encouraged to take over groups of failing schools, independently of local authorities if they so wished, in the hope that they would provide solutions where LEAs had failed (Dickson, Germitz, Halpin, Power, & Whitty, 2002, p. 185). Later, Labour sought to formalise business inputs into state services through the expansion of specialist schools, first introduced by the Conservatives in 1994 as city technology colleges, and the launch of city academies in 2000. In addition to contributing to the running costs of these schools, the government hoped that business partners would "bring a new focus and sharpness" (Dfee, 2000, p. 4) to more autonomous governing bodies in which they would occupy a majority of the seats.

Such moves paved the way for even more radical proposals, starting in 1999, that facilitated wholesale takeovers of failing schools by outside bodies, including for-profit private companies. A number of LEAs have subsequently volunteered, or have been forced, to contract out all or part of their educational services to private firms. In a similar demonstration of its confidence in business to produce solutions to failing public services (even in firms that had not previously worked in similar areas), in 2003 the government awarded a £1.9 million contract to the construction firm Jarvis to set up a network that would advise and support failing schools in England and Wales (Slater, 2003).

Given that the government has sought to increase the voice of business where it was previously relatively weak, it is no surprise to find that Labour has done little to weaken business where it had already established a strong voice. In opposition, Labour had been highly critical of the dominance of business and other elite interests on the management boards of Training and Enterprise Councils (TECs), but Labour's replacement of them by the Learning and Skills Councils (LSCs) was designed to "give employers unprecedented influence over the education system and promote a better match between demand and supply for skills" (Dfes, 1999, p. 10). Although trade unions and locally elected constituencies were represented on the executive body of the new LSC, employers have retained a dominant voice. Of the 15 members of the LSC's National Council in 2005, six had held senior roles in business, including: Digby Jones, Director General of the CBI; the Chief Executive of ATL Telecom; the former Managing Director of Coca Cola Great Britain; and a former Finance Director for BT. The rest of the members were made up of various educationalists and government workers, along with the Deputy General Secretary of the TUC. The vast majority of the local LSC Chairs and Executives are also occupied by senior business people (Learning and Skills Council, *Who's Who*, 2002/3). Moreover, since the responsibilities of the LSCs were extended to cover education-business partnerships and to Further Education, in addition to post-16 vocational training, the scope for business influence on provision has been widened still further under these new bodies.

The problem is that, beyond advocating a business presence in the governance structure of schools, exactly what the government expected business people to contribute was unclear. As a result, business representatives have often been uncertain about what role they are expected to fulfil, and many have felt unable to speak for the business community (BiiC, 2002; IiE, 1995, p. 6), which increases the risk that they will simply represent their own narrow interests. And even where business engagement has been placed on a more formal footing, the apparent benefits of business involvement have been limited. In their examination of the EAZs, for example, Dickson et al. (2002) found that the private sector contributed relatively little—either by way of innovative ideas or additional resources—to the improvement of local education, casting doubts on Labour's continuing optimism that business has "the willingness, energy, creativity or know-how" to radically transform education and other services (Dickson et al., 2002, p. 195). Also noteworthy here is that, in cases where the private sector has assumed a greater role in the delivery of educational services, senior management posts were predominantly filled by former public-sector workers rather than private-sector "gurus."

> Regarding the impact of private-sector involvement in service delivery, the evidence is rather mixed. In 2007 the Chief Inspector for OfSTED stated that the academy and specialist school initiatives had not improved standards overall (BBC, 2007). Even the government's own evaluations reported that, of the nine LEAs that had been forced to hand over services to the private sector, a majority were rated as "poor improvers," while a minority (10 out of 15) were rated as "good improvers" (Slater, 2003). Several of the private companies that took over LEA functions subsequently faced heavy penalties for failing to make improvements as set out in their contracts. Cambridge Education Associates (CEA) faced annual fines between 2000 and 2004 for failing to meet its agreed targets in Islington (Clement, 2004: 8), and SERCO, the company running educational services in Bradford, failed to meet 47 out of 52 targets in 2002, the first year of its contract. The perverse response to this failure by Islington and Bradford Local Authorities was to adjust the targets downwards (ibid.). At the same time, SERCO asked the government for additional support to help make the improvements that were supposed to result from private-sector engagement. Ultimately, of course, private-sector successes result in high financial fees; but if they fail, the government ultimately has to pick up the pieces, as happened when WS Atkins unilaterally decided to terminate its contract to run educational services in Southwark, at a cost of at least £2.2 million to the government. (Toolis, 2003)

Not surprisingly, business has hit back at its critics. In 2005 the Confederation of British Industry defended business involvement in education, and published evidence that it stated proved that the "privatised" LEAs had significantly outperformed publically run LEAs between 2000 and 2004 (CBI, 2005a). Digby Jones, who was at the time Director General of the CBI and subsequently a Labour Minister with a seat in the House of Lords, argued that "where the government has intervened directly using the private sector, standards have improved markedly" (CBI, 2005b, p. 5), and that the net result was that educational standards had been "driven up" (CBI, 2005a, foreword). This conclusion was used by the CBI to argue for an expansion in outsourcing and the marketisation of state services. In publishing the results, the CBI (2005b) argued that, in order to achieve sustained improvement in education, more private-sector involvement would be needed in future.

> The successful use of the private sector in turning around failing local education authorities (LEAs) will be difficult to replicate in future public service reforms if the government fails to adopt a more sustainable approach to outsourcing. (CBI, 2005a, Foreword)

The report was warmly welcomed by government and by the private companies in charge of the outsourced LEAs, and it appeared to silence some of the critics of outsourcing. However, a more detailed analysis of the same data used by the CBI to reach its conclusions in 2005 reveals that, on the basis of "success" measured by the CBI, if anything, the public sector outperformed the private sector (for detailed examination of the evidence see Farnsworth, 2006). This analysis reported four key findings, as follows. First, although the data on growth in examination performance between 2000 and 2004, which is the source of the CBI's claims, indicates that the outsourced authorities outperformed the nonoutsourced authorities, none of the outsourced authorities were actually managed by the private sector between 2000 and 2004. Only one contract, for Hackney, was awarded at the beginning of the 2000–2004 period. Thus, many of the "improvements" claimed by the CBI to have been made by the outsourced authorities were actually made while they were still managed by the public sector. Moreover, all of the subsequently outsourced authorities performed better in the year prior to outsourcing, when they were still under LEA controls, than they did following the imposition of private-sector management. Second, one of the most important determinants of the rate of growth in examination performance is the starting position. Whilst it is true that the outsourced authorities appear to have outperformed the public sector between 2000 and 2004, those same authorities also dramatically outperformed comparable authorities in the years prior to outsourcing. The key reason for this is that it is far easier for poorly performing authorities to make rapid gains in examination success than it is for better performing authorities (the deviation to the mean factor). Third, the majority of the top performing authorities during this period, taking into account starting point, were publically run LEAs. Fourth, as the performance of the outsourced authorities moved closer to the mean, their apparent successes have tended to diminish. If we consider later evidence, public LEAs easily outperformed the outsourced authorities during the 2004–2005 period. Based on this analysis, it is possible to conclude that LEAs appear to perform better under the management of the public sector, although the analysis needs to be broadened beyond examination success to other indicators of achievement in order to adequately test this thesis. However, these findings do question the necessity and wisdom of the government's strategy of bringing the private sector in to rescue failing LEAs.

One last point that is pertinent here is that the Blair government generally failed to fully recognise the strengths of the public sector. Its policies have largely been built on the assumption that bringing business into state services was a positive-sum game—i.e., that it would have positive effects and few, if any, negative effects. However, business principles and values run counter to those held in the public sector. At the most basic level, the welfare state was established precisely because the private sector fails to provide public goods efficiently and equitably. As a key public good, education provision should be based on need rather than ability to pay. It should also be provided for noneconomic reasons—i.e., education fulfils basic needs that should be satisfied independently of the economic benefits (I. Gough, 2000, Introduction). Incorporating narrower private-sector values into the welfare state risks undermining the noneconomic functions of education and the "ethos" of the public sector (Grimshaw et al., 2002, p. 480).

Conclusion: Increased Corporate Power

When Tony Blair was elected Prime Minister, he promised evidenced-based reforms and a policy agenda that would be informed by "what works" rather than by ideology. If we consider the weight of evidence, education policy appears not to have been driven by "what works," but rather to have been driven by an almost dogmatic approach that has consistently overvalued the contribution of the private sector and undervalued the public sector.

During Tony Blair's period in office, there was an effort to drive education forward on the basis of business' needs, despite the fact that no definitive picture of what these needs are has ever emerged. Openings on management boards and opportunities to establish more formal partnerships have been provided in a range of educational services for a business community that has often been reluctant to take them up. And where business people and firms have become embedded in educational services, in whatever form this has taken, the net result has been at best neutral, and at worst disruptive and financially costly in terms of its impact. Despite the rhetoric, Blair's education policy was not evidence led. Whilst New Labour has been able to identify problems within the public sector, it has been both blind to the failings of the private sector and naive in its approach to business. It has failed to demonstrate a clear understanding of what motivates business interests, informs business views, and influences levels of business involvement in social policy.

And what of Blair's legacy? Despite the problems highlighted above, Gordon Brown has continued to place business centre stage in a whole range of reforms. This isn't surprising given that, during the Blair years, it was often Brown who led the way on initiatives to engage the private sector in education. It was telling that one of Brown's first acts as Prime Minister was to establish senior government posts for several prominent businessmen (*sic*), including Digby Jones and Johan Eliasch, Chairman of the Head sportswear corporation. Few of the lessons of the past have been learned. Yet, following the post-2007 financial crisis, government may yet come to regret its pursuit of business-led solutions to educational failure. After a decade of reforms that looked to the private sector to rescue public services from failure, the state has had to come to the rescue of a private sector in crisis to the tune of billions of pounds. This crisis has, if nothing else, exposed the folly and risks of business-led education reforms.

References

Adburgham, R. (1997) Financial Times Survey: Bristol, *Financial Times*, pp. 13–14.

Audit Commission. (2003) *PFI in Schools: The Quality and Costs of Buildings and Services Provided by Early Private Finance Initiative Schemes*, London: The Audit Commission.

BBC. (2007) *Specialist Schools "No Guarantee"* London, British Broadcasting Corporation. Retrieved January 2010 from http://news.bbc.co.uk/2/hi/uk_news/education/7119022.stm.

BiiC. (2002) *Improving Secondary Education in London: The Business Contribution*, London: Business in the Community.

Blair, T. and Shroeder, G. (1999) *The Way Forward for Europe's Social Democrats*, London: The Labour Party.

CBI. (2005a) *The Business of Education Improvement*, London: Confederation of British Industry.

CBI. (2005b) *Dramatic Educational Improvement Through PPPs Undermined by "Short-Sighted" Government Policy, News Release, 5 January*, London: Confederation of British Industry.

Clarke, J. and Newman, J. (1997) *The Managerial State*, London: Sage.

Clement, B. (2004) "Potters Bar Firm to Get Bonus Just for Doing Its Job," *The Independent* 20 March, p. 8.

CPS. (2003) *Mortgaging Our Childrens' Future*, Sheffield: Centre for Public Services.

Cutler, A. and Waine, B. (1998) *Managing the Welfare State: The Politics of Public Sector Management*, Oxford: Berg.

Dahl, R. (1961) *Who Governs? Democracy and Power in an American City*, New Haven: Yale University Press.

Davies, H. (2002) *A Review of Enterprise and the Economy in Education*, London: HMSO.

DCSF. (2009) 200th Academy Opens a Year Early as Ministers Set Out New Plans to Open Up Programme to New Sponsors, Retrieved September 2009, from http://www.dcsf.gov.uk/pns/DisplayPN.cgi?pn_id=2009_0158.

Department of Social Security. (1998) *New Ambitions for Our Country: A New Contract for Welfare*, London: The Stationary Office.

DfEE. (1998) *The Learning Age: A Renaissance for a New Britain*, London: Department for Education and Employment.

——— (2000) *City Academies: Schools to Make a Difference: A Prospectus for Sponsors and other Parties*, London: Department for Education and Employment.

DfES. (1999) *Survey of School-Business Links in England in 1997/8*, London: TSO.

——— (2001) *Education Action Zones: Annual Report*, London: Department for Education and Skills.

——— (2003) *21st Century Skills, Realising our Potential: Individuals, Employers, Nation*, London: HMSO.

Dickson, M., Germitz, S., Halpin, D., Power, S. and Whitty, G. (2002) Partnerships, New Labour and the Governance of Welfare, in C. Glendinning, M. Powell and K. Rummery (eds), *Education Action Zones*, Bristol: Policy Press.

Falconer, P. K. and McLaughlin, K. (2000) Public-private Partnerships and the "New Labour" Government in Britain, in S. P. Osborne (ed), *Public-Private Partnerships: Theory and Practice in International Perspective* (pp. 120–133), London: Routledge.

Farnsworth, K. (1998) Minding the Business Interest: The CBI and Social Policy, 1980–1996, *Policy Studies*, Vol. 19, No. 1, pp. 19–38.

——— (2004) *Corporate Power and Social Policy in Global Context: British Welfare Under the Influence?* Bristol: Policy Press.

——— (2006). Business in Education: A Reassessment of the Contribution of Outsourcing to LEA Performance, *Journal of Education Policy*, Vol. 21, No. 4, pp. 485–496.

Farnsworth, K. and Gough, I. (2000). The Structural Power of Capital, in I. Gough (ed), *Global Capital, Human Needs and Social Policies*, London: Palgrave.

Farnsworth, K. and Holden, C. (2006) The Business-Social Policy Nexus, *Journal of Social Policy*, Vol. 35, No. 3.

Gosling, T. (2004). *Openness Survey Paper*, London: IPPR.

Gough, I. (1979) *The Political Economy of the Welfare State*, London: Macmillan.

———— (2000) *Global Capital, Human Needs and Social Policies*, Basingstoke: Palgrave.

Grimshaw, D., Vincent, S. and Willmott, H. (2002) Going Privately: Partnership and Outsourcing in UK Public Services, *Public Administration*, Vol. 80, No. 3, pp. 475–502.

Hatcher, R. and Hirtt, N. (1999) The Business Agenda Behind Labour's Education Policy, in M. Allen, C. Benn, C. Chitty, M. Cole, N. Hacher, N. Hirtt and G. Rikowski (eds), *Business, Business, Business: New Labour's Education Policy*, London: Tufness Press.

HMSO. (2003) *Lambert Review of Business-University Collaboration: Final Report*, London: HMSO.

IiE. (1995) *All Their Tomorrows: The Business of Governing*, London: Industry in Education.

Institute of Directors. (2002) *Education and Training: A Business Blueprint for Reform*, London: Institute of Directors.

Korten, D. C. (1995) *When Corporations Rule the World*, London: Earthscan.

Longstreth, F. (1979) The City, Industry and the State in C. Crouch (ed), *State and Economy in Contemporary Capitalism*, London: Croom Helm.

Mann, M. (1993) *The Sources of Social Power. 3 vols. Vol. II: The Rise of Classes and Nation-States, 1760–1914*, Cambridge: Cambridge University Press.

Miliband, R. (1969) *The State in Capitalist Society*, London: Quartet Books.

NEF. (2004) *Degrees of Capture: Universities, the Oil Industry and Climate Change*, London: New Economics Foundation.

Offe, C. (1984) *Contradictions of the Welfare State*, London: Hutchinson.

Offe, C. and Ronge, V. (1984) Theses on the Theory of the State in Offe, C. (ed), *Contradictions of the Welfare State* (pp. 119–129), London: Hutchinson.

Ofsted. (2002) *Inspection of Newcastle Education Action Zone*, London: Office for Standards in Education, HMCIS.

Peck, J. and Tickell, A. (1995). Business Goes Local: Dissecting the "Business Agenda" in Manchester, *International Journal of Urban and Regional Research*, Vol. 19, No. 1, pp. 55–78.

Pike, G. and Hillage, J. (1995) *Education and Business LInks in Avon—Final Report*, Sussex: Institute for Employment Studies, University of Sussex.

Pollock, A. (2004) *NHS PLC*, London: Verso.

Pollock, A., Shaoul J., Rowland D. and Player S. (2001) *Public Services and the Private Sector: A Response to the IPPR*, London: Catalyst.

Ruane, S. (2002) Public-Private Partnerships: The Case of PFI. In C. Glendinning, M. Powell and K. Rummery (eds), *Partnerships, New Labour and the Governance of Welfare*, Bristol: Policy Press.

Sklair, L. (2001) *The Transnational Capitalist Class,* Oxford: Blackwell Publishers.

Slater, J. (2003) *Enemies of the State in Retreat.*

Toolis, K. (2003) Will They Ever Learn, *The Guardian,* November 22.

Treasury Select Committee. (2000) *Fifth Special Report. The PFI: The Government's Response to the Committee's Fourth Report of Session 1999–2000,* London: HMSO.

Wetherly, P. (2005) *Marxism and the State,* London: Palgrave.

Wintour, P. (2003) Brown Urges Universities to Cash in on Business Links, *The Guardian,* December 4.

Chapter 4

Valorisation and the Role of the University under New Labour: Reclaiming the Commons in a Knowledge-based Economy

Molly Bellamy

Introduction

There has been a widely recognised transformation in Higher Education (HE) over the past 12 years under New Labour. It has taken place in relation to a broader picture of transition to a new economic paradigm that has been referred to in epochal terms such as the *knowledge industry, digital capitalism,* the *virtual economy,* and the *learning age.* These terms point to the perception of productive forms that are postfordist, which promote knowledge production and diffusion, and which signpost a consciousness that "material processes in today's economies are increasingly replaced by immaterial processes" (Hermann 2008:1).

Jessop (2002) has theorised an emerging postfordist paradigm as *the knowledge-based economy.* He describes it as the paradigm that "reflects the general importance attributed rightly or wrongly to knowledge as a factor of production in the postfordist labour process, accumulation regime and mode of regulation" (2002:97).

Jessop identifies the need for *different* forms of valorisation in a knowledge-based economy that operates within a complex, globalised, spatial context, in what he refers to as "Economic cyberspace." "Overall this involves re-drawing the boundaries between the economic and extraeconomic such that more of the latter are drawn directly into the process of the valorisation of capital" as part of the emergent commodification of everyday life (2002:188).

In this context, the university is a "social formation," an "extra-economic" dimension playing a role. The modularisation of university programmes and the conversion to credit points, the diversification of qualifications, the public-private partnerships with industry and the business sector, accreditation and validation of organisational learning—all may be seen as vehicles of accumulation that embed the valorisation role of the university.

The state has underwritten risk for capital moving into a previously nonmarket field by providing funding and an assemblage of strategies to drive the sector into a market sphere. This project is delivered in Higher Education through an interpretative framework in what will be referred to as the *learning* lexicon.

More broadly, I argue that New Labour has made some very contentious but clear choices; not least in relation to an economic policy that "was the fatal division that facilitated the triumph of neoliberalism" (Phalley 2004:3), in relation to a contentious foreign policy in 2001, to the nonregulation of the market and a granting of autonomy and collapse of the banking system, and management of the credit crunch crisis since, to the current "industrial reserve army" of students, and in relation to Higher Education; for *lifelong learning* could have gone in a social democratic direction (Frost and Taylor 2001). New Labour has consolidated its neoliberal agenda through the opening up of markets for expanded reproduction through processes of accumulation by dispossession (Harvey 2005), a policy that has closed much of the civil liberty commons of the public sphere and the intellectual commons of education.

Leys's (2003:4) template identifies four stages in the transition of a field from a nonmarket to a market sphere:

> firstly the goods or services must be reconfigured in order to be priced and sold,....Second people must be induced to want to buy them) Third the workforce involved in their provision must be transformed from one working for collective aims with a service ethic to one working to produce profits for owners of capital and subject to market discipline,Finally, capital moving into a a previously non market field needs to have the risk underwritten by the state.

This chapter deploys Ley's template to mark the transition of Higher Education from a non market to a market sphere, under New Labour.

We now turn to the relevance of Marx's Value Theory for the labour process in the knowledge-based economy.

Historicising Marx and Value Theory

A distinct type of labour process characterises the knowledge-based economy that involves flexible production and flexible systems of working. The pressure to extend working hours has increased in relation to a neoliberal restructuralisation of the working day, which entails simultaneous compression and extension of working time for knowledge workers in relation to the new work order (Jessop 2002:108).

According to Marx, an extension of working time and a greater effort on the part of the worker constitute "absolute surplus value." "Surplus value" is the basis for profit in a capitalist mode of production. The basic mechanism of capitalism is the law of value. In his theory of value, Marx establishes two sorts of value: "use value," or the utility of something, and "exchange value," which is determined by the amount of commodified labour incorporated into the object. Without "exchange value" commodities would not be produced for sale, and without "use value" they would not be purchased (Jessop 2002).

As Hermann makes clear (2008) , some postmodern Marxist critics have argued that Marx's "Value Theory" can no longer apply in a knowledge-based economy, as units of knowledge cannot be measured like units of labour in terms of a "socially necessary labour time," because knowledge is an immaterial phenomenon for which there exists no value-creating mechanism. "In post modern capitalism there is no longer a fixed scale that measures value" (Negri and Hardt 2001:356 in Hermann 2008:1). Similarly, Gorz argues (2004: 31 in Hermann 2008:1) that it is not possible to measure the size of "socially necessary labour time" when the nature of that labour is knowledge based, so "the immeasurability of labour leads to the immeasurability of value...." and "thereby brings a crisis of the measurement of value."

There are two points worth pursuing here, in relation to a body of criticism that has arisen around Marx's theories; one that is specific, to do with the "immeasurability of value," implying the crisis of Marx's Value Theory, and one more general, to do with a form of "austere historicism" that attempts to historicise Marx's concepts out of all significance. I shall address these in turn. Firstly, the "immeasurability of value" is a point that Marx raises in relation to Value Theory, when he differentiates between the qualitative aspects of labour such as creativity (abstract labour), and the quantitative aspects of labour (concrete labour), and he claims that they are in effect incommensurable: The work of individuals participating in the same branch of activity and the different kinds of labour are not only quantitatively but also qualitatively different. What is the precondition of a merely quantitative difference between things? The fact that their quality is the same. Thus units of labour can be measured quantitatively only if they are of equal and identical quality(KMSW 1977:361 in McLellan1995:72)

This distinction between "abstract" and "concrete" labour alludes to the character of certain immaterial processes embedded within a capitalist mode of production, which critics such as Negri, Hardt, and Gorz have not here taken into account; in the same way that "abstract" labour is collapsed down into "concrete" labour at the point of exchange—that is, at the point where it becomes a commodity and assumes a value, so "abstract" knowledge, in the form of creativity or innovation, is collapsed down into "concrete" knowledge (such as a data base) at the point of exchange, when it becomes a commodity.

Similarly, Marx challenges the premise of "exchange value" for assuming "the same amount of labour (the worker) has given to society in one form, he receives back in another" (KMSW 77:568). Here, according to Marx, the premise takes an equal standard of labour for granted, whereas workers' capacities, situations, or contexts are not all the same. Once again, Marx's point is that inequality and immeasurability are built into the premise of "exchange value" itself.

In other words, having anticipated the "immeasurability of value" issue that Gorz and Negri and Hardt raise, Marx goes further to emphasise its effect, which is that value gets deflected, for wages are not the value of labour but of labour power, as what the labourer sells is not his labour, nor labour time, but labour power, which:

> both reproduces the equivalent of its own value and also produces an excess, a surplus value which may itself vary, may be more or less according to the circumstances. (Marx *Capital*, Moscow 1954 1:209 in McLellan 1995)

This variation is the rate of surplus value. Variation is also the concept that constructs capitalism as not a static system but a *historically relative system,* according to Marx, wherein value is determined by the circumstances of production, not just demand.

The wider point here, however, is that immaterial processes are part of every capitalist mode of production, whether it is a fordist system or a knowledge-based one. The point missed by Negri, Hardt, and Gorz is that "surplus value" is not created by exchange value, but by the fact that the development of the means of production, including incorporation of knowledge under capitalism, enables the capitalist to "enjoy the use value of the worker's labour power and with it produces values that far exceed the mere exchange value of his labour power" (McLellan 1995:82, emphasis added).

Hence, in the university, the labour power *value* of knowledge workers depends not on knowledge being a commodity in itself, as Negri, Hardt and Gorz assume, but as having acquired a commodity form that operates as *fictitious* capital.

Marx's use of terms such as *fictitious* capital, *abstract* labour, and labour *power* inscribes principles of indeterminacy and uncertainty into the very laws that he himself proposes; note his use of qualifiers in the following statement about the law of value: "the *general* law of value acts as a *prevailing tendency only* in *very complicated and approximate* manner as a *never ascertainable average* of *ceaseless fluctuations*" (*Capital*, 1971, 111:161, emphasis added).

In this sense, Marx's use of linguistic nuance does not reflect so much as construct his theoretical points about immaterial processes, immeasurability, uncertainty, and, more generally, the indeterminacy of laws. If, then, Marx's writing is put into the straitjacket of a stolidly literal translation, or put through the vice of metaphysical dualisms, which serve to reify his ideas, his theoretical points may be misrepresented or missed altogether; *traduttore traditore. (translator-traitor)*

Secondly, a significant corpus of postmodern, post-Marxist criticism often centres around a form of "austere historicism" (Morton 2007:15–38), questioning the possibility of theories or texts that have meaning beyond the historical moment in which they are received. Says Skinner, "The classic texts cannot be concerned with our questions and answers only their own" (1969:50 in Morton 2007:26).

Laclau and Chantal Mouffe (2001:4) argue along just such austere historicist lines in an attempt to reject historical materialism: "it is no longer possible to maintain the conception of subjectivity and classes elaborated by Marxism nor its vision of the historical course of capitalist development."

However, these standpoints are themselves circumscribed by specific historicist interests in relation to the changing critical fashions of the late twentieth century of postmodernism and poststructuralism, against which these critics define themselves (Hamilton 2003). In other words, by projecting an historical essentialism or determinacy, not inscribed by Marx himself, critics may be historicising Marx out of all significance in an effort to promote their own vantage point.

The paradox here lies in what may be lost in the pursuit, which is the way in which Marx's theory presents itself as "open to the indeterminacy and movement of history."

> You cannot make old laws the foundation of a new social development any more than these old laws created the social conditions…Any attempted assertion of the *eternal validity* of laws continually clashes with present needs, it prevents commerce and industry, and paves the way for social crises that break out with political revolutions. (McLellan 1983)

And whilst we can't vault over the project of contemporary theory and its problematising of the grand narrative and totalising theories, as though it had not happened or had not brought fresh insights, neither can we jettison all that took place before the postmodern, poststructuralist project, for that would be to subscribe to the same totalising tendency of which many post-Marxist critics accuse Marx—a tendency towards "austere historicism." Both critics and advocates of Marxism as "a totalising theory," who try to either jettison or preserve Marxism on that premise, do a disservice to Marx, who can still *speak to us* in the particular, if released from the austere historicist vice of the true/false binary.

It is, of course, the case that nineteenth century Western thinkers viewed the world through a different lens than the ones we view it through today. At that time, there was a different consciousness and cognitive framework available through which to read and be in the world that was based on the metaphysical gaze of the Cartesian dualism, which sees language as reflecting a preexisting reality, or as a supplement to the thing itself.

This binary form is a deterministic mode, as it usually privileges one of its terms over the other in a hierarchical relation. The binary literacy was bequeathed to us as part of a legacy from classical philosophy, and it inscribes a set of ontological and epistemological dualisms as part of its cognitive framework: *Reality vs. Appearance, Being vs. Consciousness, Subject vs. Object, Thought vs. Language.*

Necessarily then, Marx writes within this cognitive framework or world view of nineteenth century classicism, so that the literacy and language he uses to explain and argue his theory may well use the binary mode. Hence, the metaphor of the "base and the superstructure" to refer to "being and consciousness" as aspects of a social and economic system of social relations that are linked to a mode of production in a binary relation that privileges "being" (base) over "consciousness" (superstructure). However, contemporary theory has delegitimised the project to which this conceptual scheme belongs; the "grand narrative" and its claim to overarching theoretical apparatuses, its universalising ambition that inscribes an ontological dualism, that privileges the "real" over the "representation," or "being" over "consciousness," or the "base" over the "superstructure," has been deconstructed as a cognitive framework by the postmodern and poststructuralist project of critique, through notions such as the "discursivity of the real" (Bennett 1990). Hence, (Marx's) primacy of the real over the mode of representation is no longer a given theoretically, though it is still struggled over. The implication here is that ideology (superstructure) is not perceived as being produced out of, or emanating from, an a priori set of real economic processes (base) that are external to it, so much as partially constitutive of that process. In other words, according to the poststructuralist canon of critique, ideology is not perceived exclusively as a manifestation of an underlying social and economic reality, so much as being interconnected with it. In effect, contemporary economists use the metaphor of a "network" to refer to our system of social and economic relations "as component parts." As metaphors, the "base and superstructure" and "network" adhere to different conceptual frameworks that inscribe a different historical consciousness, and articulate a different "spatio temporal fix" (Harvey 2005). Their difference frames an ontological distinction, however, both metaphors refer to a system of social and historical relations interconnected with power: the point here is that whilst the concept of "historical materialism" may not be interpreted exclusively in terms of the premise it has traditionally been attributed—that is where in "the capitalist mode of production is the founding of all social conflict"—it continues to articulate the *ways in which* socialising and historicising processes are interconnected with power (Foucault 1980a), and social relations are interconnected with and coconstituted by the mode of production (Hermann 2008), and subjectivities remain (partially) constituted through and constitute the mode of production (Rose 1998, Fairclough 2006, Morton 2007).

In this sense, the concept of "historical materialism" continues to retain a complex and compelling sense for us today (Hall 1983, Jameson 1981, Eagleton 1983, Anderson 1983), just as the limitations of economic determinism were anticipated by Engels in a letter to J. Block on 21 September, 1890: "the economic situation is the basis but the various elements of the superstructure...also exercise their influence upon the course of historical struggle and in many cases preponderate in determining their form. There is an *interaction of all the elements*."[1]

Rather than historicise Marx out of significance then, it is surely more useful to think of the ways in which his ideas clearly *do* speak to us, the value of which may vary from one platform or institution (Bennett 1990, Morton 2007). For me specifically, the "use value" of Marx's theory is in the way it offers a conceptual "coat hanger" and a set of critical tools that do in part and in particular transfer across to the contemporary context of the university; I use Marx's theory here not as a single unifying theory, but as "a co-ordinated set of theoretical strategies" (Ryan 1984 in Bennet 1990), which will help me to analyse the capitalisation of HE under New Labour, and attempt to reclaim the intellectual commons that have been further enclosed by the neoliberal agenda of New Labour.

On another level, the scale and rigour of the empirical research that Marx uses to base his theory on, which inscribes ethical consciousness in economic theory, is unique.

It is therefore not necessary to have to align with or reject Marxism in a totalising way, as we are not tied to a conceptual framework that inscribes a Cartesian binary vice, so it possible to reconceptualise the socialising and historicising system of relations, which Marx articulates with recourse to the metaphor of "the base and the superstructure," through other related lens. In effect, Marx's historical materialist critique of capitalism rests on a *dialectical* understanding of historicism that "austere historicism" negates, wherein the present interacts with the past in relation to the continuities, as well as discontinuities of its legacies, in order to generate new meanings in different contexts; as Femia says: "an insistence on history is one thing; an *a priori* determination to fossilise all past is quite another" (Femia 1981:17 in Morton 2007:32).

Working Time and the Role of the Knowledge Worker

In this dialectical and historical materialist context, Hermann (2008) argues for the validity of value theory as an insight into the *transformation* of work in a digital economy. He states that in the case of low-qualified knowledge workers, the efficient application of labour power can be assured via "bureaucratic control and Tayloristic work organisation... *but for highly qualified knowledge workers* (emphasis added), who are supposed to use their creativity and experience to achieve new tasks or find new solutions to old problems" (2008:3), the assurance of adequate labour power performance is harder to achieve.

Here, employers use performance indicators as a form of measure, but as they are based essentially on attempts to quantify a qualitative dimension, they are not so successful. Other regulative means for valorisation are needed. Thus, strategies of Continuing Professional Development (CPD) are vital. In this sense, Hermann illustrates how value arises not out of material production but out of *immaterial* production, which is an historically contingent phenomenon.

He identifies how contemporary labour processes can be intensified through strategies of benchmarking, lean production management, intensification of deadlines, restructuralisation of departments and redundancies, part-time staff staffing, flexi work, and cutting back on human and other resources in order to reduce the proportion of concrete labour time per unit of output (2008:8). "Cut backs in resources and the reduction of paid working hours to have a job completed along with performance measures have led both to an intensification of work place pressures and a deregulation of workers rights" (Hermann 2008:8).

Regulation is the system that enables these mechanisms of "valorisation" to be effective. Responsibilisation is part of this discourse, wherein highly qualified knowledge workers are more autonomous and take greater responsibility through a work ethic that conflates self with work, and where workers are identified with the results of their work. Given the choice between the hierarchical approach of traditional managerial control and the "self-organisation" option, such workers prefer the latter, even with added stress and unpaid overtime (Hermann 2008:8). This mode of work organisation operates through a set of self/work regulatory techniques to affect a deeply penetrative "self-organised extension of working time."

In the "network paradigm" of the knowledge-based economy, "self-organisation" acts as an organising principle for the economic structure. Self-organisation and self-reliance strategies for organisations, partnerships, and individuals provide interactive ways of participating in "economic cyberspace" that circumvent the potential for or fear of market failure (Jessop 2002). According to Castells, in a network economy, this principle of self-organisation enables networks to share decision making and to decentre performance (Castells 2000 in Jessop 2002:237). It is part of the discourse of "flexibilisation" that appears to work along a continuum of *flexiploitation to flexicurity*, marked, however, by the needs of "the demand side" of industry in the new work order.

Interestingly, "flexibilisation" is also a *fordist* form of work organisation that characterised the poorly paid or unpaid work that was

associated with women in the caring professions and other marginalised sectors, marked by notions of altruism. According to Baines,
women were co-opted into a passive response in relation to their
own working conditions and rightssomething which was problematised by feminists as core to the domination of the labour market by
men (Fraser 2009. Second wave feminists and union activists sought
to contest the practice, calling on Marxist concepts of a gendered
division of labour to argue against the devaluation of "women's work"
and the women themselves. Many of these women workers openly
resisted workplace rules and union policy, *in defiance* of a system that
did not adequately cater for those in need of care. However, it was
these women who established an unpaid overtime culture and a self-
managed workload that has foregrounded the current practice of "a
self-organised extension of working time."

Paradoxically, strategies of intensification of labour, flexibilisation,
unpaid overtime, and self-management—in other words, a *feminised*[2]
labour practice that was considered exploitative—now inform the pre-
ferred work organisation of the knowledge-based economy. What is
of interest here is the manner in which a "feminised" (soft), altruistic,
fordist work ethic is appropriated by a postfordist culture of "workfare" (Jessop 2002) in order to legitimise a policy of *flexiploitation*.
Andrew Sayer has expressed this phenomenon succinctly in terms
of "a soft capitalist mode for achieving hard economic goals such
as profit through the harnessing of cultural norms" (Ray and Sayer
1999:17). It is a nice example of how a formerly problematised work
ethic has been resignified under New Labour as a neoliberal *ideal* of
labour practice. According to Rose (1998), it is "a neoliberal form of
governance that governs through culture". It uses narratives of "turn
to life," "work-life balance," and "lifestyle" to imbue a different kind
of postfordist *work ethic*—to replace the subjectivity of the "suffer-
ing worker" with that of a "satisfied consumerist" (Jackson 1994),
wherein work is construed as a "creative outlet" rather than a "form
of alienation."

Paradoxically also however, the neoliberal ideal of work as a "creative outlet" is the same as Marx's utopian idea of work as "creative
activity." This is at the heart of Marx's vision, in which he sees labour
as the main vehicle for fulfilling a worker's potential as a human
being.[3] What makes his idea utopian is that he wishes it for all workers; in effect, it still remains the privilege of an elite few, potentially
the *highly qualified knowledge workers*, and it is not the experience of
the majority. The horizontal structures of the "network economy" do
not eclipse hierarchical power structures in terms of a global division

of labour, to produce a workforce made up of *lower* and *higher* quali-fied knowledge workers.

This is a nice example of how the "self-organisation extension of working time" in a fordist paradigm, deployed as an exploitative prac-tice for extracting surplus value, is reworked in a postfordist "network paradigm" as an organising principle for the new economy, as a hege-monic mode of regulation or governance and neoliberal ideal. The resignification of this work *ethic* illustrates the historically contingent nature of immaterial production, and extends Marx's genesis of capi-talist modes of production.

There exists a further paradox, wherein the felt *anxiety* that mate-rial processes in today's economies are being replaced by immaterial processes, which operate through a form of digitial capitalism, and speculative finance within a spatio-temporal matrix that accentuates the *virtual* character of our global economy is contained by recourse to *quantifiable measures* for inscribing labour value.

In this audit society, *technes* such as benchmarking, outcomes, performance indicators, and deadlines work collectively to reify the immaterial processes of the knowledge-based economy in ways that reproduce a "methodical distribution of working time between the various branches of production" (KMSW 77:361). As a result, a divi-sion of labour continues to characterise our "knowledge industry," and the legacy of nineteenth century logo-centrism, based on a metaphysi-cal binary of materiality/immateriality, still holds us to account. Marx's insight into the way in which *immaterial processes produce material effects* in a capitalist mode of production brackets this binary concept, in a way that is never more salient than for today's "virtual economy."

To summarise, the section above illustrates how the university valorises working practices that secure the conditions for it to produce an "absolute surplus value" that enables the capitalist or employers to enjoy a use value of the knowledge worker's labour power, *which far exceeds the mere exchange value of their labour power* in a knowledge-based economy.

More broadly it has explored the way in which Marx's Value Theory, applied to the contemporary labour process in Higher Education, extends our understanding of how, according to Leys's template, a shift towards a market sphere has been achieved; by *transforming the workforce* of the university *"from one working for collective aims with a service ethic to one working to produce profits for owners of capital and subject to market discipline."*

We now turn to the universities' role in the commodification of knowledge.

The Commodification of Knowledge and
the University

In the second half of *Capital,* Volume One, Marx contextualises his own era through an historical genesis from a feudalist to a capitalist mode of production that he locates mainly in Britain.

Marx charts the ways in which the "forcible expropriation of the people" takes place in relation to a capitalist mode of production over three centuries, from the 1500s to 1800s, through the spoliation of the Church's property, the theft of the common lands, and the usurpation of feudal and clan property, and he observes: "the clearance and dispersion of the people is pursued by proprietors as a settled principle, as an agricultural necessity, just as trees and brushwood are cleared from the wastes of America or Australia; *and the operation goes on in a quiet business-like way,* etc.—as so many idyllic methods of primitive accumulation" (*Capital* 1990:893, emphasis added).

The relevant point being that primitive accumulation precedes capitalist accumulation, "it is an accumulation which is not the result of the capitalist mode of production but its point of departure," and as such, Marx adds ironically, "plays approximately the same role in political economy as original sin does in theology" (Marx *Capital* 1990, 1:874).

Alternatively "accumulation through dispossession" is the phrase that Harvey (2005) uses to translate Marx's theory of primitive accumulation and its alignments with the enclosing of the commons. The "dual character," says Harvey, of expanded reproduction and accumulation by dispossession "are organically linked, dialectically intertwined" *in Marx's view, so* that where expanded reproduction takes place so too does primitive accumulation. Harvey offers a distinction, however, in saying that opening up paths to expanded reproduction is one thing, accumulation by dispossession is another, and he asks whether the two can be separated. The question is pertinent to the sphere of Higher Education. The adoption by the UK Higher Education of the U.S.-style modular system, which operates through an accumulation of credit points that lead to a qualification, and the upgrading of the UK polytechnics into universities in 1992, combined to create both a framework and an impetus for a "new university" model of Higher Education. This model provided the first step towards the commodification of knowledge, which served as a basis for a "new economy."

For knowledge to acquire a commodity form that is something which *can be priced and sold*, it has to, in some way, be rendered "material." This simple conversion of knowledge into measurable units of credit points has made it possible to turn knowledge into a commodifiable entity, as a form of academic capital.

Along with the credit point system, the introduction of a strategy called Credit Accumulation Transfer Scheme (CATS) opened the way for the transfer of credit points across universities in England, wherein credit points count like promissory notes in a system of exchange. Although slow to gain acceptance by the Higher Education sector, and despite remaining uneven (some universities still do not accept the transfer of credit even amongst its own faculties), the CATS initiative established a framework for credit exchange that has served as the prototype for the Bologna Agreement (ECATS), facilitating learner mobility across Europe, and in turn facilitating labour mobility.

In the same way that Marx speaks of the fictitious nature of the commodity, of capital, of the monetisation of exchange, of the enclosure of land, and the commoditisation of labour power, the commoditisation of *knowledge* is also an example of "fictitious capital."

In themselves, said Marx, in *The Secret of Primitive Accumulation*, "money and commodities are no more capital than the means of production and subsistence are. They need to be transformed into capital" (Marx, *Capital* 1990, 1:874).

Reconfiguring knowledge as a *"goods or service which can be priced and sold,"* then redefines the purpose of both education and knowledge in a *knowledge-based economy* as one designed to:

> ...put the UK ahead of the rest of the world in using new technology to improve *learning* and skills....It will act as a hub of a brand new learning network, using modern communication technologies to link businesses and individuals to cost effective, accessible and flexible education and training. (DfEE 1998:18)

The question here is not whether a different kind of education and training is needed for a knowledge-based economy and a digital age, but whether it can achieve a democratisation rather than a commodification of knowledge.

The section above illustrates the ways in which the university has valorised a system that consists in the modularisation of its programmes and a conversion to credit points, which constructs knowledge as capital, in a move that, according to Leys's template, facilitates a further shift towards a market sphere in which *"the goods or services in question be reconfigured so that they can be priced and sold"*.

We now turn to the capital accumulation regime.

The Qualification Explosion and Market Logic in HE

The transforming of knowledge into a credit system requires a vehicle that can frame its use value. This is in part provided by "the qualification" as a legitimising form that is valorised by the university as a "currency" in the job market of the knowledge-based economy. A "qualification explosion" has accompanied the conversion of knowledge into a commodity form. It serves as a form of diversification and competetivity in a knowledge-based economy, as a screening mechanism for employers.

Credentialism is a term used by American sociologists, along with "qualificationism" or "qualification earning," to signify a utilitarian application of and motivation for the qualification as "a means to an end," "a process of certificating," a "passport to a job," or "status." Dore (1997) uses these terms in a critical account of how the project of education was harnessed to the objective of economic growth in modernisation programmes for developing countries in the 1950s and 1960s. In a strategy of human investment, the notion of a "social rate of return" provided the legitimising discourse that tied education into economic growth in much of the adjustment programmes policy. The logic was based on an assumed correlation between the amount of time invested in an individual's education and their (future) earning power and economic value to society. Rhetorically, the investment metaphor expresses the logic that education through certification "enhances the capacity to alter the price at which an individual can sell their labour" (Dore 1997:93).

What is of particular relevance about Dore's research to us is the extent to which the underlying logic of human resource as *investment* has been reproduced and reapplied in contemporary Higher Education, in the "Modernisation of Higher Education" White Paper (2004), albeit resignified within a neoliberal discourse.

The notion of investment coincides with the new managerialist discourse that "more is better"—a *techne* that is perceived to operate, irrespective of context, on the premise that "more and better management" can "fix" the problem (Clarke 2000). This has become a very powerful discourse which constructs itself as *value free*, as acting *transparently* by *reflecting* the degree of applied good management to the context. This function of management, as panacea having universal applicability, appeals at a common sense level. "Managerialese" inscribes ethics of economy, efficiency, effectiveness, and *disinterest*. It is the "best practice" with which to imbue a very plausible set of goals for *transforming* the economy. Thus, the more (*learning*) one invests in humans, the better they will perform as resources for the nation or global economy. Human "worth," therefore, is construed in the same "social rate of return" logic that inscribed an economistic purpose and premise for education, which was used in what used to be termed "Third World Development," and which, in Dore's account, was seen to have failed. The contemporary version of this stolidly literal "human investment" logic may be summarised thus: the more learning an individual, organisation, or country possesses, the more competitive, productive, or successful it will be (CIHE *Workforce Development* 2005).

In a climate of credentialism, in which the qualification counts as a "positional good"—something whose value is not intrinsic but depends on how many other people have it (Dore 1997)—we witness the same kind of "qualification inflation and deflation" trends as experienced by developing countries in the twentieth century. In both instances, qualifications are produced within a market discourse of competitivity in relation to a need for a complexity of qualifications that differentiate status and provide a screening mechanism for employers. For instance, "Qualification inflation-deflation" has occurred throughout the post-14 sector, in relation to *the demand from industry* for a basic requirement of five A-C GCSE passes from pupils in school (Allen and Ainley 200:8, and a demand from industry for a basic requirement of graduate skills to make graduates employable, which affect a reordering of the HE sector along neoliberal lines.

Tens of thousands of graduates are facing unemployment, to which the government has responded with a "rescue package" of an internship scheme, wherein graduates work at a wage just above the current loan system (£2,835) to gain experience. Predictably, major companies are narrowing their search for graduates to a small number of "elite" universities: *Oxford, Cambridge, LSE, UCL,* and *Imperial* (not those attended by British Minority Ethnic [BME] groups, migrant, or working-class students). Competition is extremely high, and it has a knock-on effect on those with no or lower qualifications in a climate predicting that three million people of all ages will be unemployed by the end of 2009, 40 percent of whom will be under the age of 25 (Guardian 10/1/09).[4]

As we witnessed with the subprime mortgage phenomenon in the recent credit crunch, devalued assets in one circuit can be turned around as a fresh basis for capital accumulation in another. So we see with our graduate population via the government's short-term use of a "rescue package" internship scheme; here, the government pays graduates below minimum wage to "gain experience" in industry, which effectively serves to hold down wages in the primary circuit by releasing an immediate set of assets in the form of labour power. This can be turned into immediate profitable use by creating what Marx called an "industrial reserve army" of highly qualified cheap labour, whilst deferring the graduates' entry into the real job market, and so redirecting capital into the secondary or tertiary circuits. In this way, the state has *underwritten the risk of an overaccumulation crisis* that may affect industry by creating a "rescue package," which will benefit both the employers and the circulation of capital, through a process of accumulation by dispossession, by disenfranchising graduates and devaluing graduate*ness*.

Similarly, the diversification of qualifications acts as a strategy to produce a qualification *market* that operates according to a capitalist *logic* of uneven and combined development across circuits—by producing an *overaccumulation* of qualifications (amongst young graduates particularly in the new university), and by identifying "new outlets" for qualifications amongst the predominantly white, male middle-aged middle classes through the introduction of professional doctorates,[5] effectively producing a surplus of educated labour power. Diversification has occurred in relation to a recruitment drive for teaching assistants in 2004, which drew predominantly from the former colonies; these professional teachers had to retrain in England at international fee and visa rates, whilst effectively being dispossessed of their own intellectual capital as professionals by not having their overseas qualifications recognised. The diversification strategy has also produced a *scarcity* of qualifications amongst the economic migrant classes, through the closure of free English as a Second Other Language (ESOL) programmes in 2007 (Mackney 2007).

These closures serve to freeze migrant labour mobility in an economic crisis leading to a loss of labour rights, which are enshrined in European labour law, for adequate training. The move reflects the increasing restrictions on immigration at a national and global level. In 2007 the enforced closure of institutions for adult *learning* led to 750,000 adult places being lost (Mackney 2007), in a move which has rescinded the right to an education that is not based on "qualification"; the distinction that Harvey offers between the opening up of paths to expanded reproduction and accumulation through dispossession is not evident here.

Rather, the uneven and combined development of the "qualification market" reflects the geopolitical character of a neoliberal global economy wherein "the surpluses of capital and labour power that exist in one area can be sent elsewhere to find outlets for profitable realisation where the surplus that is available in one territory is marked by the lack of supply in another" (Harvey 2005). In effect, the flows of "knowledge capital" in the form of qualifications may be likened to those of "money capital," and operate similarly according to a model explained as "capital bondage" (Harvey 2005). Here, capitalism depends on the ability of (financial or state) institutions to switch the flows of capital between three primary secondary and tertiary circuits in this uneven yet combined way. The qualification explosion valorised by the university operates according to this market logic.

New Technologies for Capital Accumulation: The University as a Spinning Jenny

Market logic is also inscribed through Higher Education research policy, as a Society for Research in Higher Education (SRHE) conference theme makes clear.

> ...the University prescribes an increasingly "bespoke and work based curriculum" which "demands flexibility and informal structures" and promotes "relationships between universities and employers," and redraws "the boundaries between the University and other learning institutions such as Further Education colleges," in order to "expand provision through private and corporate universities and other organisations," so as to redraw the "connections between education employment and trade," and reconfiguring knowledge in terms of "knowledge as created in its applied context (mode 2 professional). (SRHE conference theme 2009)

New vehicles for this capital accumulation come in the form of the accreditation and validation of organisational and sector-based learning. Within this project, the university accredits or validates the in-house "know-how" of organisations or sectors. Programmes are written and delivered by the organisation or sector, which then seeks formal recognition from the university. Accreditation and validation of organisational learning may involve "staff development schemes" or Continuing Professional Development (CPD) content, such as *"Leadership, Management, and Change"* or *"Coaching and Mentoring,"* accredited at the undergraduate or postgraduate level. The organisations need validation from the university, plus valorisation that is *recognition* from a bonafide authority, for "brand-name" status, which will make their product marketable. HEFCE funding dovetails with employer-led education projects, so as to have the risk run by the organisations of moving capital into what was formerly a nonmarket domain, underwritten by the government.[6]

At the time of writing, *state* universities have the monopoly on degree-awarding powers, though this is changing, precisely because of the uneven and combined dynamics that the capitalisation of the sector entails. The state university's role of valorisation already competes with many of the professional associations and bodies that characterise a distinctly British profile of what a profession is deemed to be (Lester 2003).Architecture (RIBA) and accountancy (ACCA) propose alternative routes to the world of work through apprenticeship schemes that run parallel pathways independent of the university, and which attract school leavers as well as graduates. These professions are capitalising on the current capping of university places which seriously restricts access to thousands of potential students and on the increased costs of a university degree, which leaves a bigger market for the professions from which to recruit and progress young people. This competition, coupled with HEFCE's planned, phased withdrawal of funding, nudges the new university towards engaging with market sphere initiatives, such as these public-private partnerships (PPPs), in an attempt to find *independent sources of income* that come neither from HEFCE nor the student fee source. HEFCE funding has made provision for specialised business and marketing teams to become part of the university structure, with the specific task of developing this kind of PPP with the business sector and industry.[7]

Organisational learning accreditation activity often brings a redistribution of the knowledge capital because the tacit knowledge that is possessed by the knowledge workers of the organisation is made explicit, and it is turned into a form of intellectual property for the organisation. It happens as part of a market discourse that is encapsulated by the theory of "Structural Capital" (Stewart 2001), the objective being that the "know-how" of the organisation remains in-house, and is not "lost" if the knowledge worker leaves. This creates a form of *learning* power that provides a basis for surplus capital to be utilised by the employing *organisation*. The knowledge workers themselves gain certificates of academic credit, deemed to hold "currency" (or subsidence) in a knowledge-based economy, and to be exchangeable in a Credit Accumulation and Transfer Scheme (CATS).

In effect, the knowledge worker becomes dispensable to the organisation itself.

Sector-based learning provides a discrete sphere for expanded reproduction as emerging professional fields present themselves for accreditation. Here, whole sectors may seek to establish a qualification structure to represent professionals at undergraduate and postgraduate level in a bid to professionalise their sector through CPD directives from the European Union (Driver Education Sector), or from UK statutory bodies (Teaching Development Agency), or from the private/corporate sector drivers for innovation and creativity (National Outsourcing Association).[8]

This is a nice example of how a social democratic value has been spun into a neoliberal ideal, shifting emphasis in accreditation— hitherto a potentially emancipatory mechanism that facilitates access to those individuals who are conventionally excluded from the sector of Higher Education, as used in 1997—to accreditation as a vehicle for capital accumulation and source of independent revenue. This gives voice to industry through sector-based and organisational learning claims. An attractive feature for the second and third tiers of the Higher Education sector is that in this form, accreditation brings increased revenue beyond the usual intellectual property terrain of copyright and licences (e.g., of biochemistry), more usually the terrain of the elite universities, and it provides an independent stream of income for the sector.

Thus, the university acts as a modern-day "spinning jenny," turning the base metal of tacit knowledge, or the *learning power* of the knowledge workers, into gold for the employers, in an employer-led education sector.

Like the wood of Marx's table, once knowledge becomes commodified, it changes into "a thing which transcends sensuousness and begins dancing of its own free will," wherein it becomes reified and alienated. The impact of capitalism on the raw material turns "the sensuous thing"—be it wood or *learning* capacity or already working knowledge—into "something grotesque" and ascribes, says Marx: "a mystical character not arising from its use value but its commodification"....."I call this the fetishism which attaches itself to the product of labour as soon as they are produced as commodities" Marx (Capital 1990:163).

These new vehicles of accreditation are made possible primarily through the valorising role of the university, which, in these ways, enables a shift towards a market sphere, wherein, according to Leys's template, "*the goods or services in question must be reconfigured so that they can be priced and sold and people must be induced to buy them*".

We turn now to the pedagogical framework of the university.

Commodified Self and Higher Education:
The *Learning* Lexicon

One of the key ways in which the university is responsible for securing the conditions for the valorisation of knowledge capital in a knowledge-based economy has been through the embedding of a framework for a new pedagogy. A different pedagogical lexicon was needed for New Labour to achieve a successful transition from a nonmarket to a market sphere, which, according to Leys's template, involves producing services *people must be induced to buy.*

Learning has provided the lexicon through which to deliver this project.

"Flexibility" is what most characterises the *learning* lexicon. Here, the stem of the verb *to learn* acts as a flexible touchstone for the entire user-friendly schema. *Learning* heralds a new nomenclature to "do" or "be" in Higher Education, which is through performing the self: *the autonomous learner, the distance learner, the learner-managed learner, the lifelong learner, the e- learner, the reflective learner,* in the learning organisation and learning society.

The *learning* lexicon specifies student subjectivities through the academic and professional literacies of lifelong learning. These literacies inscribe a combination of a citizen/stakeholder subjectivity, an entrepreneur of the self-subjectivity, and a self-regulatory subjectivity, in which the self is often written in the (pro)active voice through the use of *I* .The *I* of many of the "learning style" technologies is cousin to the *I* of the 'fast capitalist literacies' (Gee and Lankshear 1997) of market democracy that inform the work place, the social sphere of citizenship, and the institutions of education that our students frequent. Repeated practice of this *I* creates and reinforces an ethic for self-agency in a discourse that construes the self as a fixed and continuous subject through history. Self-agency, as inscribed by the active voice through the use of *I*, is the imperative that informs the essentialist mode of the learning style questionnaire instruments, such as those designed variously by *Honey and Mumford, Dunn and Dunn , Chris Jackson , Ehrmanand Learer,* which generally identify the four "VAKT" cardinal styles: visual, auditory, kinaesthetic, and tactile.

Compare below an example from a learning style questionnaire, and a claim for experiential learning made by an undergraduate student in work-based learning.

Table 1   Entrepreneur of the Self Subjectivity

Learning Style Questionnaire	Claim for experiential learning
My plans almost always lead to success. I am sure of achieving most of my goals. I am confident that I will succeed. Experience suggests I achieve hard goals.	During my role as Head Teaching Assistant, undertaking a degree in work-based learning to develop professional practice, I have gained an ability to organise my time and energy to optimum effect along the way. This time-management skill is something which I have also been able to transfer over to my personal life, for example I know how to spend quality time with my children and family, choose the best options for their education, and take a proactive role as a parent-governor. In this way, I ensure I achieve a good work-life balance, which is crucial for a professional woman and mother.

Note: Both inscribing Goal oriented achievement![9]

Here, the "bullet-point," "self-help," "twelve-step" literacy of personal/professional *agency* that characterises market democracy converges with the formulaic schema that characterise *audit* and *new managerialism*, through strategies of "self-managed learning" and through "diagnostic tools" such as the *learning style questionnaire*.

This "can-do," "pop" literacy that informs the knowledge-based economy eschews all complexity and differentiation, wherein the *I* worker, *I* learner, and *I* citizen become "enjoined" across the spheres of work, education, and citizenry to realise "techniques of the self." The essentialising character of this literacy affects a quasi-behaviouralist trope. The effect is achieved in the way that the "student" in the former field of education, as a social practice, is reconfigured in this discourse as an individual learn*er*, practition*er*, stakehold*er*, through academic literacies inscribing a disinterested positionality and economistic subjectivity. Here, the spheres themselves appear to collapse into one economistic mode (du Gay 1997) as these new literacies interpolate a *will to selfhood* that makes available a new site for the expanded reproduction of academic capital, by providing a new portfolio of narratives through which to *valorise the self* as a worker-learner-citizen.

Governmentality is a Foucauldian notion concerned with the ways in which internal structures of knowledge and discourse are produced in relation to power, and the effects of power on

individuals. Rose (1998) brings this notion into the present debate
of education through a focus on "the regime of selfhood." Thus,
after Foucault, selfhood is at the centre of contemporary systems
and formations of regulatory practice, such as those outlined in
this chapter. These "technologies of self" are the vehicles for "the
conduct of conduct." If the principle *ethic* of the *learning* lexicon
inscribes *self*-regulation (in the guise of self-agency), the principle
effect is articulating governance. It construes learning, teaching,
and assessment as a system for meeting targets, which are identified in relation to learning *deficits,* specified against curriculum
benchmarks, audited via assessment criteria that are linked to learning outcomes, and institutionalised by statutory frameworks such
as *Learning, Teaching, and Assessment Strategies* (LTAS). This
triangular framework allows no space for unanticipated learning
or teaching, in a closed system , where emergent learning is not
permitted or does not count —because in order to count, it must
be anticipated, measured, and auditable. It perpetuates its own
practice and preserves institutional structures that lend themselves
to practices of self-regulation. Designed to "raise standards," it
effectively standard*ises,* not only the curriculum that is aligned to
employability, but pupil and teacher *behaviours* also.[10] In effect, it
is a framework rather than a curriculum that draws on the regulatory structures of accounting—at the heart of which is fraud. Says
Power (1994): "Audit constitutes a normative influence—its power
is in its benchmarking potential for all other practices involving
constant checking and verification as the ruling principle."

Under New Labour, audit has become a driving force for modernisation, implemented in HE chiefly through human resource
management and quality assurance practice, which has inscribed
an Eichmann-like propensity for instrumentation over the past
12 years: *Institutional Audits, Reviews, and Quality Monitoring
Reports* are part of the familiar infrastructure for monitoring faculties across the university. At a microlevel, *Learning, Teaching, and
Assessment Strategies* provide a vehicle for administering a plethora
of customer satisfaction instruments, such as the national *student
feedback questionnaire,* which is fed into university *league tables* all
over the country and used as criteria for funding. LTAS also provide
a plethora of standardised instruments to regulate individual performance through *appraisal forms, mentoring templates, peer-review
frameworks, teaching observations, work-programme plans, shared
online diaries,* and *teaching fellowships*—means of micromanaging
the knowledge worker through a system of *learning, teaching, and*

assessment in a discourse that conflates transparency with self-agency and excellence.

> Regulatory practices which seek to govern individuals in a way more tied to their self hood than ever before...wherein...the ideas of identity and its cognates have acquired an increased salience in so many of the practices in which human beings engages.... (Rose 1998: 4)

At a macro level, regulatory practice is best framed by three key shifts in HEFCE policy: from a *lifelong learning* (1997–2004) emphasis on the individual as *homo economies*, to a *workforce development* (2004–2006) emphasis on national competitivity in a global society, to, more recently, an *employer-led education* (2006–2008) emphasis on a neoliberal model of "workfare" (Jessop 2002) that privileges the supply side of industry, in a project enshrined by the *Leitch Report* of 2006.

These policies signpost a gradual shift in emphasis from employ-*ment* to the employ*er*, synonymous with a shift of education as a sector from a *non*market to a market sphere. Such molecular shifts in emphasis in HEFCE's policy over the 12 years in office of New Labour have achieved far-reaching and material effects. At a European level, this practice is implemented through *lifelong learning* policy, which embeds Quality Assurance (QA) as one of its key strategies. The European Association for Higher Education (EAHE) identifies an aim for "mutually shared criteria and methodologies on quality assurance" (Fairclough 2006).

In this way, HRM and QA act as the *machinery* at the centre of the *new* global technology through which academic and human capital is put into motion and governed. It is part of the mode of production of the knowledge-based economy, and the "extraeconomic" social formation that the university embodies. Says Marx: "every special historic mode of production has its own special laws of population historically valid within its limits alone" (62) (Marx's *Grundisse* (ed) McLellan 1971:62 in McLellan 1995). This is what Harvey (1999) calls the "spatio-temporal fix," a matrix that has to do with the circulation of (knowledge), capital within the temporally and spatially contingent cycles *that are specific to each epoch*.[11]

More broadly, the postfordist mode of production *combines* the means for "capital flows" as the vehicle for expanded reproduction *with* governance—across the UK, Europe, and beyond—via the donor agencies of the European Commission and the World Bank.[12] In a project that articulates the global market, *lifelong learning* embeds and embodies *the* interpretative framework for its accumulation regime.

The principle effect of the *learning* lexicon has been to produce a distinct proselytisation of learning that has accompanied the objective of widening participation; whereas the project of lifelong learning was initially felt to be an emancipatory discourse (Frost and Taylor 2001), it has increasingly become the framework through which to deliver the neoliberal project that has taken Higher Education from a nonmarket to a market sphere. It has served to resignify the social practice that formerly characterised the field of education, by flattening out all contours and complexity of the social, and collapsing education into one single signified stem so that, for example, in terms of its nomenclature, in place of *student, pupil, child, scholar,* we have "the learne*r*," and in place of *English as a Second Other Language student,* we have the "distance learner." In place of *teacher, lecturer, academic, professor,* we have the "learning facilitator," and in place of *study, research, education, epistemology, pedagogy, theory,* and not least the *curriculum,* we have the simple collective noun "learning."

A material effect of the *learning* lexicon is that the *social legacy* of all the "cumbersome" terms in italics above—with their condensed associations of historical struggle, intellectual engagement, political movement, economic and academic status, and *lived* context—becomes eviscerated by its grammar, banalised, as the social dimension, the geopolitical and the historical dimension that has characterised Higher Education in the UK as having a social purpose, is effectively removed.

In this way, the learning lexicon has served to restructure a pedagogical framework around an organising discourse of *selfhood,* which, under a neoliberal mantle, inscribes a self-interested, individualistic, consumerist ethic. In a postfordist, capitalist mode of production, the *self* acts as the new "opium of the masses" after Marx, or the site for "governmentality" after Foucault, or the "governance of the soul" after Rose.

The focus of the section above shows how small regulatory practices act as forms of valorisation and governance for the "molecular process of capital accumulation" (Harvey 2005:90). It extends our understanding following Leys's framework about how a further shift by the sector of Higher Education towards a market sphere has been achieved. It goes some way to explaining why the academic *workforce* has so little resisted the transformation. *Trasformismo,* according to Gramsci (1975) explains the phenomenon of *passive revolution,* through which it was the passive nature of the Italian majority that enabled a minimal hegemony to be sustained in 1920 Italy as the vehicle for the rise of fascism (Morton 2007). It is not hard to draw a parallel between such minimal hegemony and the rise of neoliberalism in twenty-first century England.

We now turn to the legacy that New Labour inherited, and has left to us.

New Labour's Legacy

In a critical account of neoliberalism, Harvey notes, "the genius of Reagan and Thatcher was to create a legacy and a tradition that tangled subsequent politicians in a web of constraints from which they could not easily escape....so that those who followed like Clinton and Blair could do little more than continue the good work of neoliberalisation, whether they liked it or not" (Harvey 2005:63).

However, the section below summarises some of the distinct *choices* made by New Labour, in relation to the transition of the sector of Higher Education from a nonmarket to a market sphere.

The tripartite project amongst the state, industry, and the university has secured the conditions for the valorisation of capital and the reproduction of labour power for the "molecular process of capital accumulation" (Harvey 2005, after Marx) in the following ways:

The state has underwritten any risk for capital being moved into what was formerly a nonmarket sphere. It has achieved this by choosing a neoliberal economic policy that "was the fatal division that facilitated the triumph of neo liberalism" (Phalley 2004:3), which facilitates strategies for expanded reproduction through accumulation by dispossession. It has withdrawn HEFCE funding from the new university and established alternative funding schemes that promote employer-led initiatives, which have increasingly tied the university into PPP projects that produce surplus value in ways that privilege industry. It has produced policy initiatives, such as the *Dearing Report, the Leitch Report, CETLs, workforce development, employer-led education,* and a series of *White Papers,* designed to drive the sector of Higher Education into the market sphere. It has abandoned the idea of a training levy or tax on companies or industry in an "employer-led" education system. It has established regulatory labour practice within the university via vehicles of HRM and QA designed to produce a distinct type of labour process that creates a "self-organised extension of the working day." It has promoted intellectual property rights by enclosing the intellectual commons to create further opportunity for accumulation by dispossession. It has used direct intervention via initiatives such as compulsory "graduate skills" or internship schemes, which protect industry from the problems of overaccumulation. It has sought to change the culture of Higher Education via discursive and regulatory practice, producing material effects that go beyond "just discourse" (12).

The main concern here is the way in which it has underwritten risk for capital being moved into what was formerly a nonmarket sphere by privileging an accumulation regime over the educational project. As Higher Education is the last hurdle within the nonmarket sphere, after health and broadcasting, this move to introduce strategies for profit and commercial practice into a sector that had previously been spared is significant, as it shifts the balance of power between government and the corporate sphere to consolidate a neoliberal hegemony.

Against this background, it has been difficult for the project of "widening participation" to achieve the democratisation of Higher Education that the left had hoped for when New Labour came to power, for although there *has* been a widening of participation in Higher Education than ever before, in terms of the number of people who can now access Higher Education in the UK (and this is most welcome), the expansion has been uneven, as we have seen, and everywhere accompanied by new enclosures of the intellectual and educational commons, both in terms of who gets included and who gets excluded—as the prognosis of 200,000 would-be students who are likely to be left without places in UK universities this year tells us. In this system, new forms of capital accumulation, new forms of valorisation, and new sites for governance, such as credentialism, quality assurance, and citizenship, combine to effect a reordering of the HE sector along neoliberal lines.

Industry has ensured that its voice has grown in the sector of HE in order to meet its own short-term needs, through polices that range from *flexiploitation to flexicurity* (Jessop 2002) in a culture of "workfare" that privileges the demand side. The main concern, however, is the way in which it has used this freedom to expand reproduction via methods of accumulation by dispossession, without impunity.

The university has acted as an "extraeconomic social formation" a catalyst through which to *valorise* a wide range of economic enterprises and practices for the knowledge-based economy culminating in *the embedding* of a new pedagogical framework for a global economy. What is in question here is the extent to which its role as "extraeconomic" has been colonised by a market logic wherein the university serves like a "spinning jenny" to *spin* social democratic values (of emancipation) into neoliberal ideals. And the extent to which, in securing the "extraeconomic" conditions for capital accumulation, it has contracted into a division of labour that is modelled on an increasingly global division of labour, characterised by unequal working conditions and a deeply penetrative "self-organised extension of working time." The chief concern here is the extent to which it has contributed to a commodification rather than a democratisation of knowledge. This raises the question of the extent to which the "extraeconomic" role of the university has helped to achieve a minimal hegemony that is neoliberal in character, not least by conceding leadership of the university to the employers. Also in consideration, of course, is the extent to which the university has engaged with this market logic *in ways not always according to its choosing.*

The discursive effects of what has come to be called the "spin factor" is perhaps what most characterises the legacy that New Labour has left us; it is a paradox, like the allegory of the empty wheelbarrow, as whilst we are all checking the wheelbarrow for the stolen tools being smuggled out of the building site, what is actually being stolen from us are the wheelbarrows themselves. Here, the wheelbarrow serves as a metaphor, in true Marxist tradition, for the intellectual, educational, and civic liberty commons, which have been become increasingly enclosed under New Labour's four terms. The transitional space that New Labour has represented, between one century and another, one government and another, one form of capitalism and another, and one proposed sphere and another, has offered the left potential points of entry to smuggle in change—hence the reelections of New Labour over four terms. There were moments in these transitional spaces when we might have claimed certain freedoms. But, like the "free workers" in Marx's account of the movement from a feudal to a capitalist mode of production, no sooner were we emancipated from the "fetters of the guilds" of Thatcherism and Reagan, the free market, and an Ivory Tower elitism in the UK university *by New Labour,* than we were robbed of our commons *and* lost the guarantees of welfare afforded by the old arrangement. Working-class students had access to Higher Education for the first time in history *only after* the grant system turned to a loan system and the fees were increased. Workers were able to take ownership of their work through "self-organisation" frameworks *only after* the introduction of new regulatory measures of "flexiploitation." Access and the democratisation of Higher Education through the route of "experiential learning" and work-based learning were formally established *only after* employer-led education policy was introduced with funding. The university was able to engage in creative partnership with business and industry *only after* HEFCE funding had been withdrawn. And lifelong learning was hijacked by the neoliberal stagecoach before it had a chance to go in a different direction. Marx's genesis, a history of the worker through different modes of production, is extended through these contemporary forms of expropriation.

Genesis is a metaphor for legacy, for the way transitions to a new order exist along a continuum wherein some traces of the old order are retained and refashioned, and others are discontinued. According to Marx's theory, the economic structure of contemporary capitalist society has grown out of the economic structure of Thatcher's and Reagan's society; "the dissolution of the latter set free the elements of the former." (Marx *Capital* 1990 1:875)

In effect, whilst different models of capitalism emphasise different roles for the market and the state (fordism, liberalism, neoliberalism) and produce different structures of horizontal or vertical chains of command and control (the Keynesian model or Castells's global net-working model), and whilst different modes of production operate within a different "spatio-temporal matrix," which compresses time and space and capital flows in ways that are historically contingent, these variations of capitalism also share certain immutable character-istics that can be evoked with recourse to Marx's enduring metaphors. Not least of these is capitalism as an indomitable force, as contem-porary economists continue to construe it in terms of *unleashed, unstoppable, unbridled,* or in terms of "vulture capitalism," a modern expression of the predatory nature of accumulation by dispossession, and a derivative of the passage in *Capital* in which Marx denounces the synthesis between capital accumulation and the exploitation of the labourer, who is "riveted to capital more firmly than the wedges of the Vulcan (did) Prometheus to the rock" (Marx, 1954: 645 in McLellan 1995: 85).

In terms of its legacy, whether New Labour has achieved its *Third Way* ideal of free market economics and social justice will be judged by history and/or the coming elections. In terms of the university, New Labour has achieved a capitalisation of the HE sector and a valo-risation role that is constitutive of a qualification and accreditation *market* process, which articulates a neoliberal global economy.

Conclusion: Reclaiming the Commons

In this chapter, I have indicated the ways in which the knowledge-based economy provides the framework for a market-led transition towards a new capital regime under New Labour, in the form of "a primary accumulation regime, a mode of societalisation, and mode of regulation" that is neoliberal in character.

I have discussed the ways in which the university has acted as an "extraeconomic" dimension in the knowledge-based economy, securing the conditions for the valorisation of capital and the reproduction of labour power, in relation to a market logic that produces accumulation by dispossession strategies that culminate in the enclosing of the intellectual and civic liberty commons.

I have considered the ways in which a lexicon of *learning* provides the interpretative framework for this accumulation regime, by inscribing both an economistic subjectivity and a mode of regulation and labour process that produces "a self-organised extension of working time."

I have argued that New Labour governance has resignified the "emancipatory promise" of social democratic values as neoliberal ideals; ideals that are enshrined in HEFCE policy via "molecular shifts of emphasis" that produce "molecular processes of capital accumulation," which have moved Higher Education towards a market sphere over the four terms of New Labour. I indicate, following Leys (2003:224), that what is at stake in this shift is the project of democracy itself—"if the collective services on which democracy depends, gradually decay."

On another level, I have tried to reclaim some of the Marxist commons that we have lost in the move to a market sphere by using some key Marxist concepts for an analysis of contemporary Higher Education under capitalism, not least in relation to the labour process. I have illustrated, after Hermann, how *Value Theory* remains a significant point of reference for an understanding of the regulatory practice of knowledge workers in the new work order. I have argued against the rhetorical practice of "austere historicism" that seeks to fossilise Marx's ideas out of all significance, and against the use of a Cartesian binary lens that inscribes a totalising perspective. I have argued that the concept of "historical materialism" continues to hold relevance for the twenty-first century as a socialising and historicising system of relations, and I have celebrated the way in which, for Marx, economics and ethics are inextricably linked.

I have argued that the current neoliberal project of education in the UK is hegemonic, in the Gramscian sense, in that the abstraction of the social is assumed to be natural. It cannot, therefore, be addressed through a proposal for an alternative kind of university *model,* such as the "liquid university," the "therapeutic university," or a "new kind of metaphysical university" (Barnett 2009). A different *hegemonic* paradigm to the current neoliberal one has to be achieved, as the university cannot be split off from the economy, nor is there an option to return to the elitist system of the so-called "Ivory Tower." It has to be possible to combine research and curriculum with business development and enterprise, in a new economy and a digital age that *opposes a capitalist logic for all spheres of life*. For this to occur, the university, and not the employers, has to lead on the project of education. Our particular task as academics is to confront the neoliberal turn of the university whilst remaining part of Higher Education and embracing the digital age. We have to foster a critical, reflexive position towards the market forces that have penetrated Higher Education, which reproduce an increasingly global division of labour, and redress the current narrow, instrumentalist vision of *employer-led education* that tilts towards a market ideology. We have to find a new lexicon and academic literacy for education that reclaims the social and establishes a curriculum that sustains the principle of democracy, whilst engaging with industry in ways that democratise rather than commoditise learning.

The role of the university in the new economy is surely to work towards an hegemony that is *not* based on a neoliberal market logic, but which looks to a knowledge-based *society* and the reclaiming of the intellectual commons; only in this case might expanded reproduction without accumulation by dispossession, or in Marx's terms, without primitive accumulation, be achieved. The recession and its management are unlikely to enhance the prospects for reclamation without wider social movement.

Notes

1. Engels's letter to J. Block on September 21, 1890, cited in N.I Bukarin, *Historical Materialism* New York 1925 London. Quoted in *The Fontana Dictionary of Modern Thought* edited by Alan Bullock and Oliver Stallybreass and Stephen Trombley 1988.
2. The term "feminised" is usually used in relation to a sphere of work or profession that has become populated by women (Leys/Fraser/Baines). I intend it here in terms of a "feminised" work ethic, or practice, such as altruism.
3. For a fuller discussion of this point please see Sayer, S. 2003 in *Creative Activity and Alienation in Hegel and Marx* in Historical Materialism 11.1.
4. As we have seen this prognosis has been borne out, whilst the demand for university places increases and supply decreases as the net reduction

in student numbers for 2010–2011 has been confirmed by HEFCE , the result it says of the government's decision to withdraw the 10,000 unfunded emergency places. Lord Mandelson's cuts will affect the young people from the disadvantaged areas first as thousands of places are lost. (THES Times Higher Education Supplement, 4–10 February 2010).

5. In the introduction to this book Professor David Boud and Alison Lee (2008) state how Professional Doctorates and other practice-based doctorates are commonly profession specific, and more generally aimed at midcareer professionals, or used as advanced training grounds for professional groups; they offer a range of alternatives for knowledge making and credentialising. The predominance of white, middle-class and middle-aged males in Professional Doctorates is evidenced in the Standard Reports on student profiles from Middlesex University.

6. The accreditation of organisational and sector-based learning dovetails with one of the prime ways in which HEFCE allocates its funding, providing one way for the new university to "grow its contract" by bidding for cofunded "additional student numbers" in the **cofunded** area of employer-led education. These cofunded numbers are currently ring fenced, like a separate contract. (HESA's return guidance document HEFCE website)

7. "MODNet" stands for Middlesex Organisational Development Network. It is a Middlesex University project funded by HEFCE, which is part of the Corporate Plan of the University. Its aim is to increase engagement with the business sector. Its vision is that by 2012, Middlesex University will be the foremost workforce and organisational development university in the country. It seeks to develop partnerships with employers and specialist private providers through new routes to qualifications and accreditation activity. It has a regional, national, and international reach. www.mdx.ac.uk/ schools and departments/IWBL/MODNet.

8. Driver Education is a field led by the Driver Instructor Association (DIA). This body and other associated ones in the sector are subject to the Driving Standards Association regulations on driver instructor practice and policy, which is informed by European Policy on driver training.

Teacher Development Agency (TDA) is a government body that produces and valorises the training practice and policy of state school teachers.

The National Outsourcing Association (NOA) is an agency that produces professional training and networking opportunities in Outsourcing activity.

9. *Goal oriented Achievement!*—the quality identified by Professor Frank Coffield in relation to this *learning style questionnaire* at Conference at Institute of Education, 2005.

10. For a fuller discussion of education and audit practice please see "Modernising Managerialism in Education" by Ross Ferguson in: Clarke, J. Gewirtz, S. and McLaughlin, E (Eds) 2000 *New Managerialism New Welfare* The Open University/Sage.

11. Projects of Sustainability in developing countries funded by UNESCO, the World Bank, and the European Union, designed in relation to strategies of Good Governance, are implemented regularly by Non Governmental Organisations (NGOs) that use European theories of research to inform their practice. These theories are taught in many European University Courses of Development. One example is "A Societal Learning Perspective for Sustainable Chain Management and Good Governance" led by an NGO associated with the Agriculture Centre in Wakening Netherlands proposes: "Community participation and empowerment" for a group of tribal villages in the Extreme North of Cameroon in 2005. Its objective: "The design and facilitating Complex Multistakeholder Processes." (MSP) The framework and approach used for the MSP-related training, facilitation, and consultancy work of the International Agriculture Centre (IAC), and comprehensive database of methodologies and tools can be found on the MSP Resource Portal (www.iac.wur.nl/msp).

The "TRIPs agreement," Trade Related Aspects of Intellectual Property Rights, promoted by the World Trade Organisation, identifies a set of guidelines for the funding of research and copyright and licences in the field of biochemistry and other areas that the University engages with.

12. Beyond "just discourse": The project of Cultural Political Economy (CPE) by Norman Fairclough seeks to identify the ways in which discursive and regulatory practice produces material effects. Fairclough applies a form of critical discourse analysis to texts such as leading politicians' speeches, and government policy with a view to illustrating how discursive practice works. Fairclough, N. 2006 *Language and Globalisation* Routledge. Fairclough's theory of CPE, Foucualt's "governmentality" and Rose's "governance" and Gramsci's "normative grammars" sustain very similar views on the way in which governance is achieved through discursive practice.

Abbreviated References

CIHE: The Council for Industry and Higher Education produces consultation documents for staff development and policy between Industry and Higher Education. The "investment theory" trope discussed in the chapter informs the CIHE publication on *Workforce Development*. 2005 ISBN 1 874223 53 X

RIBA: Royal Institute of British Architecture

ACCA: Association of Chartered Certified Accountants
HEFCE: Higher Education Funding Council for England
CETLs: Centres for Excellence in Teaching and Learning
DfEE: Department for Education and Employment.

References

Allen, M. and Ainley, P. (2008) *A New 14+: Vocational Diplomas and the Future of Schools, Colleges and Universities,* National Union of Teachers' Pamphlet.

Anderson, P. (1983) *In the Tracks of Historical Materialism,* London: Verso.

Barnett, R. (2009) Article in *Times Higher Educational Supplement (THES),* November.

Bennett, T. (1990) *Outside Literature,* London: Routledge.

Boud, D. and Lee, A. (2008) *Changing Practices of Doctoral Education,* London: Routledge.

Castells, M. (2000) *The Rise of the Network Society* (2nd edition), Oxford: Blackwell.

Clarke, J. Gewirtz, S. and McLaughlin, E. (eds) (2000) *New Managerialism New Welfare,* London: Sage/The Open University.

Department for Education and Employment (DfEE) (1998) School Standards and Framework Act. London: HMSO.

Dore, R. (1997) *The Diploma Disease* (2nd edition: first published in 1976 by George Allen and Unwin), Institute of Education, University of London.

Du Gay, P. (1997) *Doing Cultural Studies: The Case of the Sony Walkman,* London: Sage/The Open University.

Eagleton, T. (1983) *Literary Theory: An Introduction,* Oxford: Basil Blackwell.

Fairclough, N. (2006) *Language and Globalisation,* London: Routledge.

Femia, J. V. (1981) *Gramsci's Political Thought: Hegemony. Consciousness and the Revolutionary Process,* Oxford: Clarendon Press.

Foucault, M. (1980a) *Power/Knowledge: Selected Interviews and Other Writings 1072–1977,* New York: Pantheon Books.

—— (1980b) "Nietzsche, Genealogy, History"' in *Language, Counter Memory, Practice,* Ithaca: Cornell University Press.

Fraser, N. (2009) Feminism Co-opted from *Feminist Contentions: A Philosophical Exchange,* London: *New Left Review no 56.*

Frost, N. and Taylor, R. (2001) Patterns of Change in the University: The Impact of Lifelong Learning and the World of Work, *Studies in the Education of Adults,* 33 (1) (April).

Glyn, A. (2007) *Capitalism Unleashed Finance, Globalization and Welfare,* Oxford: Oxford University Press.

Gramsci, A. (1971) *Selections from the Prison Notebooks,* ed. and trans. Q. Hoare and G. Nowell Smith, London: Lawrence and Wishart.

———. (1975) *Quaderni del carcere IV*: 962–963, 1238 di V Gerratana Einaudi.

Gorz, A. (2004) *Wissen, Wert und Kapital. Zur Kritik der Wissensokonomi,* Zurich: Rotpunktverlag.

Hall, S. (1983) The Problem of Ideology—Marxism without Guarantees, in Mathews, B. (ed) *Marx 100 Years On* London: Lawrence and Wishart.

Hamilton, P. (2003) *Historicism,* London: Routledge.

Harvey, D. (1999) *The Limits to Capital,* London: Verso.

——— (2005) *The New Imperialism,* Oxford: University Press.

Hermann, C. *Value and Knowledge Insights from Marxist Value Theory for the Transformation of Work in a Digital Economy* Conference Paper "Many Marxisms" Fifth Historical Materialism Annual Conference November 2008, at School of Oriental and African Studies, London, November 2008, SOAS University.

Jackson, L. (1994) *The Dematerialisation of Karl Marx: Literature and Marxist Theory,* London: Longman.

Jameson, F. (1981) *The Political Unconscious,* London: Methuen.

Jessop, B. (2002) *The Future of the Capitalist State,* Cambridge: Polity Press.

Laclau, E. and Mouffe, C. (2001) *Hegemony and Socialist Strategy: Towards a Radical Democratic Politics* (2nd edition), London: Verso.

Lankshear, C. and Gee, J. P. and Knobel, M. and Searle, C. (1997) *Changing Literacies,* Open University Press.

Lester, S. (2003) What Is a Profession? Qualifications in Professional Development: A Discussion with Reference to Conservators in the UK and Ireland, *Studies in Continuing Education,* 25 (3): 264–283.

Leys, C. (2003) *Market Driven Politics: Neoliberal Democracy and the Public Interest,* London: Verso.

Mackney, P. (2007) *New Visions for the Future of a Changing Higher Education System,* Keynote Speech Given at NAICE, University College Union and College Union.

Marx, K. (1867/1990) *Capital* (2nd edition), Harmondsworth: Penguin.

McLellan, D. (1983) *Karl Marx: The Legacy,* London: British Broadcasting Corporation.

——— (1995) *The Thought of Karl Marx,* London: Papermac.

Morton, A. D. (2007) *Unravelling Gramsci: Hegemony and Passive Revolution in the Global Economy,* London: Pluto Press.

Negri, A. and Hardt, C. (2001) *Empire,* Harvard MA: Harvard University Press.

Phalley, T. (2004) *From Neo Keynesianism to Neo Liberalism: Shifting Paradigms in Economics,* tpalley@osi-dc.org British Library.

Power, M. (1994) *The Audit Explosion,* London: Demos.

Ray, L. and Sayer, A. (1999) Introduction, in L. Ray and A. Sayer (eds) *Culture and Economy after the Cultural Turn,* London: Sage.

Rose, N. (1998) *Inventing Our Selves: Psychology, Power, and Personhood,* Cambridge: Cambridge University Press.

Ryan, M. (1984) *Marxism and Deconstruction: A Critical Articulation,* Baltimore: Johns Hopkins University Press.

Sayer, S. (2003) Creative Activity and Alienation in Hegel and Marx, *Historical Materialism,* 11 (1).

Skinner, Q. (1969) Meaning and Understanding in the History of Ideas, *History and Theory,* 8 (1): 3–53.

Stewart, T. (2001) *Intellectual Capital: The New Wealth of Organizations,* New York: Doubleday-Currency.

Chapter 5

The Professional Imagination: Remaking Education Policy in a Neoliberal Context

Denis Gleeson

Introduction

This chapter, located in a mainly English context, addresses the recent resurgence of interest in the remaking of public policy through a "new professionalism" (Cabinet Office 2008). As a case in point, this contribution explores the shifting nature of public professionalism in Further Education, a sector that has arguably been exposed to more market experimentation than any other in the public sphere.[1] It draws parallels with wider areas of public policy analysis that chronicle the effects of centralised deregulation on professionals as the subjects of reform. The research that informs the main argument addresses two interconnected processes of regime change (policy and periodisation) and technologies of control (audit, inspection, and peformativity) that impact on the identities and cultural practices of professionals (agency and mediation) in the contexts of their work (Strathern 2000). In exploring the paradox of generating policy through professionalism (Cabinet Office 2009), this chapter analyses how invisible pedagogies of professional practice and power both challenge and reproduce classic elements of purity and danger (Douglas 1966; Bernstein 1996; Bourdieu 1998). The approach taken challenges modernising agendas that seek to reprofessionalise or empower professionals without examining the changing conditions of their work or the neoliberal policies that frame their practice. It also questions the assumptions through which Labour's *Third Way* politics seek to reconcile tensions and conflicts between professionals and stakeholder interests, markets, and civil society, through a customer services approach.

The chapter is subdivided into three main parts: the first explores the recent interest in modernising public-sector provision through *reforming* the relationship between professionals, the state, and civic society. The second examines exemplars of this process in FE through the perspectives and experiences of professionals working in the sector.[2] The final section considers the notion of a professional imagination that reflects and informs wider configurations of democratic accountability and governance in civic society (Mills-Wright 1968).[3]

The Politics of Professionalism

Professionalism within education and the wider public sector is a complex and elusive concept. Renewed interest in the way professionalism is being constructed and contested has its roots in recurring tensions that surround changing relations between the state, professionals, and socioeconomic performance (Grace 1995). Historically, English liberal notions of the professions surrounded the freedom to define their relationship with their clients without any mediation from third-party or external organisations. Such autonomy is traditionally associated with the "free professions," law, medicine, and the city, where the power and privileges of self-regulation defined their independence and distance from "semiprofessions" (teaching and nursing), employed by the state (Etzioni 1969; Johnston 1977). Two contrasting views of the professional as either self-serving, with powers to define their own conditions of work, or as subjects answerable to external rules and constraints, underpin past and present constructions (Weber:see Mills-Wright 1948;1968). The first focuses on issues of *agency* in the way professionals construct power and identity in their work, either through self-employment, restrictive practices, or resistance, or altruism or critical engagement. The second denotes issues of *structure* that are associated with how professionals, as "employees," are conditioned by labour processes and working practices, through audit cultures, targets, inspection, and performance management (Pollitt 1993; Power 1997) In reality, the absorption of lawyers and medics into government, national health, and corporate bureaucracies has eroded their independence as globalisation, state, and market interventions have become more invasive (Gewirtz et al. 2009)

In practice, public-sector professionals have never been in the position to define their relationship with the public they serve, despite growing union representation, which is regulated through the state or its agencies as the employer of the services provided. This lack of power to define the relationship between the provider and customer of public services does not, however, mean that all public professionals are of the same status or that hierarchies of pay, gender, status, expertise, and power do not exist (Evetts 2009). However, in terms of the broader picture, the main source of power that defines the relationship between professionals and the public remains the state. In turn, this relationship is not static and is constantly changing over time. Most recently, this includes the subcontracting out of education, health, social, and welfare services to trusts, agencies, and private-sector provision. The process involves the state shedding significant dimensions of its employer and provider function—a role described as "steering not rowing" public provision—signalling a shift in the role of the state from provider to *guarantor* of rights to public services (Rhodes 1995; Clarke and Newman 2009)

Underlying such regulative change there remains a recurring disenchantment amongst successive governments with a public sector that is seen to be policed by self-serving professional interests, lacking speed and flexibility in response to the threats of global change. In connecting *deficit* notions of professionalism to market reform, both conservative and labour governments have been able to reinforce professional stereotypes that legitimate the exercise of greater control over the professional labour force. This was the reasoning behind the Thatcher government's interventions in the 1980s, to deregulate and audit the professions in order to eradicate restrictive practices that interfered with "free competition" as the main driver of service quality in the market place. Ostensibly designed to increase efficiency and raise standards, subsequent reform has been contingent on altering the power relations between the state and local governance, and realigning professional and managerial cultures around private rather than public ethics (Clarke 2004). Increasingly, such accountability practices have become normalised in everyday professional practices that mask their central role in the reinvention of government. While not surprising, "what is novel about this is the role such techniques are given in how knowledge is defined in knowledge producing organisations" (Strathern 2000, p. 286). The process also forms part of a wider distancing of municipal public authority away from welfare, trade union, collective, and civic values towards an enterprise culture that promotes individualism, choice, and a consumer-driven economy. However, the shift toward a contract culture has not been achieved by ideology alone, but through new technologies of public management based on quasi-market principles. Policy interventions over several years have involved a combination of outsourcing, privatisation, and franchising of public services, coupled with external monitoring (categorical funding, audit, targets, and inspection) and internal surveillance (self-assessment, performance-related pay, and league tables, linking service delivery with compliance). What complicates this process is the unaccountable proliferation of agencies, think tanks, and consultancies that now fill the "institutional void" created by the deregulation of "old" public-sector systems of provision, accountability, and governance (Ball 2008).

While market and audit cultures have, over time, been heralded as necessary to prevent professional self-interest eclipsing public management reform, there are unintended consequences—one of which is that the state has become dependent on agencies that it once controlled (Ranson 2003). Another concerns the backlash of industrial action and the downgrading of public services that proved politically costly to both the Thatcher and Major governments. In different ways, both consequences provided the space for New Labour's "Third Way" principles to reform public services on lines that had much in common with Giddens's (1998) vision of reconciling the discipline of the market with principles of social justice. However, the combination of Keynsian principles as a means of humanising the excesses of new right reform, while at the same time advocating *modernisation* (individualism, devolution, and consumer choice), suggests continuity rather than difference between New Right and New Labour policies. According to Marquand (2000), there has been little disruption between the Thatcher and Blair regimes in terms of continuing the modernising agenda of promoting self-discipline, self-help, and personal responsibility amongst UK citizens. The seamless web connecting both regimes has been described by Hall as "Mrs. Thatcher had a project and Blair's historic mission was adjusting to it" (Hall 1998). For Travers (1999), "...of all the policies that New Labour have lifted wholesale from the Conservatives, the use of audit and inspection in the public services is one of the most visible" (p. 12: cited in Cope et al. 2003 p. 209). While the more recent transition from Blair to Brown (2008) makes reference to the limiting effects of micromanagement on public services—with calls for a *new professionalism* based on a "shared commitment between government and professionals" (Cabinet Office 2008, pp.26–34)—self-regulation, demand-led reform, and customer-led reform remain the same policy drivers as before (Cabinet Office 2009).

A continuing feature of this adjustment from Blair to Brown has been the continued proliferation of multiple agencies and stakeholder participation, including greater employer and business access to public sector funding through subsidies, tax breaks, sponsorship, and political lobbying (Keep 2006). Historically, changes in funding that were previously brokered by levies, local authorities, civil service, and government departments have gradually been replaced by market levers, direct funding to employers, agencies, trusts, foundations, think tanks, and third-sector bodies (Ball 2008). By contrast, trade unions now have almost no formal input to national policy decisions that affect employment conditions, including the education and training of the work force. According to Gleeson and Keep (2004), this situation reflects the dismantling over time of tripartite structures that once afforded employer, union, and government interests a formalised role in national policy formation. It also finds expression in the transformation of education and training into a skills-led agenda, predominantly defined by employers in both education and the workplace (Coffield et al. 2005). A key focus of skills-based reform is largely behavioural rather than employment related: the dominant pedagogy is based on competencies and learning styles that subject teaching and learning to a secondary status (James and Biesta 2007). The lack of restraints on employer and managerial decision making has consequently had considerable effects on the education labour process, including the design and content of teachers' work, learning, and the curriculum (Reid 2003). As Keep (2006) points out, more than two decades of employer-led voluntarism have created neoliberal expectations, norms, and targets that make greater real partnership and accountability extremely difficult to contemplate or deliver. One effect is to marginalise professionals from accountability in circumstances where they, rather than the audit culture, can be held responsible for system failure (Avis 2009). While such a deficit view is administratively convenient, it has also proved fertile territory for a range of neoliberal market reforms to attack the autonomy and confidence of professionals in the public sector. Though cultures of audit and accountability have become increasingly normalised, very little is known about the practitioners who are their target, in terms of who they are and how they interpret or mediate such influences in their professional practice (Gleeson and Knights 2006). Similarly, there is considerable investment in training leaders and professionals for the future, but with little apparent understanding of how leadership and professionalism is exercised in the everyday conditions of public-sector work (Grace 1995).

At the same time, notions of self-regulation and demand-led reform continue unabated and remain couched in progressive rhetoric that links accountability and value for money with devolved powers of decision making. While the official rationale for such reform is to improve the efficiency of public services in a knowledge economy, in practice, it places organisations in a constant state of fending off impending crises. The object of such accountability, the demands of data, performance, and compliance overrides and disrupts the subject's life course (Power 1997; Strathern 2000). This tends to portray the professional as either "part of the problem"—as determined by either *structures* of government, employers, and policy makers funding priorities, inspection timetables, and targets—or as an *agent* seeking to comply, resist, or modify such demands. This apparent dualism explains the emphasis in recent research on the deskilling (and reskilling) of professionals through technologies of audit and control, and the reworking of self and professional identity in and through the contradictions of neoliberal reform experienced on the ground (Gleeson and Knights 2006). Such distinctions, however, tend to reinforce stereotypes that, in the contested conditions of professional practice, are more complex and socially situated (Colley et al. 2006). In the section which follows, the analysis turns to explore professionalism as a culturally produced process, through illustrative examples of the experiences and practices of those working in the FE and training sector.

New Professionalism in Context

The nature of professionalism in the Further Education and training sector is currently high on the policy agenda (Cabinet Office 2009). In response to a combination of factors ranging from historic high levels of underfunding, mismanagement, low morale, industrial action, and casualisation, FE is at the heart of the government's skills and employment reforms (Coffffield et al. 1995). Though recently described as the neglected "middle child" of English education (Foster 2005)—wedged between school and Higher Education—FE's voluntaristic and entrepreneurial traditions have proved attractive to market capture in order to create closer economic partnerships between business, employers, colleges, and workplace (DFES 2002; 2004; 2005; p. 2). According to Lord Foster's Review of Further Education, such employer-driven partnerships constitute a *"new discourse of FE"* that realigns FE with its historic mission as the handmaiden of British industry (Foster 2005).

There has since followed a range of additional policy initiatives (Leitch 2006; DFES 2006; DIUS 2008) that advocate improvements in leadership and teacher education, governance, workforce reform, professional development 14–19 reform, and self-regulation.

While such unprecedented investment and growth has placed FE at the centre rather than the periphery of education reform, it remains historically contested terrain. At root, one tradition defines its purpose as training young people with the skills to secure labour market competitiveness in the global knowledge economy. Another tradition promotes FE to achieve a renaissance in learning that provides young people and adults with the broader capabilities to participate as citizens in renewing and sustaining their communities as places to live and work (Cabinet Office 2008). Remaking civil society through such expansive learning requires the social inclusion and cohesion that is necessary for economic regeneration. This tension remains at the heart of UK public policy, in which the skills policy agenda has become noticeably market and employer led (Foster 2005; Leitch 2006).

Increasingly, the locus of FE provision, professionalism, and governance is shifting from the traditional communities colleges (as guardians) to a stakeholder model (as social partners) that embraces the wider access and influence of government, employers, commercial, business, and third-sector organisations (Gleeson et al. 2009). If, ostensibly, the model appears to be progressive and to embrace modernist principles of transparency, consumer demand, and efficiency, the reality is one of a continuous neoliberal turn following incorporation in 1993 (Avis 2009). This gradual shift is captured in the following heuristic snapshot of FE periodisation that mirrors wider shifts in the centralised deregulation of public services.

1993–1997: *deregulation,* whereby colleges became independent corporations that are run on business lines, moving from local authority restrictions to market-based freedom through funding led reform (FEFC)

1997–2001: *reregulation,* whereby checks and balances are put into place to regulate unchecked growth, sleaze, and corruption, including the return of representational and community governance

2001–2009: *centralised deregulation,* or marginalisation, whereby the planning role of FE governance is replaced by LSC funding and a cycle of resourcing, based on external inspection, audit, and target cycles

2009 onwards: *self-regulation,* whereby colleges operate through a Further Education agency and stakeholder framework (FSA, DIUS, SSCs, LAs) that involve *single voice* and *demand-led* elements, i.e., self-regulation via employer, business, and third-sector governance (Gleeson, Abbott and Hill 2009)

While such policy gyrations are, in practice, less linear and more complex than portrayed here, the typology exemplifies what Clarke and Newman (2009) describe as the "dispersed state." This involves constant reorganisation and the proliferation of agencies and bodies involved (see Appendix 1)—private providers, professional bodies, employers, representatives, sponsors, regulators, funders, and inspectors—that define what has essentially become the private governance of public provision (Ball 2008). While the locus of such devolved powers keep changing, how does FE meet the twin aims of what Brown (see Cabinet Office 2008) calls the basic framework of public policy, in promoting the preconditions of social and economic opportunity?

In addressing this question, the analysis turns to how professionals who work in the sector interpret such policy shifts in the contexts in which they work. While early research accentuated the structural effects of market reform and regime change on professionals who work in the sector (pay, contracts, conditions of work, casualisation, deprofessionalistion, and mangerialism) (Randle and Brady 1997), more recent research has accentuated issues of agency through which professionals mediate technologies of control (audit, inspection targets, and performativity) in the contexts of their work (James and Biesta 2007). The two are not exclusive. However, the objective here is not to reconcile such differences between agency and structure in the sense of Giddens's (1998) or Blair's "Third Way" (equating principles of social justice with those of the market), but to illustrate its critical mediation (brokerage and trade-offs) in the contested conditions in which FE practitioners work. A recurring theme in the narratives that follow is that while roles and positions in the sector may vary, professional perceptions of the "new discourse" have more in common than one might expect. In contrast with research that, for example, tends to stereotype distinctions between managers and practitioners, the data demonstrates a more nuanced and critical understanding of the wider effects of audit cultures on policy and professional cultures across FE. If the nature of such understanding remains contested, the ways in which policy is experienced on the ground, in relation to ethics, pedagogy and power, reveal rich narratives that capture the professional tensions involved in mediating contradictory policies at the college level. One such example from John, a college governor and policy analyst who is working in the sector, assesses the ethical impact of cuts in adult funding on the college where he is a governor.

> If colleges are left alone they know what to do but they have been
> blown around by different funding and audit streams. They are adept

at dealing with it but if they don't get funding for adult provision or for what they define as their priorities...if it doesn't meet with funding council or government approval...there's an issue. What is the governor's role in such circumstances? In my view governors are expected to challenge what is going on: asking what are we doing about this...supporting the college in defining its curriculum, values and priorities....

In a different context, Ian, a trade union official, comments on buzz word concepts that have little meaning in the real world of FE practice.

Self-regulation is a buzz word. It's a conceptual ideal that is not clarified—a wonderful ideal or another form of regulation? In fact self-regulation is a bit of a myth as the (lack) of balance between central and local powers will remain. Demand-led is also a bit of a dream concept when employers often don't know what they want, yet demand a voice....Demand is also led by government priorities when it wants to turn off or on provision through cuts or additional funding...

In different ways, both John's and Ian's accounts exemplify familiar tensions between policy and practice experienced by professionals (Stronach et al. 2002). In exploring the accounts and strategies that professionals adopt in order to survive, the analysis draws on a cultural approach that focuses attention on who practitioners are, how they construct professional meaning in their work, and what, if any, new constructions of professionalism are emerging as a result (Gleeson and James 2008). Following on earlier and more recent research in FE, the main focus of what follows is on the way that FE professionals position themselves in and around various creative tensions in the diverse contexts of their work. This involves how practitioners understand, interpret, and intervene in contradictory conditions that simultaneously enhance or restrict their professional room for manoeuvre (Clow 2001).

In seeking to determine what constitutes FE professionalism, it is important to understand the contested contexts in which FE professionals work. Even then, the task is not straightforward, as professional identities in FE derive from a wide range of academic, professional, business, industrial, and trade backgrounds, and operate across a diverse range of sites (college, community, employer and work-based, third sector). They also occupy different titles—lecturer, advanced practitioner, trainer, mentor, assessor, tutor, and instructor—that reflect the wider complexity of the learning and skills sector. Recent research, therefore, emphasises the term *professionality*, rather than *professionalism*, to accentuate the fluid (rather than static) ways in which professional identities are reworked, constructed, and understood in the dynamics of everyday practice. One argument for taking a cultural approach, exemplified in recent research (James and Biesta 2007), is that of capturing the multidisciplinary nature of FE practice. Another derives from the work of Bourdieu (1998) and a broader interest in situated learning (Lave and Wenger 1991). According to James and Diment (2003), Bourdieu's concept of habitus and field are key concepts that offer a distinctive view of learning cultures that include reference to the shifting positions and dispositions of professionals in the FE work place. They argue that habitus *names* the characteristic disposition of the social subject and is deeply ingrained in habits and behaviours, feelings, and thoughts that find expression in the tensions of everyday working practices. Such thought processes also engage with the field that involves a structured system of social relations—in this case, FE's relationship with society at micro and macro levels—in ways that interconnect agency and structure .The dialectical nature of such relationships allows insight into how certain sets of policy-practice assumptions prevail in various learning situations, and how they inform the practices of tutors, students, and managers in maintaining, reproducing, and challenging the status quo (Colley et al. 2006).

This critical and constructionist view of professional knowledge contrasts with cognitive definitions of professionalism based on the acquisition of learning styles, competencies, and skills. It emphasises the importance of agency, context, culture, and identity in the way professionals handle diversity in the immediacy of the work place and their everyday interactions with students. This often involves the pragmatic management of priorities, roles, and identities, as indicated by Stronach et al.'s (2002) study of teachers and nurses.

> It's a bit like juggling—you have to please your manager and the Trust, you have to please the clients and at the same time you have to keep yourself updated professionally (community educator). (Stronach et al. 2002, p. 118)

According to Wahlberg and Gleeson (2003), identity is another way in which practitioners both define their sense of professionalism and at the same time feel threatened by it. In the case of George, a business studies tutor in FE, he points out that "with the younger kids" he is no longer a teacher and more like a "welfare officer." This shift in status is seen by him as a consequence of badly thought out and poorly funded social inclusion policies that involved colleges recruiting ever younger and marginal students into a variety of vocational programmes that were not appropriate to their needs. The nature of such inclusion involves unresolved tension between teaching your specialised subject to motivated students and addressing principles of equality and social justice. While the "wake of status" for George relates to uncertainties about a loss of professional identity and status, which involves the transition from being an accredited subject specialist (lecturer) to becoming a key skills tutor, his response is symptomatic of a wider policy change in the sector. In another example, Rachel expresses her exasperation with the way external inspection focuses narrowly on teacher performance rather than student learning. In her diary, she describes a lesson that had been observed by a senior colleague in preparation for a forthcoming inspection.

> …a lesson in which I did absolutely no teaching but the outcomes were great in learning terms…It was amusing to be told that as no teaching had taken place she (the senior colleague) could not give me adequate feedback on the "lesson" as a whole, though she could not fault the activities, the students' commitment and dedication to the task, and the outcome was clearly that a high degree of learning had taken place. This latter point was endorsed by the students who said that they had learned a lot and it was helpful towards being able to complete a written assignment.

In addressing the idea that teaching always involves observable talk, action, and direction of students, Rachel is questioning the ways in which inspection practices become normalised in everyday collegial relations. Here, Rachel is also challenging the notion that student learning as enshrined in measurement is unrealistic, unhelpful, and contrary to the evidence of her experience working with the group. In a different example that deals with measurement through audit, Celia, an experienced FE lecturer and personal tutor, experimented with the use of mobile text messaging as a way of improving student communication in the college on what she calls "her terms" (Wahlberg et al. in James and Biesta 2007). Faced with the difficulties of involving so-called "hard to reach" students attending college, Celia encouraged her tutor group to use text messaging as a way of recording lateness or absence that met registration, inspection, and audit criteria sanctioned by the college. For Celia, this was more than just the routine use of mobile technology, but a way of building trust with students in order to encourage them to recognise their responsibilities and seek advice. Once in touch, Celia felt better able to watch out and help students in difficulty and, at the same time, relieve pressures that can be threatening to both student and tutor.

There are close parallels with the example of Gwen, cited by James and Diment (2003), whose role as a National Vocational Qualification (NVQ) "assessment only" practitioner is resisted in her work. Confronted with students who needed learning support over and above assessment, and whose weaknesses and employment futures were being closely scrutinised by their employers, Gwen found it impossible to pretend that she was just an assessor. According to James and Diment, the separation of learning from competency-based assessment placed on work-based assessors such as Gwen, whose working practices went well beyond her official contractual obligations. They cite examples of her coaching and mentoring students in the workplace, providing learning materials, giving her phone number to students with difficulties, and negotiating with employers to support their learning development (James and Biesta 2007). Such interventions, described by James and Diment as "underground working," both overcame recognised weaknesses associated with NVQ provision and at the same time rendered Gwen's professional support for students invisible. Whilst the emotional capital involves skill, care, and flexibility, it is also gendered and exploitative, given that her added value—or, in Marxist terms, her *surplus value*—was not officially recognised in the eyes of employers, government, and the college (see Avis 2009; Rikowski 2004). Though apparently mundane and ordinary, such examples draw attention to the dilemmas faced by professionals in creating room for manoeuvres that both challenge the impact of audit and inspection cultures and create space for some autonomy. Thus, it would be a mistake to assume that professionals are simply passive or compliant when dealing with external surveillance and performance measures.

The analysis so far suggests that professional knowledge in FE is situated in a recurring set of unstable and volatile conditions. While it would be misleading to exaggerate the degree of radical professional reinvention from such vignettes, they nevertheless provide insight into forms of mediation that involve what Stronach refers to as *restorying* professional narratives and identities "...in and against the audit the culture" (Stronach et al. 2002, p. 130). The significance of this analysis reveals the ways in which professionals draw on biographical resources to reassert their identities through resistance and contestation on the ground. Parallel research in wider contexts of public management, in schools, social work, probation, medicine, nursing, and health, indicates the ways in which professional identity and knowledge is being constructed through tensions and contradictions in market reform that are experienced in the micropolitics of the workplace (Kitchener et al. 2000; McDonald and Harrison 2004). In addition to the underground working already referred to, notions of "tacit knowledge" (Eraut 2000), "invisible trade" (Kitchener 2000), "added value" (Robson, Bailey, and Larkin 2004), and "cultural-political fit" (Newman and Nutley 2003) define ecologies of practice (trade-offs) that frame the contexts in which professionals often "walk both sides of the street" in order to protect or promote their pedagogic and professional values (Farrell and Morris 1999). This, according to Hoyle and Wallace (2005), is more than just strategic compliance or heroism (Althusser 1971). It is directly associated with the struggles and consequences of market reform that professionals have adopted to provide learners with experiences that they value and know are important over and beyond tests ,targets, and performance indicators. Referring to the concept of mediation as more appropriate than compliance, Hoyle and Wallace argue that mediating professionals:

> ...express what we regard as *principled infidelity.* Infidelity follows from not fully adhering to policy-makers' expectations, and principled follows from attempting to sustain their professional values instead of embracing the alternative values under-girding reforms. (Hoyle and Wallace 2005, p. 12)

As successive governments continue to promote managerial, audit, and market interventions as the key drivers of educational reform, they have largely ignored the nature of educational practice that learners and professionals inhabit. Ironically, this has drawn critical attention to claims that the quality of teaching and learning is at the heart of VET reform (Coffield 2005). This absence—or invisible pedagogy of power (Bernstein 1996)—has opened up the possibility for professional intervention in the spaces generated by pedagogic neglect. While such forms of professionalism are hidden from view and operate as underground working practices, there are costs involved. It is an exploitative process that passes by largely unrecognised and unrewarded by institutions and "busy" government agencies. Thus, whilst invisible pedagogies of professionalism struggle to make the transition from underground to overground, they often remain pinned down by low trust technologies of control and accountability at the national and local levels (Kitchener et al. 2000). Reflexive professionalism in such circumstances is easier said than done. At the same time, the work of professionals operating in such contexts should not be under-estimated for two reasons: first, in challenging the unrestricted influ-ence of markets in the public domain of teaching and learning and, second, in promoting examples of more democratic forms of profes-sionalism *in* and *for* civic society that are relevant to current debate.

The Professional Imagination Redefined

Professionalism is a culturally located and contested labour process. A key argument so far connects professionalism with market and audit hegemony over democratic forms of accountability and governance. Missing in much of the contemporary analysis is a relational under-standing of political and regime changes that intersect professional and public issues in time, place, and context. A key question aris-ing from the vignettes considered so far concerns where professional authority and accountability lies. In addressing this question, profes-sionals have a significant ethical role to play in mediating "private troubles" and "public issues" at the interface of citizen, state, and society (Mills-Wright 1968). While notions of mediation and the individual restorying of professional identities offer grounds for opti-mism, they are equally located in volatile and fragmented conditions that restrict opportunities for shared collegial experience (Strathern 2000).

Gaining a stronger sense of professionality requires a more fun-damental shift in the relationships that produce it through higher levels of trust and accountability that embody the term *professional*. This draws attention to both unequal power relations in FE and defi-cit assumptions about learners and professionals underpinning their practice. This has been promoted through the imposition of prescribed skills, competencies, and learning styles delivered through pack-aged programmes that can be measured and inspected (Ball 2007). Underlying such prescriptive principles rests an antagonism toward dialogical, cultural, and constructionist views of pedagogy that leads to expansive learning beyond narrow vocationalist principles. Despite the prevailing rhetoric of learner voice and personalisation, the domi-nant skills agenda accentuates what learners do not know, rather what they do. This *banking* rather than *conscientised* (dialectical) model of learning (Freire 1971) contrasts with a pedagogy that is based on developing learners *capabilitities*—their knowledge, potential, well-being, trajectory, expression, justice, and citizenship—as a way of remediating critical and reflexive professionalism (Sen 1999).

Thus, seen through a lens of cultural understanding of learning, professionalism does not simply occur in a social context, but also operates as a political practice within a wider political-economic framework. Put simply, a cultural theory of learning does not dwell on cognitive or mentalist notions of learning, but on social arrangements and material artefacts that are purposeful and constructed. The idea, for example, that external technologies of power (audit, inspection targets, funding, and performance management) do not shape the cultural contexts and frameworks that impact on teachers work ignores recognition of professionalism as part of, rather than separate from, wider labour processes (Reid 2003; Rikowski 2004).This calls for an engagement with a wider politicised notion of teachers work that has become increasingly defined in terms of audited performance and market realism. As a consequence, the nature and purpose of public education and the role of public educators has been marginalised, but, at the same time, open to challenge. Many of the key issues confronting professionalism today involve conflict and struggle rather than consensus and trust. The alternative involves establishing forms of professional autonomy that are accountable, not just in terms of market and audit cultures (that work in different ways), but are located through more vibrant democratic and civic practices that define its ethical, moral, and public legitimacy (Durkheim 1961).

Conclusion

The conclusion can be drawn that this analysis paints an overly pessimistic picture of Labour's policy achievements in the field of Further Education and training over the past decade. Yet, following *Success for All* (DFES 2002), there have been no fewer than seven major policy initiatives (DFES 2004; 2005; 2006; Foster Report 2005; Leitch Report 2006) that have placed FE at the centre of social and economic reform. In a positive fashion, the initiatives involved have been designed to improve skill levels and learner participation in post-compulsory education, including the quality and professional standards of the workforce. These include reforms in teacher education and qualifications, governor training, and continuing professional and leadership development, to be delivered through a number of newly created agencies: Lifelong Learning UK (LLUK), Institute for Learning (IfL), and the Learning and Skills Improvement Service (LSIS). Running alongside such reform, Labour has initiated a further raft of initiatives that include a new inspection framework, changes to the funding of learning and skills provision (from the

Learning and Skills Council (LSC) to the Skills Funding Agency (SFA), extended "compulsory" education to 18, 14–19 reform, and the return of local authorities to the policy mix (Nuffield Foundation 2008).

On the face of it, Labour's commitment to expand and invest in the neglected field of Further Education and training addresses longstanding and neglected issues. However, less convincing are the consequences of poor policy finishing and increased regulatory and fiscal control over the lifelong learning sector, through the continued reinvention of multiple agencies with competing interests and contradictory agendas. Closer analysis of what has become a permanent skills revolution reveals Labour's ideological adherence to employer- and market-led priorities over principles of equality and social justice. Whether such a demand-led system is based on the assumed needs of employers—who often do not know what they want and traditionally view skills as a fourth order priority—is at the core of the current skills crisis (House of Commons 2009). As rising unemployment continues to derail the Leitch skills agenda, Further Education and training is once again in danger of becoming a substitute for employment, suggesting the need to redistribute grants and subsidies away form employers and private training agencies into colleges and the local economy, as part of the wider regeneration initiatives. Two decades of conservative and labour *policycism*—one initiative and quango following another—has not only failed to break the cycle of a low-skill, low-wage economy, but also managed to load the effects of market and policy failure onto the lifelong learning sector (Keep 2006).With the return of recession, the danger is that across the continuing raft of neoliberal reforms, the narrowest notions of skill, professionalism, and learning will continue to prevail. The analysis and vignettes explored here illustrate how important an expanded concept of professional practice is, even in the face of repeated and pervasive challenges to the autonomy and scope for self-determination of its practitioners (Avis 2009). The alternative involves rethinking the role of professionalism in a wider public context (Durkheim1961; Newman 2007), not in terms of a nostalgia for old municipal or bureau professional authority, but on lines that foster public confidence in the purpose of education and training in a context of social and economic regeneration. At the centre of this professional imagination, to paraphrase Mills-Wright (1968), is the meaning of citizenship at the interface of *private troubles and public issues*, in which critical pedagogy and professionalism exposes principles of power and social differentiation in education to greater public scrutiny.

Notes

1. The chapter draws on a number of recent projects (ESRC, NASUWT, CEL, and LSIS) that I have participated in with colleagues. The work involves various collaborative research, writing, and publishing activities. I am especially grateful to Farzana Shain, Kim Diment, Madeleine Wahlberg, Helen Colley, Jennie Davies, Eunice Wheeler David James, Phil Hodkinson, Stewart Ranson, Ewart Keep, David Knights, Ian Abbott, and Ron Hill for allowing me to cite references to ideas and examples from our collaborative work.
2. The term Further Education is used generically to encompass college, work-based, and community provision of vocational education and training (VET), which is part of the wider learning and skills sector. Further Education Colleges (FECs) are similar to Institutes of Technical and Further Education (TAFE) in Australia and, to a lesser extent, Community Colleges in North America. Different systems of FE exist in Scotland, Wales, and Northern Ireland. This chapter refers exclusively to the English context.
3. The 361 FE Colleges in England have a total income of £6 billion, employ over 230,000 staff, and educate approximately 3 million students each year (Source Association of Colleges: AOC London).

References

Althusser, L. (1971) *Ideology and Ideological State Apparatuses: Lenin, and Philosophy and Other Essays*, New York Books, pp. 123–173.

Avis, J. (2009) *Education, Policy and Social Justice*, London: Continuum Books.

Ball, S. J. (2008) New Philanthropy, New Networks and New Governance in Education, *Political Studies*, 56, 747–765.

——— (2007) *Education Plc.: Understanding Private Sector Involvement in Public Sector Education*, London: Routledge.

Bernstein, B. (1996) *Pedagogy, Symbolic Control and Identity*, London: Taylor and Francis.

Bourdieu, P. (1998) *Practical Reason*, Cambridge: Polity Press.

Cabinet Office. (2008) *Excellence and Fairness: Achieving World Class Services*, London: HMSO.

——— (2009) *Working Together-Public Services on Your Side*, London: HMSO.

Clarke, J. (2004) Dissolving the Public Realm? The Logics and Limits of Neo-liberalism, *International Social Policy*, Vol. 33, No. 1, pp. 27–48.

Clarke and Newman. (2009) Elusive Publics; Knowledge, Power and Public Service Reform, in Gewirtz, S. et al. (2009) pp. 43–53.

Clow, R. (2001) Further Education Teachers Construction of Professionalism, *Journal of Vocational Education and Training*, Vol. 53, No. 3, pp. 407–419.

Coffield, F., Steer, R., Hodgson, A., Edward, S. and Findlay, Y. (1995) A New Learning and Skills Landscape? The Role of the Leaning and Skills Council, *Journal of Education Policy*, Vol. 22, No. 3, pp. 173–193.

Colley, H., James, D. and Diment, K. (2006) Unbecoming Teachers; Toward a More Dynamic Notion of Teacher Professionalism, *Journal of Education Policy*, Vol. 22, No. 3, pp. 173–193.

Colley, H, James, D, Tedder, M. and Diment, K. (2003) Learning as Becoming in Vocational Education and Training: Class, Gender and the Role of Vocational Habitus, *Journal of Vocational Education and Training*, Vol. 55, No. 4, pp. 471–497.

Cope, S., Goodship, J. and Holloway, D. (2003) Regulating the New Governance: The Case of Further Education, *Journal of Vocational Education and Training*, Vol. 55, No. 2, pp. 183–207.

Department for Education and Skills (DfES). (2002) *Success for All: Reforming Further Education and Training*, London: HMSO.

—— (2004) *Equipping Our Teachers for the Future: Reforming Initial Teacher Education for the Learning and Skills Sector*, London: HMSO.

—— (2005) *Education and Skills*, London: HMSO.

—— (2006) *Raising Skills and Improving Life Chances*, London: HMSO.

Department for Innovation Universities and Skills. (DIUS) (2008) Further Education Colleges—Models for Success, DIUS: London.

Douglas. M. (1966) *Purity and Danger; an Analysis of Concepts of Pollution and Taboo*, London: Routledge and Kegan Paul.

Durkeim, E. (1961) *Moral Education*, Glencoe: Free Press (first published in French 1925).

Eraut, M. (2000) Non-Formal Learning: Implicit Learning and Tacit Knowledge, in Coffield, F. (ed) *The Necessity of Informal Learning*, Bristol: Policy Press.

Etzioni, A. (1969) *The Semi-Professions and Their Organisations: Teachers, Nurses and Social Workers*, New York: Free Press.

Evetts, J. (2009) The Management of Professionalism: A Contemporary Paradox, in Gewirtz et al. (2009), pp. 19–30.

Farrell, C. and Morris, J. (1999) Professional Perceptions of Bureaucratic Change in the Public Sector: GPs, Headteachers and Social Workers, *Public Money and Management*, Vol. 19, No. 4(3), pp. 31–36.

Foster, A. (2005) *Realising the Potential: A Review of the Future of Further Education Colleges*, London: DFES.

Freire, P. (1971) *Pedagogy of the Oppressed*, Harmondsworth: Penguin.

Gewirtz, S., Mahony, P., Hextall, I. and Cribb, A. (2009) (eds) *Changing Teacher Professionalism*, London: Routledge.

Giddens, A. (1998) *The Third Way: The Renewal of Democracy*, London: Macmillan.

Gleeson, D. and James, D. (2008) The Paradox of Professionalism in English Further Education, *Educational Review* Vol. 59, No. 4, pp. 451–467.

Gleeson. D. and Keep E. (2004) 'Voice without Accountability: The Changing Relationship between the Employer, the State and Education.' *Oxford Review of Education* Vol. 30, No. 1 (September), pp. 137–162.

Gleeson D. and Knights D. (2006) Challenging Dualism: Professionalism in "Troubled Times," *Sociology*, Vol. 40, No. 2, pp. 277–295.

Gleeson, D., Abbott, I. and Hill, R. (2009) *Creative Governance in Further Education: The Art of the Possible?* London and Coventry: Learning and Skills Development Agency.

Gleeson, D., Davies, J. and Wheeler, E. (2009) On the Making and Taking of Professionalism in the Further Education Workplace, in Gerwirtz et al. (2009).

Grace, G. (1995) *School Leadership: Beyond Education Management*, London: Routledge—Falmer.

Hall, S. (1998) The Great Moving Nowhere Show, *Marxism Today*, Vol. 1, pp. 9–14.

House of Commons. (2009) Select Committee. Reskilling for Recovery: After Leitch—Implementing Skills and Training Policies. Vol. 1. House of Common Innovation, Universities, Science and Skills Committee. London: Stationery Office Ltd.

Hoyle, E. and Wallace M. (2005) *Educational Leadership: Ambiguity, Professionals and Managerialism*, London: Sage.

James, D. and Biesta, G. (2007) *Improving Learning Cultures in Further Education*, London: Routledge.

James, D. and Diment, K. (2003) Going Underground? Learning and Assessment in an Ambiguous Space, *Journal of Vocational Education and Training*, Vol. 55, No. 4, pp. 407–422.

Johnston, T. J. (1977) *Professions and Power*, London: Macmillan.

Keep, E. (2006) State Control of the English Vocational and Education Training System: Playing with the Biggest Train Set in the World, *Journal of Vocational Education and Training*, Vol. 58, No. 1, pp. 47–64.

Kitchener M., Kirkpatrick, I. and Whipp, R. (2000) Supervising Professional Work Under New Public Management: Evidence form an "Invisible Trade,' *British Journal of Management*, Vol. 11, No. 3, pp. 213–226.

Lave, J. and Wenger, E. (1991) *Situated Learning: Legitimate Peripheral Participation*, Cambridge: Cambridge University Press.

Leitch, S. (2006) *Prosperity for All in the Global Economy: World Class Skills*, London: HM Treasury.

Marquand, D. (2000) The Rise and Fall of Civic Culture, *New Statesman*, Vol. 13, No. 11, pp. 4–8.

Mills-Wright, C. (1948) *From Max Weber: Essays in Sociology*, London: Routledge and Kegan Paul.

——— (1968) *The Sociological Imagination*, Harmondsworth: Penguin.

Newman, J. (2007) Rethinking "The Public" in Troubled Times, *Public Policy and Administration*, Vol. 22, No. 1, pp. 27–47.

Newman, J. and Nutley, S. (2003) Transforming the Probation Service: "What Works," Organisational Change and Professional Identity, *Policy and Politics*, Vol. 31, No. 4, pp. 547–563.

Nuffield Foundation. (2008) *14–19 Review: Final Report*, London: Nuffield Foundation.

Pollitt, C. (1993) *Managerialism and the Public Services*, Oxford: Blackwell.

Power, M. (1997) *The Audit Society: Rituals and Verification*, Oxford: Oxford University Press.

Randle, K. and Brady, N. (1997) Managerialism and Professionalism in the Cinderella Service, *Journal of Vocational Education and Training*, Vol. 49, No. 1, pp. 121–139.

Ranson, S. (2003) Public Accountability in the Age of Neo-Liberal Governance, *Journal of Education Policy*, Vol. 18, No. 2, pp. 197–214.

Reid, A. (2003) Understanding Teachers' Work: Is There Still a Place for Labour Process Theory? *British Journal of Sociology of Education*, Vol. 24, No. 5, pp. 559–573.

Rhodes, R. A. W. (1995) The *New Governance; Governing without Government*, Swindon: Economic and Social Research Council.

Rikowski, G. (2004) Labour's Fuel: Lifelong Learning Policy as Labour Production, in Hayes, D. (ed) *The Routledge-Falmer Guide to Key Debates in Education*, London: Routledge-Falmer.

Robson, J., Bailey, B. and Larkin, S. (2004) Adding Value: Investigating the Discourse of Professionalism. Adopted by Vocational Teachers, *Journal of Vocational Education and Training*, Vol. 17, No. 2, pp. 183–194.

Sen, A. (1999) *Development as Freedom*, New York: Knopf.

Strathern. M. (2000) Afterword: Accountability and Ethnography in Strathern, M. (ed) *Audit Cultures: Anthropological Studies in Accountability, Ethics and Academy*, London: Routledge.

Stronach, I., Corbin, B., McNamara, S., Stark, S. and Wrawne, T. (2002) Toward an Uncertain Politics of Professionalism: Teacher and Nurses Identity in Flux, *Journal of Education Policy*, Vol. 7, No. 1, pp.110–138.

Travers, T. (1999) The Day of the Watch Dog, *Public Finance*, October 16–22, pp. 12–14.

Whalberg, M. and Gleeson, D. (2003) Doing the Business: Paradox and Irony in Vocational Education—GNVQ Business Studies as a Case in Point, *Journal of Vocational Education and Training*, Vol. 55, No. 4, pp. 423–445.

Chapter 6

Curriculum Change and the Blair Years

Terry Wrigley

Introduction

In analysing the political workings of an education system, it is important to think about cultural and ideological as well as economic effects (see Endnote). Although much sociology of education has been focussed on questions of reproduction in terms of the *filtering of people*—the ways in which the education system variously promotes or filters out students from different socioeconomic or ethnic backgrounds and functions to maintain and reproduce class structures and hierarchies—it is equally important to raise questions about the *filtering of ideas*.

> The knowledge that now gets into schools is already a choice from a much larger universe of possible social knowledge and principles. It is a form of cultural capital that comes from somewhere, that often reflects the perspectives and beliefs of powerful segments of our social collectivity. (Apple 1979:8–9)

The great pioneer of this mode of curriculum analysis in the UK was Raymond Williams, who built on a Gramscian analysis of hegemony to examine how some ideas and ways of thinking are privileged, whilst others are obscured.

> Hegemony supposes the existence of something which is truly total...which is lived at such a depth, which saturates the society to such an extent, and which, as Gramsci put it, even constitutes the limit of common sense for most people under its sway. (Williams 1976:204)

Williams shows how this operates in terms of curriculum, through assertions and assumptions that a particular set of texts or ideas is self-evidently the norm, *the* tradition, literature or science or history per se. A literary canon, for example, receives the stamp of authority through an examination syllabus, and becomes the mainstay of what is taught; the process, likewise, includes establishing which particular ways of responding to texts are acceptable.

> There is a process which I call the selective tradition: that which, within the terms of an effective dominant culture, is always passed off as "the tradition," *the* significant past. But always the selectivity is the point; the way in which from a whole possible area of past and present, certain meanings and practices are chosen for emphasis, certain other meanings and practices are neglected and excluded. Even more crucially, some of these meanings are reinterpreted, diluted, or put into forms which support or at least do not contradict other elements within the effective dominant culture. (ibid.: 205)

It is the intention of this chapter to examine how Blair's governments and their educational apparatus, building on the previous Conservative government's school reform, have transformed curriculum within the wider politics of neoliberalism and, to some extent, neoconservativism. This process has been attempted to the point of hegemony, i.e., never total—there is always some resistance—but so that it often appears to teachers and students that the curriculum is merely technical, merely common sense, and politically neutral. More than this, the governance of education has been transformed in ways that create the assumption that it is entirely appropriate for curriculum and teaching to be mandated downwards by government, and that the role of teachers is simply to "deliver."

As with many other policy areas, it is impossible to discuss curriculum change under Blair's government without focussing on the continuities with the Thatcher years. These are substantial, though it would be misleading to think that little has changed. However, a description of the Thatcherite heritage is not simply "background" in this chapter. It was an important political act for the Blair government to perpetuate the structures they inherited.

The Education Reform Act (1988)

For a large part of the twentieth century, it was widely accepted that teachers had the freedom to determine their own curriculum, and this was largely true, though never absolute. The syllabus of external examinations at age 16 determined the curriculum of the last two years of compulsory schooling. The final year of primary school, from 1945 until the introduction of comprehensive schools and abolition of the 11-plus selection tests, was dominated by test preparation in English, mathematics, and "intelligence." Of course, practising doing "intelligence tests" was somewhat paradoxical, since they supposedly tested *innate* ability. Beyond this, what teachers actually taught was heavily influenced by tacit assumptions, collective habits, and school and subject norms, as well as school textbooks, but there was no central authority dictating subject content or age-related objectives.

From the 1960s to the early 1980s, a significant minority of teachers used this freedom to engage in thoughtful curriculum reform and to question traditional norms. This was also officially encouraged through the government-funded Schools Council, the organiser of many innovative curriculum reform projects (Schools Council 1973). Typically, these took the form of a pilot, which involved volunteer schools, followed by a dissemination stage that involved the sale of project materials. The process of dissemination was voluntary and partial, and depended on the willing participation of teachers. Many primary and a few secondary schools during this period broke through established subject boundaries in favour of a thematic curriculum (e.g., Brown and Precious 1968), and placed a greater emphasis on "pupil-centred learning." Although this concept was often theoretically unclear, and does not easily fit with a social constructivist psychology of learning (Vygotsky 1978), it served rhetorically to help shift practice away from transmission modes of teaching. With the added impetus and challenge of an extension of compulsory schooling to age 16, new subjects such as environmental studies, modern studies, and media studies were developed with an added sense of relevance (Goodson 1983), and partly with the intention of reaching out to a wider section of the population than had previously completed secondary education. Although progressivism was loosely defined and insufficiently theorised, as well as impacting consistently only on a minority of schools and classrooms, the characterisation of this period in terms of "progressive" rather than "traditional" methods is a helpful starting point. As Ken Jones and colleagues put it:

> We use "progressive education," not to designate a theoretical position, nor a coherent body of practice, but rather a loose collection of economic and social assumptions, philosophies, classroom practices, political alliances and strategies and professional orientations which

together formed the dominant educational ideological complex of the mid-century. Given some rough unity by principles of child-centred learning and cultural relevance, progressivism in this broad sense was constituted as an antidote both to the traditional humanism of academic education, and to the narrow curriculum and harsh pedagogic regimes of mass schooling. It was an international movement. Drawing, often eclectically, from a variety of intellectual backgrounds—from Montessori to Freire, Froebel to Vygotsky—it spoke of reshaping the content of education, and of a new relationship between teachers, students and communities. It presented itself as the matrix of curricular and pedagogical reforms, which—driven by the decentralised initiative of educational professionals—could engage with the mass of students and resolve the problems of an educational expansion that was taking place unaccompanied by any systematic programme of curriculum change. On this basis for a short period it gained the acceptance of governments that sought to match education to what were perceived as new social and economic needs, and which lacked the capacity to generate responses of any other kind. (Jones et al. 2008:109–110)

Whilst resisting and seeking to reform the subsequent curricular regime, it is important to acknowledge the limitations of this progressive movement. Jones et al. (2008:118) point, in particular, to a failure to pay sufficient attention to the tail of low achievement. At the core of the theoretical weakness was a reliance on the individual constructivism of Piaget, rather than the social (historical, cultural) constructivism of Vygotsky and his successors.

"The child," argued the influential Plowden Report on Primary Education, "is the agent of his own learning"; children learned through "individual discovery, first-hand experience and opportunity for creative work." The curriculum should be thought of in terms of activity and experience rather than "knowledge to be acquired and stored" and the school's role was to "devise the right environment for children" in which they could "be themselves and develop at the pace appropriate to them." (Jones et al. 2008:111, quoting Plowden Report, 1967:194 and 188)

After a number of moral panics (Whitty and Menter 1989; Landman and Ozga 1995; Ball 1990) about runaway progressivism, anarchic schools and accusations that "standards" were slipping, and moves towards a "core" or "common" curriculum that would still be flexible and respect local professional judgement (DfES 1980, 1984, 1986), Margaret Thatcher and her Education Minister, Kenneth Baker, put a decisive end to this period of relative freedom by imposing a National

Curriculum covering the 11 years of compulsory schooling. This had a number of important structural features:

i) it was organised in terms of 10–11 subjects, taught separately, and in parallel to each other from year one through year 11;
ii) each was defined in terms (largely) of lists of content that had to be covered in each "key stage" (lasting two, three, or four years);
iii) progression in each subject was also defined in linear terms mapped as 10 (later eight) levels, with subjects being subdivided into different strands (DES 1989; Kelly 1990).

The centralisation of authority over the curriculum was an important issue, giving an individual minister enormous power over what was taught in schools. (The legislation delegated considerable powers to the Secretary of State.) Ironically, this was packaged, in the Education Reform Act of 1988, amongst reforms that supposedly gave schools greater autonomy. In reality, it gave the headteacher and governors power over organisational matters, while centralising control of the curriculum and holding the head and governors to account for effective curriculum "delivery."

However, it soon became apparent that more was at stake than the location of power. Firstly, the list of subjects had ideological implications. This was almost identical to those of the 1904 Secondary Regulations (Lawton 1992:49; Aldrich 1988:22), but with a greater emphasis on science and with additional subjects added in the interest of modernisation, particularly design and technology and information technology. In fact, the mathematical, scientific, and technological subjects covered more than half the curriculum time. Opportunities to develop a critical understanding of contemporary society and culture were minimised; for example, there was no place for contemporary social or political studies, and the Education Minister, Kenneth Clarke, presented the view that history did not include events of the past 20 years (Graham 1993). Haydn explains the significance and absurdity of this decision.

> The decision came in the wake of a series of right-wing pamphlets...criticising what was seen as the "politicisation" of school history, as it moved away from its traditional "Whiggish" mode. Part of Clarke's rationale for this rule was that there should be a clear delineation between history and current affairs (not that current affairs was to feature elsewhere in the National Curriculum)...Given that one of the stated purposes of the teaching of history is that it should enable young people to understand the present in the light of the past (DfEE

1999:148), this hiatus seems a strange one. In terms of "telling a story" about the history of the country they are growing up in, it is like "pulling up the drawbridge." Ingenuous attempts to "de-politicise" history, to separate the past from the present, and to rip the last chapter out of the story of the nation's past, do not make it easier for history teachers to persuade pupils of the importance and relevance of history to their lives. (Haydn 2004:93)

These tensions in the National Curriculum can be understood in terms of a fusion between neoliberal and neoconservative education reform. In the wider political arena, neoconservatism complements and reinforces the neoliberal attempt to increase exploitation and profit by providing an ideological justification for strong state control, for example, through nationalist or authoritarian ideologies. (Of course, there is irony here: capitalism is arguing simultaneously for a diminution of the state insofar as it safeguards workers' interests, and for the strengthening of the state insofar as it serves to repress opposition to capitalism.) Within the sphere of education, apparently contradictory policies can often be understood as the working through of these two macropolicy strands (see Apple 1996; Lawton 1992: 2; Gabbard ed. 2008). Young people were to be equipped with up-to-date productive knowledge, but denied the opportunity to understand the world socially and politically.

This was reinforced in the detail of many subjects. There were, in fact, important positive features in the reform of science and technology. For example, by combining physics, chemistry, and biology into a single subject, with double weighting, old gender biases were largely overcome. The new model of design and technology, replacing former craft subjects, gave students greater agency, since they were no longer in the role of operatives carrying out other people's designs (Eggleston 1996; Kimbell 2004). However, in the humanities, it became much more difficult to find a space for learner engagement or critical thinking. English had previously had little defined content, enabling teachers to organise learning around texts and themes that connected with learner interests and lives. Suddenly (with some variations over the ensuing years), there were lists of writers and linguistic terminology to be covered, and a distinct shift towards language as a technical skill. A number of writers have pointed to the Eurocentric or Anglocentric character, particularly of subjects such as English and history (Burton and Weiner 1990; Ball 1993).

The impact of some of these changes also needs to be described in terms of framing. I am using this word in a rather broader and less technical sense than Bernstein (1971 and elsewhere) to signify the way in which an action statement or policy is presented, the context in which it acquires a particular inflexion or significance, or the institutional or governance structures in which it materialises. For example, the anxiety created by lists of content to be covered and complex assessment demands that, in the beginning, were impossible to fulfil created a sense of inadequacy amongst many teachers. It focussed their attention on compliance with the standardised curriculum rather than reaching out towards learners. Although some adaptations were still possible to local contexts or ethnic cultures or youth interests, teachers were left with a diminished sense of agency: was it really permissible? Would the inspectors object? Knowledge and learning appeared as something determined from on high (Woods et al. 2001).

The designation of some subjects as "core" led to the potential marginalisation of others. This was particularly the case since the core subjects were subject to high-stakes assessment through national tests. This opened the way to a gradual marginalisation of the rest of the curriculum, whether at the national level, in terms of future changes in statutory requirements, or at the school level, in terms of the relative effort and time devoted to aspects of the curriculum.

The process whereby the curriculum was drawn up inevitably led to overload; subject panels were by ministerial appointment of the great and the good, with the headteacher of an elite school serving as proxy for the teaching profession, and no attention was paid to the practicality or coherence of the whole until it was eventually realised that the runaway enthusiasms of the separate panels had created such overload that students would need to work through the night. Lord Dearing (the ubiquitous Mr. Fixit) was wheeled in to carry out emergency pruning. Not surprisingly, the arts and humanities were the losers, particularly at key stage four (Davies and Edwards 2001:98).

Embryonic areas of study such as media were eclipsed, deserving only a subordinate clause of vague acknowledgement in the National Curriculum for English. No concession was made to the desire of many young people to explore or acquire practical work-related skills. Cross-curricular themes were very much an afterthought and had little practical importance, despite various attempts to incorporate them into documentation.

> Some...still remember the heady days of the early 1990s, the National Curriculum Council, *Curriculum Guidance 7,* and all those meetings—how we were seduced by it all! So much so that, as we were

being grateful that the government had tossed us the cross-curricular bone, we failed to notice until it was too late that the lean curriculum meat was being carved and served elsewhere. (Scott 2002; see also Whitty et al. 1994; Garratt 2000)

Thus, a curriculum was created that, while presented as a common entitlement for all, depended upon significant exclusions and omissions, and was felt by many young people to be overwhelmingly "academic." This, along with the many signals of failure given out by the assessment system, as well as the extent of setting into "ability groups," are important reasons why participation in education and training post-16 is very low in comparison to other developed countries (DfES 2004).

Blair's Reform of Literacy Teaching

In the years leading up to the 2007 election victory, a common understanding developed, supported by the promises of many election candidates and various formal policy statements, that a Labour government would reduce the tight central control of the curriculum. In 1994 they promised to value "local flexibility and the professional discretion of teachers" (Labour Party 1994:15), and that in 1995 a reformed National Curriculum would take the form of "a broad...entitlement to all children without stifling a teacher's creativity and ability to respond to pupils' needs" (Labour Party 1995:24).

On taking power, nothing was done to loosen the stranglehold, and much of the machinery of surveillance (the OfSTED inspection agency, the SATs assessment machinery, league tables of schools as the driving motor of a competitive quasi market of schools) was perpetuated intact (Smithers 2001).

However, some changes were to take place, which the remainder of this chapter will evaluate in terms of an increasingly neoliberal direction and discourse. In particular, it will examine the literacy curriculum in primary schools and the shift towards vocationalism in secondary education.

Speaking in general terms about education policy and reform under Blair, Stephen Ball (amongst others) argues:

Within policy, education is now regarded primarily from an economic point of view. The social and economic purposes of education have been collapsed into a single, overriding emphasis on policy making for economic competitiveness and an increasing neglect or sidelining (other than in rhetoric) of the social purposes of education. (Ball 2008: 11–12)

There can be no doubt that this was a conscious act of political leadership. Given a single-minded neoliberal belief that it was futile for a nation-state to try to intervene directly in investment and production, the only effective intervention would consist of making Britain attractive through high educational standards—the creation of "human capital." (In effect, this was only half of the strategy; the other half involved ensuring a low-wage economy with limited workers' rights.) Ball cites an early speech in Blair's premiership.

> Education is our best economic policy...This country will succeed or fail on the basis of how it changes itself and gears up to this new economy, based on knowledge. Education therefore is now the centre of economic policy making for the future. What I am saying is, we know what works within our education system, and we can learn the lessons of it. The key is now to apply those lessons, push them right throughout the education system, until the young children, whether they are growing up here in the constitutency of Sedgefield, or in the inner city urban estates of London, or Liverpool, or Manchester, or Newcastle, wherever they are, they get the chance to make the most of their God given potential. It is the only vision, in my view, that will work in the 21st century. (cited by Ball 2008:12)

It is clear from this speech that various discourses and ideologies were fusing together, including a meritocratic version of social justice that sits alongside the suggestion that ability is innate (i.e., "God given"). Central, however, is the place given to the economic role of education in a "knowledge economy" (see, for example, Lingard and Gale 2007; Ozga and Lingard 2007 for a critical discussion).

There is at the same time a claim that the government has authoritative knowledge of "what works," and that what is needed is to pressurise schools and teachers to implement it. This resulted in a qualitative stepping up of centralised control. The preceding Conservative governments had argued that, whilst centrally determining curriculum content and assessing outcomes, they would leave it to teachers (subject, of course, to appraisal and inspection) to decide how best to "deliver." The Blair government immediately embarked on processes involving the centralised control of teaching methods through the various "strategies."

This messianic sense of certainty, which was to mark Blair's premiership throughout, perhaps most disastrously in the decision to invade Iraq, led to the Literacy and Numeracy Strategies in primary school, followed by broader interventions across the curriculum (primary and key stage three) (DfEE 1998; DfES 2003a; DfES 2003b; Alexander 2004; Stobart and Stoll 2005). These were not absolutely compulsory, but woe betides anyone who chose an alternative approach, unless they could demonstrate excellent test scores.

> Implementation of the strategy was held to be non-statutory, but schools were to be inspected against the requirements of the programme, and those opting for alternative approaches were warned at the outset that they would be "interrogated" (Stannard 1998)…The effect of these commandments has been to greatly reduce diversity of practice, a goal which the NLS openly acknowledged in its early determination to ensure that everybody should be "working to the same blueprint." (DfEE 1997:20; Hunt 2001:52)

A regime was imposed whereby literacy and numeracy were separated off from the rest of the curriculum into their own "hours," which would take up almost all of each morning. The hour was divided into sections, which initially many teachers observed religiously. It had a predefined structure, and two-thirds of the time was devoted to whole-class instruction. This was "interactive" only in a limited sense, leading to a strengthening of the IRF (teacher *initiates*, pupil *responds*, teacher *feeds back*) patterns of exchange, criticised by Stubbs (1975) and others. The pattern sets up a pseudodialogue in which the teacher's role is to elicit prior knowledge and reward its regurgitation, while the children's contributions are limited to brief responses to convergent questions (Hunt 2001:54). This was not accidental, but rather encouraged in the training videos. For example:

> *Teacher*: Now on that page there's a word that's got two words in it. Can you find it for me? We call it a compound word. Two words together. Have you found it, Adam?
> *Child*: Moonlight.
> *Teacher*: Is he right? Are there two words in that word? Let's see everybody's finger underneath it. Right. What's the first word?
> *Children*: Moon.
> *Teacher*: And what's the last word?
> *Children*: Light.
> *Teacher*: Good. (Literacy training pack. Video 1. DfEE 1998)

Despite the claim that this will develop a greater competence through the improved appreciation of textual composition, such teaching scarcely helps children to critically appreciate texts, which requires more exploratory conversations. It also fails to engage with children in the kind of discussion which develops them cognitively and linguistically. There is research which shows that this form of interaction has increased since the inception of the National Literacy Strategy (See, for example, Mroz et al. 2000; Smith et al. 2000).

In terms of the rapid and consistent implementation of a major curriculum reform, the Literacy Hour (DfEE 1998) might well count as one of the most successful initiatives of all time; it was implemented through a unique blend of nationally directed support and intimidation (Hunt 2001). At first, it also led to a rise in attainment, as evidenced by national tests. There were a number of problems with this, however. Of course, the test scores had to go up, since Education Minister David Blunkett had promised his resignation if 80 percent of 11-year-olds didn't jump the hurdle of a level four. In order to achieve a rise in 1999, the tests were simplified. Of course, you can't easily pull that off twice, so the results then hit a plateau. Mary Hilton (2001) discovered that the Qualification and Curriculum Authority (QCA) had changed the criteria. The 1999 test involved more straightforward factual questions, and fewer that required interpretation and reading between the lines. This made it easier to classify readers who were still struggling as having reached level four. The type of text used also became less demanding: in 1998, Adele Geras's thoughtful account of her own childhood, alongside an extract from her fiction; in 1999, two straightforward factual texts and a poem about spiders (Hilton 2001). This clearly set new standards in terms of policy-based evidence.

Peter Tymms, using his considerable assessment expertise, conducted a research project that involved comparing the official test data with 11 other assessment sources and tools. The data included some very stable tests, and a sample of nearly half a million pupils. His conclusion was that there had been some real improvement, but much smaller than claimed. His estimation was that the proportion of pupils genuinely reaching level four had risen from 48 percent in 1995 to around 58 percent by 2000, rather than the 75 percent shown by the SATs. After that, the official percentage stuck at 75 percent in 2001, 2002, and 2003 (Tymms 2004).

Subsequent qualitative investigations by OfSTED inspectors confirmed an increase in basic exercises rather than meaningful reading. They called these "holding activities [which] occupied pupils but did not develop or consolidate their literacy skills," and which reduced interest and motivation. They found that some schools had abandoned independent reading, that boys in particular were responding badly to lessons, and that the curriculum was narrowing as teachers focussed more on the tests (Ofsted 2004).

The government responded to the hole they were in by digging deeper. In their search for another magic cure, they abandoned the Literacy Hour, which did at least seek to maintain a balance amongst word, sentence, and text levels of attention, for something even more restrictive, an exclusive concentration on phonics. Based on inadequate experimental research, the entire education system of England was switched to a particular approach (synthetic phonics). The justification neglects complex factors such as the phonic irregularities of English (requiring whole-word "look and say"), the importance of word shape and prediction based on syntactic patterns, and the importance of reader engagement with the meaning of the page or text as a whole. This was largely based on an experiment involving 300 children in Clackmannanshire, Scotland, which showed a rapid and sustained improvement in single-word tests that required pronunciation but not understanding. When retested several years later, the same pupils scored three years ahead in these tests, but only three months ahead in comprehension tests. As the researchers pointed out, even this could not be attributed unproblematically to the choice of a particular phonics method, since these children also experienced other initiatives, such as Philosophy for Children, the New Community Schools initiative, personal learning planning, home-school link teachers working with parents on literacy issues, story clubs, after-school homework clubs, and library visits (see Rosen 2006; Watson and Johnston 1998; Johnston and Watson 2003).

It is also important to extend evaluation beyond straightforward questions of "effectiveness." "Literacy" is not a simple and unambiguous technical term, but relates to complex cultural practices involving, for example, different degrees of critical independence in the relationship of the reader to the text. It raises questions of citizenship as well as scholarship. In addition to the question of whether progress can be sustained or genuine participation in literacy achieved, there is the hidden possibility of class discrimination: why subject those children with the least experience of enjoyable reading during infancy to a school regime that is squeezing out time for books? One might ask whether the proponents of a strict phonics regime would subject their own children to it.

Jim Cummins, perhaps the world's leading expert in the education of bilingual (ethnic minority) children, expresses the following concerns:

> Nowhere in this anaemic instructional vision is there room for really connecting at a human level with culturally diverse students. When we frame the universe of discourse only in terms of children's deficits in English and in phonological awareness..., we expel culture, language, identity, intellect, and imagination from our image of the child. In contrast...an instructional focus on empowerment, understood as the collaborative creation of power, starts by acknowledging the culture, linguistic, imaginative, and intellectual resources that children bring to school.
>
> Effective citizenship requires active intelligence, critical literacy, and a willingness to challenge power structures that constrict human possibility...Identity, intellect, imagination and power are absent from the new regime of truth because they potentially challenge the smooth operation of coercive power structures. (Cummins 2003)

The Literacy Strategy, under the Blair government, is illustrative of a number of key shifts within a broad policy continuity. It has been marked by increasing standardisation, extending beyond curriculum to the details of classroom method. Even the right-wing Conservative chair of the original National Curriculum English working group, Brian Cox, has been sharply critical of its narrow instrumentalism (Cox ed. 1998). The above quotation from Cummins forcefully expresses the cultural disempowerment involved.

Whilst there are difficulties in collapsing features of curriculum formation into macrolevel political categories, I would tentatively conclude that the attempt to increase "efficiency" of skills transmission aligns with a neoliberal policy direction, and the stripping away of the critical-cultural aspects of reading is a local manifestation of wider neoconservative political disempowerment.

The following section examines another key shift, this time impacting more on the secondary stage of schooling.

The Redefinition of Secondary Education

One of the most inexplicable acts of the final years of the Thatcher government was the abandonment of an emphasis, in the mid- to late 1980s, on technical and vocational education. The Technical and Vocational Education Initiative (TVEI) was nationally funded but locally managed within the local education authorities. It brought teachers into contact with industry and commerce, and, following locally determined plans, modernised key areas of the curriculum. It was not narrowly work preparation, and did not just affect lower achievers. It brought about a significant discursive shift, but amongst its broader effects was an emphasis on more active forms of learning. Its abandonment in favour of a rigid subject-bound academic curriculum for all pupils is indicative of the unresolved tensions in the Thatcher curriculum reforms between neoconservative and neoliberal directions. It appears that there was a swing towards the former under Thatcher's successor John Major, with the modernisers losing ground to the "cultural restorationists" or "aristocratic traditionalists."As Stephen Ball argues, this was a complex and even accidental twist within a broadly conservative policy coalition.

> The losers...were a coalition of educational "modernisers"...a loosely constituted group made up of "new progressive" educators, especially from the science and mathematics education communities, and "progressive vocationalists" representing the educational concerns of many of the UK's largest multinational companies. (Ball 1993:197)

Reference was made earlier to the pruning of the National Curriculum once politicians were made to realise that it was seriously overloaded. The Dearing Report (SCAA 1994), submitted in December 1993, in addition to slimming down content at key stages one to three, removed the compulsion behind art, music, history, and geography at key stage four, with the expectation that this would create space for vocational courses for academically less successful pupils. No serious thought had been given to how time was to be found for all four of these subjects, except at a tokenistic level, in key stage four. However, it was quite another thing to abandon an expectation, common in school planning and individual subject choice throughout the 1980s, that all students would have a broad and balanced curriculum that included a humanities subject and one of the creative/performing arts. No amendment was made to this during the early years of the Blair governments, but later, there was a further retreat from the National Curriculum subjects, namely abandoning the expectation that most students would study a foreign language.

Policy formation is not always straightforward, and sometimes a measure that is intended to fulfil one purpose gratuitously contributes to wider aims. A key shift in the direction of vocationalism, in terms of elements within secondary curriculum that are closely directed towards training for work, occurred through a strange kind of "market" mechanism, by redefining the exchange rates of qualifications. This resulted in giving greater statistical value to work-related courses. Although the unitary qualification of GCSE was established by Thatcher's previous Education Minister, Keith Joseph, the old divisions between higher and lower qualifications were resurrected by constant emphasis on A–C grades, to the neglect of D–G grades. The success of secondary schools came to depend on the percentage of 16-year-olds with five or more A*–C grades. This formed the starting point of inspection judgements, and was the basis of league tables published in local and national newspapers.

Around 2000, the decision was taken that henceforth a particular vocational qualification, the GNVQ (Intermediate), would count as equivalent to four A*–C grades. In other words, a student with a GNVQ would only need a C grade in one other subject to count as having "five or more A*–C grades." GNVQs were available in a number of broad areas such as construction, engineering, and healthcare, but the extension of these subjects in schools was slight. Ironically, in view of the importance of vocationalism to the neoliberal strategy, the vast majority of GNVQ entries by schools were in existing compulsory subjects, science and ICT. The GNVQ (since superseded) became a quick-fix way of dramatically improving a school's competitive position; schools were able to double their percentage scores of five A*–Cs within a single year, with headline-hitting praise from government agencies as the "most improved" schools in the country. It is difficult to establish a genuine equivalence—my own statistical comparisons point in the direction of an E rather than a C—but the interesting point is that no government agency appears to have worked on this systematically. The QCA then proceeded to establish long lists of equivalence, based largely on estimated time taken to study rather than qualitative considerations, until the bubble was burst early in 2005 by exposures in the national press, fuelled by complaints from elite independent schools that a distinction in cake decorating now counted for more than an A in GCSE physics. The prime measure of a secondary school's success then became "five A*–Cs or equivalent, including English and Maths." This did not displease the vocationalisers, since the Confederation of British Industry (CBI) was continuing to clamour for a greater focus on literacy and numeracy (for example, CBI 2004).

A far more radical and explicit curriculum change is now in progress, as a result of the Education and Inspections Act of 2006. There was a major backbench revolt against clauses in the preceding Bill to deregulate school admissions, which could, in their original version, have led to the end of comprehensive schools. There was minimal discussion of equally serious curriculum changes.

In brief, hidden within the depths of the Act, clauses 74 and 75 *Curriculum and entitlements* divide pupils into two distinct tracks from the age of 14 onwards. For the more academic, the 1980s version of a broad and balanced curriculum is restored, including the entitlement of all pupils to a social subject (history or geography), an art (now including media), a language, and a branch of design and technology. For others, all these entitlements are abandoned and replaced by a vocational course. Even English and maths, for these pupils, can be replaced by courses in functional literacy and numeracy.

It must be understood that there is nothing new in 14–16-year-olds following a vocational course, often in a nearby college, as part of a broad curriculum. Back in the 1970s, the school I taught in had large numbers of 14–16-year-olds who chose child care and car mechanics, which was taught in the school's flat and garage (purpose-built to create realistic environments for learning), or bricklaying and hairdressing at the local technical college. (Admittedly, the choices were usually strongly gendered.) However, in those days, nobody ever suggested that these same pupils would not also do drama, geography, or a foreign language. That is the difference between comprehensive schools of that time and the 2006 Schools and Inspection Act. The 2006 Act is a frontal attack on the comprehensive school principle, in that it divides 14-year-olds rigidly into two, the academic track and the vocational track. It amounts to a declaration that roughly a half of the population (those not aspiring towards Higher Education, and predominantly the children of the manual working class) should acquire little knowledge of history or geography, and should not experience the ability to express themselves creatively.

One of the ironies of this situation is that voices continue to be expressed by the Confederation of British Industry that cast doubts on government strategy. The CBI's response to the proposed 14–19 diploma includes reservations about the need for training in specific work skills ("Firms to not expect to appoint *oven ready* recruits"), arguing rather for attitudinal formation and for a greater priority for improving "the basics" amongst "the long tail of low achievers" (CBI 2004).

It would be incorrect to argue that there is no place for vocational preparation in the education of adolescents, and it is hard to imagine a future society—capitalist or socialist—in which this would not apply. Schools should include the development of economically useful skills and knowledge in their aims alongside other social (e.g., preparation for democratic citizenship, environmental education) and personal (e.g., leisure, health, aesthetic) aims. Language, mathematics, and the use of ICT underpin all three types of educational aims. What is significant, in terms of the Blairite neoliberal project, is the extent to which the social and personal have been marginalised in favour of the vocational for roughly half the school population.

Of course, as Ball (2008) and others argue, policy formation is often incoherent and sometimes unclear as to its end result. Policies can also be subverted by practical contingencies, as well as organised resistance. However, the intention is clearly stated, and practical arrangements, in terms of new vocational diplomas, are currently being pursued. This represents a significant shift from the rhetoric of the opening pages of the National Curriculum "Handbook" (DFEE/QCA 1999), which articulated a wide spectrum of aims and values, as a result of professional demands for a framing statement to underpin the prescriptive detail (See also White 2004:1–19).

Conclusion

It is impossible within a chapter to do justice to the curricular implications and tensions involved in the hundreds of initiatives taken by the Blair government, and some of these appear to pull in different directions. Some policy moves have been widely received as benign, for example, the more caring rhetoric of Every Child Matters. It is important to note, however, that even progressive-sounding initiatives such as Every Child Matters are articulated within and into an economic agenda with an emphasis on the production of "human capital" (see Ball 2008:189–191). This predominance of a neoliberal strategy and discourse can be seen even in the expansion of nursery education, accompanied by an expression of purpose that is clearly weighted towards preparation for basic skills learning in primary school; it is preparatory rather than developmental.

Another potentially positive curricular initiative was Education for Citizenship, which has opened a space for discussion about current social and political issues. (As noted above, the study of contemporary society was an important and deliberate omission from the original National Curriculum.) Its original introduction was tokenistic—a "half subject" requiring less than an hour a week and leading (at most) to a "half GCSE" (OfSTED 2006)—though it has grown in popularity in many schools and can now be studied to A-level. It is, however, important to recognise the ambivalent orientation of Education for Citizenship: it can just as easily be taught to encourage conformity and obedience as critical understanding and resistance, and teaching materials have been sponsored and published from organisations as different as Christian Aid and Greenpeace on the one hand, and the British Army and major banks on the other.

It is also important to note ways in which official recognition and support can sometimes be given to progressive initiatives. One examples is the QCA's espousal of the notion of "a curriculum for the future" through a website that highlights and praises schools that have embarked upon different kinds of thematic interdisciplinary curricula (QCA 2008). Similarly, the concept of "creativity" has received some official support, including through the Creative Partnerships initiative (see Thomson et al. 2009), though one needs to recognise how the concept of "creativity" has been subject to redefinitions through attempts to align it with entrepreneurial attitudes and practices, and to justify the arts in terms of their economic importance (Robinson 2001).

It is important to use the official support and encouragement provided by such initiatives, whilst recognising that they stand in acute tension with the ongoing performativity pressures of the system; the "bottom line" remains the test and exam results, a school's position in local and national league tables, and the danger of a failed inspection. These threats are heaviest in the most deprived areas—precisely those where innovation is most needed—and are likely to thrive only in schools in more affluent areas, leading to a new educational "apartheid" (Hargreaves 2003:180seq.). It is difficult for curriculum innovation to flourish in such an environment.

Whilst emphasising the predominantly neoliberal direction of Blairite policy, involving the sidelining of some traditionalist or conservative aspects of Thatcher's National Curriculum, it would be wrong to assume that curriculum policy has taken an entirely functionalist turn. As Apple has consistently argued in the educational field (e.g., Apple 2004), along with Harvey (2005) in the wider political and economic realm, neoliberalism and neoconservativism operate in tandem. Indeed, the need to combine, in mass education, functional skills with social control has been endemic to capitalism from the start (Simon 1960).

> Capitalism needs workers who are clever enough to be profitable, but not wise enough to know what's really going on. (Wrigley 2006:8)

In the present era, perhaps more intensively than ever, capitalism needs both to enhance the economic functionality of education and to instil in future employees the habitus of being a "human resource." The latter involves both socialisation into compliance and a denial of the knowledge that would enable young people to see beyond the current way of the world.

In the present era, this tension plays out in different contexts and in particular ways. For example, while many employers are taking a "back to basics" line, others "would like communication skills and initiative, but not too much of it" (Wrigley 2006:8). The attempt to cut educational "waste" (Sears 2003) seems to involve a redivision during school into those who will contribute to the "knowledge economy" and those destined for "poor work" (Brown and Scase 1991). Certainly in an era of multiple global crises—environmental, economic, military—the last thing capitalism can afford is an education that enables young people to make sense of the world, a schooling in which their voice and agency is encouraged.

The complexity of interpreting curriculum change in terms of macropolitical contexts should not be underestimated, and Jones et al. (2008:136) point to the absorption of a mix of ideologies and practices.

> The educational programme of neo-liberalism combines elements from very different traditions...Deconstruction can also suggest something of neo-liberalism's hegemonic force: it aims both to destroy previously powerful educational practices, and to assimilate them, and the social agents associated with them, into a new educational regime.

It is clear, however, that there has been a decisive shift, during the Blair years, towards a conception of curriculum as basic skills (literacy, numeracy, ICT) leading (for a large proportion of young people) to an early preparation for particular fields of work. Even those who are allowed a broader curriculum are expected to study it at such intensity and pace that the opportunity for critical thinking is squeezed out.

Despite the important work of dedicated teachers to keep spaces open for real learning, most young people now face a curriculum that is utilitarian, economistic, arid, and divisive. Even in its own terms, whereby quality is judged in terms of narrowly defined standards and competences, it is not leading to the expected "improvements." At the level of lived experience, it is proving unsustainable and "ineffective," since it fails to engage young people as citizens and learners.

Note

This chapter represents an analysis of the curriculum for England and Wales only. Scotland has throughout this period had a separate curriculum that, though frequently influenced by events south of the border, has taken a different direction, and has now embarked on a major curriculum reform, "A Curriculum for Excellence."

References

Aldrich R. (1988) The National Curriculum: An Historical Perspective. In Lawton, D. and Chitty, C. (eds) *The National Curriculum*. Bedford Way Paper 33. London: Institute of Education.

Alexander, R. (2004) Still No Pedagogy? Principle, Pragmatism and Compliance in Primary Education, *Cambridge Journal of Education* 34(1).

Apple, M. (1979) *Cultural and Economic Reproduction in Education: Essays on Class, Ideology and the State.* London: Routledge and Kegan Paul.

——— (1996) *Cultural Politics and Education.* Buckingham: Open University Press.

——— (2004) *Ideology and Curriculum* (3rd ed.), London: Routledge.

Ball, S. (1990) *Politics and Policy Making in Education: Explorations in Policy Sociology.* London: Taylor and Francis.

——— (1993) Education, Majorism and "the Curriculum of the Dead." *Pedagogy, Culture and Society* 1(2), pp. 195–214.

——— (2008) *The Education Debate*, Bristol: The Policy Press.

Bernstein, B. (1971) On the Classification and Framing of Educational Knowledge, in Young, M. F. D. (ed) *Knowledge and Control*, London: Collier-Macmillan.

Brown, M. and Precious, N. (1968) *The Integrated Day in the Primary School*, London: Ward Lock.

Brown, P. and Scase, R. (1991) *Poor Work: Disadvantage and the Division of Labour*, Milton Keynes: Open University Press.

Burton L. and Weiner G. (1990) Social Justice and the National Curriculum. *Research Papers in Education* 5(3), 203–227.

Confederation of British Industry. (2004) *The CBI's Response to Proposals for Reform of 14–19 Qualifications and the Introduction of a Diploma Framework*. London: CBI.

Cox, B. (ed) (1998) *Literacy Is Not Enough: Essays on the Importance of Reading*, Manchester: Manchester University Press.

Cummins, J. (2003) Challenging the Construction of Difference as Deficit: Where Are Identity, Intellect, Imagination, and Power in the New Regime of Truth? In Trifonas, P. (ed) *Pedagogies of Difference: Rethinking Education for Social Change*, London: Routledge-Falmer.

Davies M. and Edwards G. (2001) Will the Curriculum Caterpillar Ever Fly? In Fielding M. (ed) *Taking Education Really Seriously: Four Years' Hard Labour*, London: Routledge.

DES. (1989) *The Education Reform Act 1988: The School Curriculum and Assessment*, Circular 5/89, London: HMSO.

DfEE. (1998) *The National Literacy Strategy Framework for Teaching*, London: DfEE.

DfEE/QCA. (1999) *The National Curriculum Handbook for Primary / Secondary Teachers in England* [two versions].

DfES. (1980) *A View of the Curriculum*, London: HMSO.

—— (1984) *The Organization and Content of the 5–16 Curriculum*, London: HMSO.

—— (1986) *Better Schools*, London: HMSO.

—— (2003a) *The Key Stage 3 Strategy, Introducing the Third Year*, London: DfES.

—— (2003b) *Excellence and Enjoyment: A Strategy for Primary Schools*, London DfES.

—— (2004) *Five Year Strategy for Children and Learners*, London: DfES.

Eggleston, J. (1996) *Teaching Design and Technology* (2nd edition), Buckingham: Open University Press.

Gabbard, D. (ed) (2008) *Knowledge and Power in the Global Economy: The Effects of School Reform in a Neoliberal / Neoconservative Age*, (2nd edn). New York: Lawrence Erlbaum.

Garratt, D. (2000) Democratic Citizenship in the Curriculum: Some Problems and Possibilities. *Pedagogy, Culture and Society* 8(3).

Goodson, I. (1983) *School Subjects and Curriculum Change*, London: Croom Helm.

Graham, D. (1993) *A Lesson for Us All; The Making of the National Curriculum*, London: Routledge.

Hargreaves, A. (2003) Professional Learning Communities and Performance Training Cults: The Emerging Apartheid of School Improvement. In Harris A. et al., *Effective Leadership for School Improvement*, London: Routledge.

Harvey, D. (2005) A Brief History of Neoliberalism, Oxford: Oxford University Press.

Haydn, T. (2004) History. In White, J. (ed) *Rethinking the School Curriculum: Values, Aims and Purposes*, London: Routledge-Falmer.

Hilton, M. (2001) Are the Key Stage Two Reading Tests Becoming Easier Each Year? *Reading* 35(1), pp. 4–11.

Hunt, G. (2001) Democracy or a Command Curriculum: Teaching Literacy in England. *Improving Schools*, 4(3), pp. 51–58.

Johnston, R. and Watson, J. (2003) *Accelerating Reading and Spelling with Synthetic Phonics: A Five Year Follow Up*. Insight 4, Edinburgh: Scottish Executive Education Department.

Jones, K., Cunchillos, C., Hatcher, R., Hirtt, N., Innes, R., Joshua, S. and Klausenitzer, J. (2008) *Schooling in Western Europe: The New Order and Its Adversaries*, London: Palgrave Macmillan.

Kelly, A. V. (1990) *The National Curriculum: A Critical Review*, London: Chapman.

Kimbell, R. (2004) Design and Technology. In White, J. (ed) *Rethinking the School Curriculum: Values, Aims and Purposes,* London: Routledge-Falmer.

Labour Party. (1994) *Opening Doors to a Learning Society: A Policy Statement on Education,* London: Labour Party.

——— (1995) *Excellence for Everyone: Labour's Crusade to Raise Standards,* London: Labour Party.

Landman, M. and Ozga, J. (1995) Teacher Education Policy in England, In Ginsburg, M. and Lindsay, B. (eds) *The Political Dimension in Teacher Education,* London: Routledge.

Lawton, D. (1992) *Education and Politics in the 1990s: Conflict or Consensus?* London: Falmer.

Lingard, B. and Gale, T. (2007) The Emergent Structure of Feeling: What Does It Mean for Critical Educational Studies and Research? *Critical Studies in Education* 48(1).

Mroz, M., Smith, F. and Hardman, F. (2000) The Discourse of the Literacy Hour, *Cambridge Journal of Education* 30(3), pp. 379–390.

OfSTED. (2004) *Reading for Purpose and Pleasure: An Evaluation of the Teaching of Reading in Primary Schools,* London: OfSTED

——— (2006) *Towards Consensus? Citizenship in Secondary Schools,* London: OfSTED [www.ofsted.gov.uk].

Ozga, J. and Lingard, B. (2007) Globalisation, Education Policy and Politics. In Lingard, B. and Ozga, J. (eds) *The Routledge-Falmer Reader in Education Policy and Politics,* London: Routledge-Falmer.

Plowden Report. (1967) *Children and Their Primary Schools: A Report of the Central Advisory Council for Education,* London: HMSO.

QCA. (2008) *Futures—Meeting the Challenge.* www.qca.org.uk/qca_6073. aspx.

Robinson, K. (2001) *Out of Our Minds: Learning to Be Creative,* Oxford: Capstone.

Rosen, M. (2006) *What's Politics Got to Do with It?* Lecture at King's College, London, June 6th 2006 [www.michaelrosen.co.uk].

Schools Council. (1973) *Pattern and Variation in Curriculum Development Projects,* London: Macmillan.

School Curriculum and Assessment Authority. (1994) *The National Curriculum and Its Assessment: Final Report,* London: SCAA.

Scott, W. (2002) *Sustainability and Learning: What Role for the Curriculum?* Inaugural lecture, University of Bath. [www.bath.ac.uk/cree/resources/scott.pdf].

Sears, A. (2003) *Retooling the Mind Factory: Education in a Lean State,* Aurora, Ont: Garamond.

Simon, B. (1960) *Studies in the History of Education 1780–1870.* London: Lawrence and Wishart.

Smith, F., Hardman, F., Wall, K. and Mroz, M. (2000) Interactive Whole Class Teaching in the National Literacy and Numeracy Strategies, *Cambridge Journal of Education* 30(3).

Smithers, A. (2001) Education Policy. In Seldon, A. (ed) *The Blair Effect*, London: Little Brown.

Stobart, G. and Stoll, L. (2005) *The Key Stage 3 Strategy: What Kind of Reform Is This? Cambridge Journal of Education* 35(2).

Stubbs, M. (1975) Teaching and Talking: A Sociolinguistic Approach to Classroom Interaction. In Chanon D. and Delamont, S. (eds) *Frontiers of Classroom Research*, Slough: NFER.

Thomson, P., McGregor, J. and Sanders, E. (2009) Changing Schools: More Than a Lick of Paint and a Well-Orchestrated Performance? *Improving Schools* 12(1).

Tymms, P. (2004) Are Standards Rising in English Primary Schools? *British Educational Research Journal* 30(4), 477–494.

Vygotsky, L. S. (1978) *Mind in Society: The Development of Higher Psychological Processes*, Cambridge, MA: Harvard University Press.

Watson, J. and Johnston, R. (1998) *Accelerating Reading Attainment: The Effectiveness of Synthetic Phonics*, Interchange 57, Edinburgh: Scottish Office.

White, J. (2004) *Rethinking the School Curriculum: Values, Aims and Purposes*, London: Routledge-Falmer.

Whitty, G. and Menter, I. (1989) Lessons of Thatcherism: Education Policy in England and Wales 1979–88, *Journal of Law and Society* 16(1).

Whitty, G., Rowe, G. and Aggleton, P. (1994) Subjects and Themes in the Secondary-School Curriculum. *Research Papers in Education* 9(2).

Williams, R. (1976) Base and Superstructure in Marxist Cultural Theory [First published 1973]. In Dale, R. et al. (eds) *Schooling and Capitalism: A Sociological Reader*, London: Routledge and Kegan Paul.

Woods P., Jeffrey B. and Troman G. (2001) The Impact of New Labour's Educational Policy on Primary Schools. In Fielding M. (ed) *Taking Education Really Seriously: Four Years' Hard Labour*, London: Routledge.

Wrigley, T. (2006) *Another School Is Possible*, London: Bookmarks/Stoke: Trentham Books.

Chapter 7

Academies: Diversity, Economism, and Contending Forces for Change

Philip A. Woods

Introduction

The focus of this chapter is the UK government's academies programme in England and the contending forces that characterise this key policy aimed at bringing about transformational change in education.[1] First, a brief outline is provided of the programme's policy context, where the concern is to create more enterprising public institutions exposed to and involving new private players in education. Second, the academies programme is discussed, with particular attention being given to the developing pattern of sponsorship. Third, in the context of an emergent governance system of 'plural controlled schooling', two competing hypotheses are put forward: one suggesting that, despite an emphasis on innovation and diversity, academies tend to converge around an instrumentally driven, business-orientated model of entrepreneurialism and educational priorities; the second suggesting diversification, where meanings and practice show significant variations, including opportunities for progressive change. This second hypothesis looks for the degree to which new openings emerge in the programme, creating spaces for educational alternatives nurturing broader understandings of human potentiality and personal capacities for self-determination. The chapter concludes by drawing attention to the deficit in democratic accountability and the importance of the system's underlying philosophy. It is also suggested that the academies programme is a policy arena of contending forces within the *socialised* sphere of relationships and that consequently there is scope to evolve it towards a model of social co-production for human educational needs rather than one of individualistic influence dominated by instrumental and business rationales.

Policy Context: Bureau-enterprise Culture

In the past two decades traditional bureaucracy has come under sustained criticism, through works such as the seminal book by Osborne and Gaebler (1992). Bureaucratic hierarchical regimes imply a particular role and disposition of officials, based on 'the primacy of the traditional administrator, offering neutral and objective advice, administering state resources according to the bureaucratic rules of central or local government, and accountable upwards to ministers or local politicians' (Newman 2005: 719). The counterpart to the bureaucratic official is the sphere of the professionals who have had traditionally their own expertise, language and culture, and with this a marked degree of autonomy and discretion.

The modernising agenda pursued in the 1990s and into the new century aims to alter radically this structure of bureau-professionalism (Clarke and Newman 1997). New Labour since 1997 has been attempting to chart a new way between what it sees as the old dichotomy between state control and individualistic autonomy. Tony Blair's vision for the role of government illustrates how a *third way* orientation sees itself discriminating between 'good' and 'bad' strands within the extremes of hierarchical control and local freedom and attempting to combine the good from each in new ways:

> There will be no return to the old centralised command and control systems, which stifled innovation and responsibility, and we reject the creation of bureaucratic and pointless internal markets. Instead we favour partnerships at local level, with investment tied to targets and measured outcomes, with national standards but local freedom to manage and innovate. (Blair, 1998: 15)

This remains a pretty good description of New Labour's aspiration concerning public services. The reference to internal markets as pointless, however, underplays the role of choice and competitive pressures in public services. New Labour never did overturn the market-like features introduced into education in the late 1980s, such as parental rights to choice, diversity of schools, local management of schools and student-led funding. Private participation in education has proceeded through a myriad of ways—including the sponsoring of schools, contracting out of public functions, increased use of private consultants and so on. There has been 'an incremental process of breaking up established assumptions and modes of operation and taken for granted practices and replacing these with new "freedoms", new players and new kinds of relationships and new forms of service delivery' (Ball 2008: 195), so that 'the private sector is now thoroughly intertwined in the day-today business of decision-making, infrastructural development, capacity building and services delivery…' (196).

The drive is to make public sector organisations more flexible, to introduce or sustain features of the market, including a much more entrepreneurial culture (du Gay 2004), and to combine this with a governmental 'steering' role (Woods 2003). There is perceived to be, therefore, a move 'away from welfare and civic values toward an enterprise culture promoting a consumer-driven economy…re-aligning professional and managerial cultures around private rather than public ethics' (Gleeson and Knights 2006: 281).

The results are, however, complex and non-linear. Modernisation is played out in different ways according to local contexts and the responses of local players. Entrepreneurialism in education can take different forms (Woods et al. 2007). Bureaucracy and enterprise are not, in practice, exclusive and mutually opposed organisational logics, with one neatly succeeding the other (du Gay 2004). It is, rather, more a case of entrepreneurial principles becoming more prominent within bureaucracies which, as a result, are evolving into a modified form of bureaucracy. Courpasson and Clegg (2006) argue, for example, that whilst certain principles of bureaucracy remain intact, its administrative principles have been softened in order to incorporate a more entrepreneurial style of project management. Far from disappearing, entrepreneurial cultures rely on bureaucratic rationality to provide practical organisational arrangements which sustain their operation.

The direction of travel is, nevertheless, clear: from organisation characteristic of bureau-professionalism to organisation characterised by *bureau-enterprise* culture valuing the following features:

- a dominating instrumental rationality embodied in a flexibilised sets of organisational roles;
- a more entrepreneurial and consumer-responsive culture;
- a belief in flatter hierarchies, combined with reformed hierarchical structure and bureaucratic procedures;
- a visionary zeal to achieve system and organisational goals;
- the systematic monitoring and measurement of performance in formally rational ways.

Academies

The Academies Programme

The creation of new types of school is at the forefront of moves to facilitate diversity, innovation and the blurring of the public/private boundary (Woods et al. 2007). A critical move in this aim is the creation of a new organisational type of school—academies[2]—intended principally to replace so-called failing schools. (A further policy strand in this direction is the creation of trust schools.[3]) These are at the leading edge of change which brings private organisations, groups and individuals into influential roles in the public education system. Academies are state-funded (usually secondary) schools, which replace existing schools and are established and managed by independent sponsors, such as businesses, faith groups, educational institutions (including universities and colleges) and charitable organisations. The first group of academies opened in 2002. There are 200 academies open at the time of writing[4], and a commitment to establish 400. Outside the local authority system, they are intended to be innovative and entrepreneurial and are aimed primarily at increasing the educational attainment of pupils in socially and economically disadvantaged areas where they are usually, though not exclusively, located.

The academies programme is one of New Labour's most controversial policies, criticised for taking schooling out of the local democratic framework and transferring too much influence to unaccountable sponsors. Its scale and cost—estimated to be £5 billion (House of Commons Select Committee on Education and Skills 2005)—has fuelled critical scrutiny. Some of the key criticisms are that academies[5]:

- are a means of privatising education
- attract an unfairly large proportion of public expenditure on education
- are a costly, unproven experiment
- place too much emphasis on changing educational structures at the expense of concentrating on raising standards
- cream off higher ability students from neighbouring schools
- are 'degrading' the curriculum by introducing easier vocational qualifications to boost headline results
- exacerbate local competition between schools
- are leading to an increase in the numbers of faith schools, thus exacerbating segregation in the state school system

- are not democratically accountable at a local level
- are detrimental to teachers' terms and conditions of employment.

These continue to be keenly debated and it is difficult to come to agreed conclusions around most of them. Issues of privatising education and increasing faith involvement, for example, depend on how concepts like privatisation are defined and what perspective is taken on the positive and negative aspects of private participation and faith-influenced education. Much also depends on how academies are working in practice—for example, whether they are in practice creaming off students, raising standards, exacerbating local competition between schools, worsening employment terms and conditions, and so on. What is clear is that there is a considerable degree of diversity amongst academies—in terms of factors such as their success in improving students' measured attainment and recognition of trade unions—leading PricewaterhouseCoopers (PWC) in the final report of its 5-year study of academies to conclude that 'rather than a simple uniform "Academy effect", there has been a more complex and varied process of change' (PriceWaterhouseCoopers 2008: 8). (See also Armstrong et al. 2009.) Whilst the PWC finds some evidence of academies using their status to be flexible and creative (in curriculum matters for example), its report also concludes that 'in their efforts to improve teaching and learning, Academies are generally operating *in similar ways to improving schools in the LA [local authority] maintained sector*, namely monitoring and improving the quality of lessons, ensuring appropriate continuing professional development, and tracking and monitoring pupil progress' (PriceWaterhouseCoopers 2008: 189, emphasis added).

On measured performance, the PWC researchers come to the conclusion that there is 'insufficient evidence to make a definitive judgement about the Academies as a model for school improvement' (Armstrong et al. 2009: 123). A study by Machin and Wilson (2009: 8) of academies compared with matched schools, also concluded that it was premature to suggest any effect from being an academy: they could not find a pattern of 'short-run effects of becoming an academy on GCSE performance when long-run differences between the academies' predecessors and matched schools are taken into account'. Gorard (2009), from his analysis of official figures on academies, suggests too that there is currently no clear evidence that academies produce better results than local authority schools with equivalent intakes.

One of the issues that the PWC study raises for future consideration is the fact that, in a departure from traditional governance, academies 'are not scrutinised or held accountable to their local education and children's services or democratically elected members' (PriceWaterhouseCoopers 2008: 119). Nevertheless, whilst academies remain controversial, a number of local authorities have decided to take a strategic approach to developing academies in their area and to become co-sponsors; there is also more emphasis on and evidence of academies becoming embedded in their communities, collaborating with other schools and having a closer relationship with their local authority (PriceWaterhouseCoopers 2008, Barker and Turner 2007). This illustrates how the academies programme is an evolving policy. It has been subject to a number of changes which have 'addressed some of the deficiencies of the programme and . . . have certainly been welcomed by some observers, even while others remain unconvinced' (Curtis et al. 2008: 49).

Academy Sponsors

The academies programme is integral to a government drive to challenge under-achievement and what are perceived to be the low aspirations of disadvantaged communities. The policy is framed by a belief in the need to introduce top-down change and to bring in new, 'dynamic' players into communities which, if they are to progress educationally, are seen as dependent on external change-agents. Moreover, the dominant emphasis is on producing school leavers whose attitudes and skills will enhance the workforce of 'UK plc'. Education is predominantly framed in economistic terms.

Fitting into this agenda, a major thrust behind the academies programme is to involve business in sponsoring schools and to create more enterprising students better suited to the needs of the competitive, globalised economy. The reason given for the creation of one academy, for example, is: 'We must ensure that our children and young people—the employees of tomorrow—gain the skills and qualifications demanded by employers. This calls for a different approach to secondary education—one that is much more closely linked to business.' (Manchester Academies Consultation 2007a: 1). Another declares that 'Even the building design reflects our specialism [business enterprise], with its 'retail' street, enterprise outlets, hair salon and restaurant' (Castle View Enterprise Academy 2009: 5).

However, businesses are by no means the only or main source of sponsorship. An analysis of academy sponsors—a 'snapshot' picture, based on academies either open or in development in 2005 (Woods et al. 2007)—found that the proportion being sponsored solely by a business sponsor falling: amongst the first wave of Academies opened between 2002 and 2004, 59% (n=17) were sponsored by solo business sponsors, whilst amongst Academies opened or in development in 2005 the proportion was less than half that: 27% (n=40). Other, non-business types of sponsor are increasingly important as the range of academy sponsors has been diversified (Curtis 2009, PricewaterhouseCoopers 2008) (Table 7.1). These include faith sponsors, universities and further education colleges, with also increasing numbers of independent schools converting to academy status (Curtis 2009, Kingston 2006, Marley 2007b, Woods et al. 2007).

This evolving pattern of sponsorship is significant for the nature of schooling as 'the power of an Academy sponsor is considerable' (Curtis et al. 2008: 6). According to PWC (2008: 121–122), sponsors' contributions include *resources* (in some cases over and above the basic £2million input {now no longer a requirement from sponsors}); *support* (which includes expertise directly from the sponsor{s} and his or her business and personal associations); *ethos* (shaping and supporting the Academy's underlying values and culture); and *challenge* (helping to encourage 'an unremitting focus on improvement and…on raising attainment'). I want in the remainder of this section to illustrate the complex picture of sponsorship that is steadily developing.

As noted, some local authorities are taking a strategic approach to academy development. Manchester's Education Partnership is one such local authority driven strategy for the creation of academies. Manchester City Council's vision for partnership (Manchester City Council 2006: 7) states that 'Manchester's vision can only be achieved through innovative partnerships between schools, public services, communities and the city's businesses'. Its intention is to develop academies within an overarching city-wide strategy led by the City Council. Instead of academies being seen as stand-alone schools, the intention is to draw them into clusters of non-academy schools.

> Small, medium or large companies—either individually or together through consortia—can support the development of a new skills base for the city through sponsorship, and businesses are invited to sponsor an Academy, along with up to four schools that each Academy is itself a partner with. (7)

Companies are sought as partners which share a specified set of values, including equity (reinforcing the articulated aim of inclusion). The benefits for business are also spelt out (see Box 7.1).

Table 7.1 Sources of sponsorship in the 133 Academies open by 2008

Sources of sponsorship	Description	Total no. of Academies with sponsor type*	No. of Academies with sponsor type as sole sponsor
Business entrepreneurs	A wealthy individual sponsors or co-sponsors one or more Academy.	26	14
Companies	A company sponsors or co-sponsors one or more Academy.	16	5
Non-profit Organisations	A non-profit organisation, trust or foundation (not including those with overt religious affiliations) is established that sponsors or co-sponsors one or more Academy.	34	22
Faith-based organisations	A church diocese, or an organisation with religious affiliations or ethos, sponsors or co-sponsors one or more Academy	51	38
'Successful' Schools	A 'successful' (usually independent) school sponsors or co-sponsors one or more Academy.	7	1
Further education colleges and universities	A further education college or university sponsors or co-sponsors one or more Academy.	9	2
Local Authorities	A local authority co-sponsors one or more Academy.	8	0
CTC conversions	A CTC converts to an Academy	11	
Independent school conversions	An independent school converts to an Academy	4	

Note: *Figures total more than 133 as some Academies are sponsored by more than one sponsor type.
Source: Curtis 2009

Box 7.1 Benefits and Values of Businesses

Benefits for businesses	Values businesses are expected to share
• A diverse and skilled workforce, committed to lifelong learning and work-based training, is arguably the key to long-term economic competitiveness. • By partnering with an Academy and its partner schools, businesses will be able to reach high numbers of students and have access to an important product and service development research base. • Businesses, rightly critical of the national standards of secondary education, will have an opportunity to improve the quality and outputs of the education system. • Businesses will be able to influence both the specific and generic skills students acquire, and thus address local skills shortages—an ever-present issue within growing and new industries. • Businesses will be able to use the Academy and schools as a training or learning resource for their own staff. • Long-term engagement with schools will enable industry partners to develop outreach initiatives, such as pupil or staff mentoring—stimulating and motivating not just the recipients but the mentors themselves.	**Commitment:** businesses must be fully committed to the Education Partnership, Manchester and the region, to achieving excellence, and to working with all children from all communities across Manchester. **Ambition:** business partners must share Manchester City Council's vision of a better world delivered through engaging local communities. The Education Partnership aims to make a difference to the lives of young people, the economy and business throughout the city region. **Innovation:** by creating an education system that focuses on work-related learning, businesses should share the enthusiasm for creating an environment of lifelong learning that will build a strong and diverse future workforce. **Teamwork:** the Education Partnership seeks a shared leadership that is flexible and responsive, and that can build streamlined teams with flair, initiative and the zeal required to make the vision a reality. **Equity:** business partners must share responsibility and take equal ownership of the Education Partnership to ensure a first-class education system that everyone across the city has access to.

Source: Manchester City Council 2006: 9, 10

These benefits for business, described in the prospectus issued by Manchester, include:

- the creation of a 'diverse and skilled workforce'
- access to schools and students who will provide an 'important product and service development research base'
- influence over the curriculum, specifically the 'specific and generic skills students acquire'.

With the Manchester City Council initiative there is a *prima facie* commitment to a public ethos and public values—such as equality of opportunity and development throughout the city, collaboration between public organisations, and a sense of identity with the place and the people of that area that transcends the narrower interests of individual organisations. The strategy emanates from a democratically legitimated body which is in being to represent the locality.

However, what is also evident is the strong and explicit view of education as a means to economic success, and the privileged position being offered to business. The driving purpose of the strategy is the creation of a new kind of education to the benefit of both employers and individuals. However, in the context that this is placed, the economic goal (and the perceived magnitude of the task) is clear (Manchester City Council 2006: Foreword):

> [W]e must invest in business and the public sector, and create and sustain new jobs in tomorrow's industries. And if we are to create new jobs, we must create a different kind of education...

A different perspective is represented by the entry of the Royal Society for the Arts (RSA) into the academies programme. The RSA decided in 2006 to sponsor an academy in a deprived area in Sandwell in the West Midlands (Tomlinson 2006). It took the view that the academies initiative, although controversial, deserves to have a chance to prove itself as a policy aimed at improving education in disadvantaged areas. The RSA brings to its academy a focus on 'fostering resilient communities and moving towards a zero-waste society' (p35). It sees the academies programme as an innovative way of promoting an environmentally sensitive attitude to living and contributing to local regeneration through 'a suite of projects that have the potential to help meet the educational, social, health and economic needs of the area' (RSA 2006: 9).

The RSA also expresses a wider ambition for the academy which explicitly articulates a philosophy of education that is broader than the business-orientated perspectives associated with many academies. As the RSA's then Executive Director put it:

> There is no doubt that the skills and techniques of the business world can teach us vital lessons for later life but they are only one set of ingredients in what must be a carefully measured blend. The RSA's investigation of a number of existing academies has shown us that a disappointingly small number are striving to be innovative in the way

they provide education, relying perhaps on the grammar school models of the 'fifties and 'sixties. (Egan 2006)

She went on:

> The City Academy programme could provide local communities, businesses, statutory bodies and educators with the chance to take a collaborative, coherent approach to creating education that is relevant to the challenges of today's world. One step on the road to meeting those challenges is equipping our children for life—not just for university. (Egan 2006)

Opened in 2008 the RSA academy has a dual specialism of Health and Citizenship and describes its approach as follows:

> We focus on healthy minds in healthy bodies, embedding the values and skills which will enable our young people to grow into citizens who can participate, contribute and lead within the local community. Health is promoted throughout the curriculum encouraging and enabling students to develop and maintain healthy lifestyles. Our focus on Citizenship begins within the Academy but will always look outwards. Students have a voice within the decision making processes through a Student Council where they learn to listen to the views of others, present ideas and discuss issues. It also encompasses the local community with students having the opportunity to work with local policy makers, debating real issues which impact on themselves and their families. (RSA Academy 2009: 12)

The articulated philosophy of the RSA contrasts with the explicit business and economic focus of Manchester's strategy.

Faith organisations are prominent as sponsors, as is clear from Table 7.1. Sole sponsorship by faith groups increased from 12% of Academies opened in 2002–04 to 30% of Academies opened or in development in 2005 (Woods et al. 2007). By 2008, 29% of opened Academies were solely sponsored by a faith sponsor and, in all, 38% were either solely or jointly sponsored by a faith sponsor (Table 7.1).

The Church of England (CofE) has reinforced its commitment to involvement in the Academies programme as it looks to increase the number of CofE schools (Marley 2007a). An arm of the CofE— the United Learning Trust (ULT)—is the single largest sponsor of Academies. At the time of writing it sponsors 17 Academies with more on the way. ULT was founded in 2003 as a subsidiary charity of the CofE's United Church Schools Trust which has been providing independent (fee paying) education since 1883. ULT's stated educational priorities emphasise academic excellence, the importance of pastoral care, the value of what it refers to as healthy competition (through games and sport), encouragement of the arts, and a sense of community: 'In keeping with our general emphasis on spiritual values, we strive to ensure that every school fully engages staff, pupils, parents and local supporters into a happy community'[6]. Other faith sponsors include the Roman Catholic Church and Oasis (a Christian organisation).

A further example of an alternative approach entering the academy programme is represented by the Co-operative Movement. (The Co-operative Movement is also developing a national network of 200 co-operative trust schools {School Coop 2008}).The collaborative, partnership approach in Manchester encouraged the Co-operative Movement to become involved as an academy sponsor. It could see within this context an opportunity to promote and encourage its values in and through education—values of:

- self-help
- self-responsibility
- democracy
- equality
- equity
- solidarity.

The Co-operative Movement, and other like-minded organisations, sees education as a means to 'achieving individual and community benefits through self responsibility and mutual self-help' and as being 'the secular equivalent of faith schools, in which education is combined with commitment to a purpose, based on a shared identity' (Lochrie 2006: 12). It has taken the view that it can sponsor an academy in a way that brings its values to bear. It has committed itself to designing a curriculum that will 'inspire and excite young people' and 'help them make informed choices in terms of their career and life decisions'; and it brings to this its co-operative values and principles, a strong sense of social responsibility which means not only serving customers but making a positive contribution to the well-being and enrichment of society, and an ethical stance towards trading and environmental issues (The Co-operative Group/Manchester City Council 2007).

The values and strong ethical stance of the Co-operative Group will underpin this Academy....[C]o-operative members believe in the ethical values of honesty, openness, social responsibility and caring for others. These values mean the Academy will be developed to benefit not just their members but the wider community, allowing members to have a say in the way the Academy is run, and developing co-operative ways of working and learning. (Manchester Academies Consultation 2007b: 3)

A final illustration of the diversity of sponsorship is the Steiner movement, which is made up of schools which follow the spiritual and scientific philosophy of Rudolf Steiner. One Steiner school, previously in the independent sector, reopened as Hereford Steiner Academy in 2008. Like all Steiner schools, this a non-faith school with a strong underpinning philosophy and sense of purpose. Its foundation is spiritual, without the intention of educating children into a particular faith[7]. The decision to seek academy status arises from both a wish to make Steiner education more accessible and a recognition that state funding would improve its financial situation. The essence of Steiner education is its philosophy and understanding of human development, which involves a commitment to nurturing young people in an environment that allows all of their capabilities (spiritual, social, physical and so on) to develop at an appropriate pace and enables them to grow into independent, free-thinking individuals. It thus challenges dominant educational policy that emphasises tests and league tables, and a curriculum and pedagogy that are shaped by the perceived needs of the economy and driven by measurable performance (Burnett 2009). The school recognises that a key challenge 'will be in ensuring that we do not lose the very nature of Steiner education in the transition' to being a state-funded academy (Hereford Steiner School 2006).

Opportunities for Progressive Change?

Plural Controlled Schooling[8]

In the English education system there are strands of both control and autonomy. Increased school diversity, as in the academies programme, has to be understood in relation to and in the context of a national framework of goals, values and identities forged by centralised reforms. Educational professionals and schools are constructed within the changes emanating from the centre that have sought to re-form the content of educational experience and bring about structural change. In addition, the system created by central government has opened spaces and opportunities for different kinds of agency through the introduction of new players as sponsors of academies and partners of trust schools, by no means all of whom, as we have seen, are from the business sector. All of this introduces some degree of indeterminateness in how the education plays out in the future. Central government is not in control of all of the consequences of everything that it controls.

Arguably, a *plural controlled schooling* governance model for the school education system is emerging[9], characterised by multiple sources of control and influence on education. Whilst central government retains significant levers of control, there is also a multiplication of educational players and partners, drawn from business and other sectors. The emphasis in plural controlled schooling is on diversity of sources of control and influence, the consequent necessity for networks and partnerships, and on processes of relationship-building between educational players which involve negotiation and attention to the nurturing of connections across traditional local community, organisational and sector boundaries.

The consequence for actors in the education system is that they have, at best, *constrained empowerment.* Autonomy and involvement by educational players and partners are encouraged. Opportunities and spaces for creativity and innovation are built into the system. These occur, however, within a specific kind of regime that values detailed central evaluation and priorities that accord with the perceived demands of a globally competitive economy and maintenance of a top-down version of social cohesion. Empowerment is constrained by a context that expresses powerful valuational signals consistent with a neo-liberal agenda. The requirement to apply national tests, the intense attention given to measured performance, the operation of school inspections by the national inspection agency (Ofsted), and the strong valuation given to the priorities and needs of the market act to forge a powerful, dominant discourse defining education and its governance.

Two Hypotheses

There may be diversity of sponsors and articulated aims, but do these translate into significant differences in educational culture, practice and student experience? Two hypotheses suggest themselves. The first is the *convergence hypothesis.* Institutional theory, for example, which has been used as one framework in studies of charter schools in the US (which have similarities to academies), emphasises the power of institutional forces which emanate from educational stakeholders, policy, regulations and so on, and which act to promote conformity amongst schools despite their very divergent forms of governance and (apparent) differences in predisposition to innovation.[10] Research in the US suggests that, in line with institutional theory, charter schools are not more innovative and different as compared with 'ordinary' state schools and do not buck the conforming power of institutional forces (Goldring and Cravens 2008). As noted above, research evidence in England suggests that academies are tending to follow patterns of school improvement strategies similar to those found in other, non-academy schools.

A more specific form of the convergence hypothesis proposes that that the dominant and ultimately effective press is to conformity around an instrumentally driven business model of entrepreneurialism and innovation. The proposition with this is that there is continual change and innovation in processes and techniques: capitalism by its very nature requires 'constantly revolutionising the instruments of production, and thereby the relations of production, and with them the whole relations of society' (Marx and Engels 1967: 83). But, the underlying purpose and effective rationale remains orientated to servicing and sustaining capitalistic relationships, and the subjection of life to means-end rationality continues to be in the ascendant (Woods 2009). Educational reforms since the 1980s have forged an education system 'increasingly geared toward instrumental industrial interests', imbuing the system with an 'agenda of "realism"' that creates education 'fit for a capitalist twenty-first century' (Hill et al.: 2002). This 'realism' involves a more efficient socialisation of the classes dependent on selling their labour, so that they have a more attractive product in the labour market—a particular concern being to tie more closely erstwhile disadvantaged communities to the dominant culture and disciplines of globally competitive capitalist enterprises. From this point of view, the academies programme can be seen as a further twist in the subordination of education to the economy, instrumental rationality and the worldview of private business—in other words, a contemporary reinforcement of alienation, in which people are delimited and manoeuvred by social forces created by humankind but not under their control. In this argument, the academies programme is driven by concerns other than the holistic growth of human potentialities and development of young people's capacity for 'self-conscious self-determination'.[11] There may be efforts in this regard—which are laudable and interesting, and ostensibly challenge the materialism and instrumentalism of a profoundly economistic society—but these remain (according to the convergence hypothesis) marginal and junior partners in the dominant educational rationale.

However, the question I want to ask is whether the unfolding reality of the academies programme is more complex and nuanced than this. I want to ask this in the spirit of Marx's dialectical analysis of alienation—which I take to be about moving beyond alienation, through awareness and practical change that yields the good suppressed in the present, revealed through its contradictions. Are there goods (potential or actual) embedded in the academies programme? Is the academies programme becoming a policy territory over which social forces encouraging a larger view of education are contending with economistic perspectives on the purpose of schooling? Do some of these represent credible attempts to provide opportunities for re-enchantment—that is, education that fosters meaning in contemporary life and capabilities and predispositions to challenge domination by rationalising forces (Woods 2009).

With these questions in mind, I turn to the second hypothesis, which is the *diversification hypothesis*. This proposes that meanings and practice show significant variations, ranging from models and rationales that serve business and instrumental rationality to fundamentally different models and rationales of human development, particularly those seeking progressive change. The diversification hypothesis aligns itself with ' "new openings" theories' (Antonio 1998: 46), as developed by theorists such as Tony Giddens and Alberto Melluci, and which I shall refer to as *new openings theory* to emphasise an essential focus on the capacity and potential in contemporary society for agency, innovation and difference. Key themes in this perspective include personal reflexivity, construction (rather than inheritance) of identity, cultural diversity, active individual agency, collective action (the latter not confined to social class, but through, for example, new social movements), and choice and participation in groups and organisations (challenging traditional hierarchy). New openings theorists take the view that 'increased diversity, openness, and participation herald a more inclusive, freer and sustainable democracy' (op. cit.: 47). Class-based politics and the ultimate power ascribed to economic relationships are rejected. However, the creative social spaces new openings theory discerns as possible can be seen, in their most progressive form, as areas of interpersonal energy that encourage the 'absolute working-out of [people's] creative potentialities' and 'the development of all human powers as such the end in itself, not as measured on a *predetermined* yardstick' (Marx 1973: 488).[12] In other words, they focus on personal empowerment in the sense of nurturing and unfolding the fullest human capabilities, and offer collective challenges to education confined to skills and predispositions for people principally defined by their economic role in society.

If the diversification hypothesis is to have some credibility, it must be that the academies programme is attracting effectual agents of change which are creating educational experiences that counteract to some significant degree the narrowing of education to a system of workforce supply. In support of this, it is possible to point to interventions through the academies programme which have the aim of enlarging the content of education (addressing the full potentialities of young people to grow with a sense of autonomy, self-belief and emotional and spiritual maturity) and working explicitly as organisations on the basis of broader principles. Examples include the RSA, the Steiner movement and the Co-operative Movement, as well as some faith organisations which would count themselves in this terrain of change too. Such interventions are, to varying degrees, contributing to 'cultural progressivism' (Woods et al. 2007: 250). They challenge the narrowness of education—which governance through performative-orientated quality control (manifest in particular types of tests, inspections, etc.) and an economistic-values focus tends to promote—and the social injustices that emanate from instrumentally driven capitalist relations and socio-cultural divides. It is important to recognise that commitments to broaden education are not absent from 'conventional' state (non-academy) schools, where examples of progressive change can be found.[13] However, the interventions by sponsors aimed at enlarging education are of interest as specific forms of *public entrepreneurialism* (Woods 2007; Woods and Woods 2009, Woods et al. 2007) which test the potential for progressive change through the academies route.

The potential to access this route and take on the role of new educational players and partners is, however, unequally distributed. Inequalities in resources—human, social and financial capital—exist amongst sponsors and potential sponsors. Sponsors tend to be individual and institutional actors who already have existing structural advantages in their field, be it business (financially privileged and/or well-connected business people, or successful companies) or the cultural sphere (universities, colleges, churches and their agencies, and so on). (And the challengers who contribute variously to cultural progressivism are also characterised by substantial differences, as, for example, between the Steiner movement and the large financial and institutional mass of the Co-operative Movement—although the Hereford Steiner Academy, which is in a rural area, not the deprived urban community originally intended for academies, may represent another strand of influence, namely of middle class activists able to lobby effectively to enhance their choice.) There is overall an imbalance of power between the challengers and the dominant fixers of signs (Kratochwil 2007) moulding authoritative meanings of educational process and success and defining the parameters of constrained empowerment. Herein lies the potential predictive power of the convergence hypothesis. Despite the complex pattern of sponsorship, discussed earlier, the academies programme is part of and calibrated by an education system framed in economistic terms. It is a dimension of the contemporary trend towards 'network governance' which combines market rationalities and a governmental 'steering' role and attaches only marginalised significance and value to democratic authority and processes (Woods 2003: 149). Challenges to the dominant rationality are limited presences in the system, exercising constrained empowerment and dependent on where sponsorship resources are able to arise and coalesce.

On the other hand, the diversity of sponsorship does enable spaces to be created where genuine difference can grow. Prospects for the diversification hypothesis rest with the very complexity and relative openness of the developing plural controlled governance model—that is, the intricacy and multiplicity of potential pathways opened by the more plural system, which enable players to find niches, support and alliances that may allow alternatives to survive and flourish and to have potentially a wider influence in the system. So, for example, Steiner schooling has the potential to engage in a mutually influential dialogue with 'mainstream' educators (Woods et al. 2005); and the Co-operative movement, through engagement with the academies and trust schools programmes, is showing how values and a concern with ethics that challenge individual competitiveness can work practically in schools and is actively disseminating these alternative approaches to education (Wilson and Mills 2008). The plural system is home to a developing sub-pattern of cultural spaces (made up of a limited number of the kind of academies and trust schools espousing alternative approaches) which have roots in institutions that in varying ways and with varying ideational, institutional and financial resources take a different view of dominant instrumental and economistic rationalities. They represent possibilities for 'organic governance' (a more open type of governance than network governance). This kind of governance is one in which social actors take advantage of the fluidity of network relationships, and both work with and challenge pressures to conform to bureaucratic and market rationalities, in order to find ways of forging cultures and organisations infused by the human potential for creativity, meaning, ethical values and democratic rationalities (Woods 2003, 2004). The sub-pattern of alternatives that arises through this public and civic-minded enterprise is about creating spaces within a boundary that is both protective (so not succumbing completely to dominant rationalities) and porous (as there are connections to and dependencies on state and other institutions). The scope for the diversification hypothesis to be realised depends, *inter alia*, on how that boundary is managed.

Concluding Remarks

The academies programme is not a monolithic vehicle for business values, but an arena where contending influences and ideals are being played out. There may be a tendency amongst academies towards technical convergence around certain strategies of school improvement and ways of working that are aligned with bureau-enterprise culture, but examples of innovation in values and ethos are also evident and could represent (notwithstanding the press of network governance rationalities) the most promising area of enterprising change. Continuing research is needed to understand exactly what degree of convergence and diversification is occurring in the various kinds of academies (and other kinds of schools, such as trust schools) that are being created.

The political framework has a crucial effect on the emerging pattern. In a plural controlled system, such as that emergent in England, there are (*inter alia*) two pivotal questions. The first concerns democratic accountability. Plural control does not equate with democratic control, unless there are specific policies and procedures in place to ensure transparency, principles of equity and fairness, and community participation. These, however, are not robust enough presently in England's education system to facilitate local democratic empowerment. The precise arrangements effective and appropriate for democratic accountability of a more plural system have not been thought through. Yet, the nature or weakness of such accountability affects the flow and oversight of sponsors. A related, second question concerns the philosophy of education that underpins the system. Some philosophy—at the very least some kind of *ad hoc* perspective—will lie beneath the decisions that forge and evolve the policy framework, and what it is and who effectively decides the underlying philosophy are consequential for the kinds of schooling that emerge. A *laissez faire* philosophy, for example, leaves the question of who is allowed into the educational arena to the free play of individual and institutional decisions. It therefore cedes formation of the consequent pattern of education to existing social forces and the inequalities and power differences that are represented in them. By contrast, a progressive philosophy, in the terms defined in this chapter, has in mind to encourage and support forms of education, and hence new players in the field, that innovate in ways that advance a progressive agenda—namely, enlarging the content of education (developing creative potentialities not confined solely to skills and predispositions defined by economic roles) and founding its institutional arrangements in principles of human flourishing, social justice, participation, and so on.

A final point to note is that the intervention of sponsors—whether business or otherwise—is taking place within the socialised sphere of relationships, i.e. within a sphere that remains in public ownership and funded collectively by state finance. The boundary between academies and conventional state schools is a boundary within the public sector, within the sphere of socialised relationships. This boundary may harden or blur. Much depends on how the many actors within and influencing the arena reinforce or challenge that boundary. The implication for progressive change is to take a pro-active stance towards it as a policy arena and to try and evolve it towards a model of social co-production for human educational needs rather than one of individualistic influence dominated by instrumental and business rationalities.

Notes

1. The the key stated aims of the academy programme are to challenge the culture of educational under-attainment and produce improvements in standards, and play a key part in the regeneration of communities—helping to break the cycle of underachievement in areas of social and economic deprivation. Academies are meant to become 'leaders in innovation, adopting radical approaches to the way they address underachievement and promote excellence. The independent status of Academies will allow them the flexibility to be innovative and creative in their curriculum, timetabling..., staffing and governance. (DfES, 2005).

2. They were initially called 'city academies' but later were termed simply 'academies'.

3. State-funded schools can apply to become trust schools, which are foundation schools supported by a charitable trust. Through this arrangement, the intention is that schools build sustainable relationships with external partners (from further and higher education, business and the voluntary sector). Like academies, the policy aim

is 'to create a new source of dynamism and to help raise standards' (DCSF 2007: 95) by reforming the relationship with other agencies and organisations. The first 30 trust schools opened in September 2007; by January 2009, 124 were open, with 444 planned. Trust schools fit into the broad policy trend and theoretical discussion in this chapter, though the chapter concentrates on academies.

4. October 2009
5. See, for example, Beckett (2007), Hatcher (2009), National Union of Teachers (2007), Needham and Gleeson (2006), Titcombe (2008).
6. http://www.ucstrust.org.uk/about-us/view/40/Our-core-values, accessed February 17, 2009.
7. See Woods et al (2005) for further discussion of Steiner schools in England.
8. Further discussion of the ideas in this sub-section on plural controlled schooling is in Woods and Broadfoot (2008).
9. This does not replace or necessarily dominate other models of governance (the quality control, competitive market, local empowerment and school empowerment models, outlined in Glatter 2003 and Glatter and Woods 1995), but is inserted alongside and interacts with these.
10. See Dimaggio and Powell (1983), for example, on institutional theory.
11. Oxford Companion to Philosophy, Oxford University Press, 1995 (from website, www.xrefer.com/entry/552724). See also Meszaros's (1970: 162–168) discussion of Marx's notion of 'selfmediation'.
12. It also needs to be acknowledged, however, that spaces and potential for diversity exist not only for progressive forces. Whilst there may be opportunities for 'cultural progressivism' (Woods et al. 2007: 250), there are also forms of 'cultural restorationism' (Whitty et al. 1993: 48; Ball, 1994: 5).
13. A concern with and innovations to address emotional, social, cultural and spiritual development, and issues such as students voice and participative leadership, are evident in 'conventional', non-academy state schools. Some or much of this focus is, however, subsumed within a kind of 'subtle instrumentalism' whereby it is recognised that increased measurable performance requires attention to young people's and school staff's emotions and motivations. Having said that, much of the focus on broader educational concerns and social justice also reflects a genuine commitment within such schools to a larger and progressive vision of education. The progressive question for 'conventional' state schools and academies is how far they can buck the trend to rationalise and instrumentalize education See Woods (2005; 2009) on subtle instrumentalism and the rationalisation of education, and research such as that by Fielding (2008, 2009), Jeffrey and Woods (2003), Williams et al. (2009) and Maguire

(2005) on radical and challenging approaches to education within state schools.

References

Antonio, R. J. (1998) Mapping Postmodern Social Theory, in Sica, A. (ed) *What Is Social Theory? The Philosophical Debates*, Oxford: Blackwell, pp. 46–49.

Armstrong, D., Bunting, V. and Larsen, J. (2009) Academies: A Model for School Improvement? Key Findings from a Five-Year Longitudinal Evaluation, *Management in Education*, 23 (3): 118–124.

Ball, S. J. (1994) *Education Reform: A Critical and Post-Structural Approach*, Buckingham: Open University Press.

——— (2008) The Legacy of ERA, Privatization and the Policy Ratchet, *Educational Management Administration and Leadership*, 36 (2): 185–199.

Barker, A. and Turner, D. (2007) Academies Restored to the Local Field, *Financial Times*, 27th September.

Beckett, F. (2007) *The Great City Academy Fraud*, London: Continuum.

Blair, T. (1998). *The Third Way: New Politics for the New Century*, London: The Fabian Society.

Burnett, J. (2009) Authentic Assessment in the First Steiner Academy, *Management in Education*, 23 (3): 118–124.

Castle View Enterprise Academy. (2009) *Prospectus 2009*, Sunderland: Castle View Enterprise Academy.

Clarke, J. and Newman, J. (1997) *The Managerial State*, London: SAGE.

The Co-operative Group/Manchester City Council. (2007) *Financial and Professional Services Academy in Manchester City Council: Expression of Interest for an Academy*, http://www.dcsf.gov.uk/foischeme/_documents/DfES_FoI_371.pdf, accessed 18th February 2009.

Courpasson, D. and Clegg, S. (2006) Dissolving the Iron Cages? Tocqueville, Michels, Bureaucracy and the Perpetuation of Elite Power, *Organization* 13 (3): 319–343.

Curtis, A. (2009) Academies and School Diversity, *Management in Education*, 23 (3): 113–117.

Curtis, A., Exley, S., Sasia, A., Tough, S. and Whitty, G. (2008) *The Academies Programme: Progress, Problems and Possibilities: A Report for the Sutton Trust*, London: The Sutton Trust and Institute of Education, University of London.

Department for Children, Schools and Families. (2007) *The Children's Plan*, Cm 7280, London: Department for Children, Schools and Families.

Department for Education and Skills. (DfES) (2005) *What Are Academies?* Available online at: http://www.standards.dfes.gov.uk/academies/.

DiMaggio, P. D. and Powell, W. (1983). The Iron Cage Revisited: Institutional Isomorphism and Collective Rationality in Organizational Fields, *American Sociological Review*, 48 (2): 147–160.

Du Gay, P. (2004) Against 'Enterprise', *Organization*, 11 (1): 37–57.

Egan, P. (2006) This Week in the Media—City Academies: Innovation or Just Education? 20/01/2006, press release, London: Royal Society for the Arts.

Fielding, M. (2008) Beyond Student Voice to Democratic Community: An Exploratory Paper, paper presented at 'New Developments in Student Voice: Shaping Schools for the Future', Birkbeck College, University of London, 12th June, http://www.ioe.ac.uk/schools/efps/Beyond_Student_Voice_to_Democratic_Community.pdf, accessed 18th February 2009.

—— (2009) Public Space and Educational Leadership: Reclaiming and Renewing Our Radical Traditions, in Woods, P. A. and O'Hair, M. J. (eds) special issue on Democracy and School Leadership, *Educational Management Administration & Leadership*, 37 (4): 497–521.

Glatter, R. (2003) Governance and Educational Innovation, in B. Davies and J. West-Burnham (eds) *Handbook of Educational Leadership and Management*, London: Pearson.

Glatter, R. and Woods, P. A. (1995) Parental Choice and School Decision Making: Operating in a Market-Like Environment, in K-C Wong and K-M Cheung (eds) *Educational Leadership and Change: An International Perspective*, Hong Kong: Hong.

Gleeson, D. and Knights, D. (2006) 'Challenging Dualism: Public Professionalism in "Troubled" Times', *Sociology* 40 (2): 277–295.

Goldring, E. and Cravens, X. (2008) Teachers' Academic Focus on Learning in Charter and Traditional Schools, in M. Berends, M. G. Springer and H. J. Walberg (eds) *Charter School Outcomes*, New York: Lawrence Erlbaum Associates.

Gorard, S. (2009) What Are Academies the Answer To? *Journal of Education Policy*, 24 (1): 101–113.

Hatcher, R. (2009) Setting up Academies, Campaigning Against Them: An Analysis of a Contested Policy Process, *Management in Education*, 23 (3): 108–112.

Hereford Steiner School. (2006) Academy update, October 16, http://www.herefordwaldorfschool.org/Joomla/content/view/92/151/, accessed January 19, 2008.

House of Commons Select Committee on Education and Skills. (2005) *Secondary Education: Fifth Report of Session 2004–05*, London: The Stationery Office.

Hill, D., Sanders, M. and Hankin, T. Marxism, Class Analysis and Postmodernism, in D. Hill, P. McLaren, M. Cole and G. Rikowski (eds) *Marxism Against Postmodernism in Educational Theory*, Lanham, MD: Lexington Books.

Jeffrey, R. and Woods, P. E. (2003) *The Creative School*, London: Routledge-Falmer.

Kingston, P. (2006) Picking Up the Pieces, *Education Guardian*, 11th April, p. 1.

Kratochwil, F. (2007) Looking Back from Somewhere: Reflections on What Remains 'Critcial' in Critical Theory, *Review of International Studies*, 33: 25–45.

Lochrie, M. (2006) The Learning We Live By: Introduction, in *The Learning We Live By: Education Policies for Children, Families and Communities*, London: Capacity.

Machin, S. and Wilson, J. (2009) Academy Schools and Pupils Performance, *CentrePiece*, Spring, 7–8.

Maguire, M. (2005) 'Textures of Class in the Context of Schooling: The Perceptions of a "Class-crossing" Teacher', *Sociology* 39 (3): 427–43.

Manchester Academies Consultation. (2007a) *Business & Enterprise Academy*, Manchester: Manchester Academies Consultation; downloaded from http://www.manchester.gov.uk/downloads/business_entind.pdf, accessed February 11, 2009.

—— (2007b) *Finance & Business Academy*, Manchester: Manchester Academies Consultation; downloaded from http://www.manchester.gov.uk/downloads/finance_businessind.pdf, accessed February 9, 2009.

Manchester City Council. (2006) *Manchester's Education Partnership Launch Building Tomorrow's Workforce, Developing Tomorrow's Citizen*, Manchester: Manchester City Council.

Marley, D. (2007a) Spreading the Faith at the Double, *Times Educational Supplement*, 23 March, p. 12.

—— (2007b) 'Stand-off Over Academy Push', *Times Educational Supplement*, 5 October 2007, p. 7.

Marx, K. (1973) *Grundrisse: Introduction to the Critique of Political Economy*, Middlesex: Penguin.

Marx, K. and Engels, F. (1967) *The Communist Manifesto*, Harmondsworth: Penguin.

Meszaros, I. (1970) *Marx's Theory of* Alienation, London: The Merlin Press.

National Union of Teachers. (NUT) (2007) *Academies—Looking Beyond the Spin: Why the NUT Calls for a Different Approach* (London, NUT).

Needham, C. and Gleeson, D. (2006) *Academy Schools: Case Unproven*, London: Catalyst and Public World collaborative report for the NASUWT.

Newman, J. (2005) Enter the Transformational Leader: Network Governance and the Micro-politics of Modernization, *Sociology*, 39 (4): 717–734.

Osborne, D. and Gaebler, T. (1992) *Reinventing Government*, New York: Penguin.

PricewaterhouseCoopers. (2008) *Academies Evaluation: Fifth Annual Report*, London: Department for Children, Schools and Families.

RSA. (2006) *RSA Impact Report 2006*, London: Royal Society for the Arts.

RSA Academy. (2009) *Prospectus 2009*, Tipton: RSA Academy.

School Coop. (2008) *Co-op News Article—Trust Schools*, downloaded from http://www.beecoop.co.uk/cms/sites/trusts.beecoop.co.uk/files/news-article.pdf, accessed January 29, 2009.

Titcombe, R. (2008) How Academies Threaten the Comprehensive Curriculum, *Forum*, 50 (1): 49–59.

Tomlinson, M. (2006) Will Academies Make the Grade?, *RSA Journal*, June, pp. 32–35.

Whitty, G., Edwards, T. and Gewirtz, S. (1993) *Specialisation and Choice in Urban Education: the City Technology College Experiment* (London, Routledge).

Williams, L., Cate, J. and O'Hair, M. J. (2009) The Boundary-spanning Role of Democratic Learning Communities: Implementing the IDEALS, in Woods, P. A. and O'Hair, M. J. (eds), special issue on Democracy and School Leadership, *Educational Management Administration & Leadership*, 37 (4): 452–472.

Wilson, M. and Mills, C. (2008) *Co-operative Values Make a Difference in the Curriculum and Governance of Schools*, Manchester: The Co-operative College.

Woods, G. J., Woods, P. A. and Ashley, M. (2005) *Building Bridges Conference: Summary of Outcomes—Towards a Wider Sense of Community?*, Bristol: Faculty of Education, University of the West of England.

Woods, P. A. (2003) 'Building on Weber to Understand Governance: Exploring the Links Between Identity, Democracy and "Inner Distance"', *Sociology* 37 (1): 143–163.

——— (2004) Democratic Leadership: Drawing Distinctions with Distributed Leadership, *International Journal of Leadership in Education: Theory and Practice* 7 (1): 3–26.

——— (2005) *Democratic Leadership in Education*, London: Sage.

——— (2007) Enterprise in Education: All Things to All People?, Keynote, Co-operate to Succeed: Scottish Teachers' Conference, Co-operative Education Trust Scotland, 1st November.

——— (2009) Rationalisation, Disenchantment and Re-Enchantment: Engaging with Weber's Sociology of Modernity, in M. Apple, S. J. Ball and L. A. Gandin (eds), *International Handbook of the Sociology of Education*, London: Routledge.

Woods, P. A. and Broadfoot, P. (2008) Vers le controle pluriel de l'Ecole? La nature chageante du pouvoir dans le système educatif anglais [Towards Plural Controlled Schooling? The Shifting Nature of Power in the English Education System], *Revue Internationale de Sevres*, 48: 83–95.

Woods, P. A. and Woods, G. J. (2009) Testing a Typology of Entrepreneurialism: Emerging Findings from an Academy with an Enterprise Specialism, *Management in Education*, 23 (3): 125–129.

Woods, P. A., Woods, G. J. and Gunter, H. (2007) 'Academy Schools and Entrepreneurialism in Education', *Journal of Education Policy*, 22 (2): 263–285.

Chapter 8

Ten Years of New Labour Education Policy and Racial Inequality: An Act of Whiteness or Neoliberalism?

Alpesh Maisuria

When New Labour came to power in 1997, many people were enthused by the prospect of a new administration with fresh ideas after 18 years of Conservative government. New Labour wasted little time with its reform agenda aimed at aligning neoliberal policies with "social justice" issues (Blair, 1997), the latter being sidelined by the preceding Thatcher and Major governments. The overwhelming majority in Parliament allowed New Labour to advance initiatives, policies, and Green/White Papers apace with relatively little resistance. "Britain Deserves Better" was the slogan for the election campaign, and education was flagged by the new government as a priority for reform (Labour Party, 1997). More than a decade on, the then Prime Minister's focus on "Education, Education, Education," with eight education acts and hundreds of initiatives (Walford, 2005) from a series of Ministers responsible for education, has made it a target for evaluation. The key aspects of this policy agenda will be extrapolated and outlined here.

The first section of this chapter focuses on three broad policies: *widening participation, choice and stratification,* and *educational attainment.* Each policy is taken in turn and briefly evaluated in terms of its announced and actual impacts.

Using section one as context and an empirical backdrop, the second section of this chapter draws on Critical Race Theory (CRT) to analyse New Labour policy in the context of "race" equality in education.[1] CRT is used to theorise the themes and topics outlined in section one, employing its tenet of "white supremacy," and the centralising of the concept of "race."

The third section will show the relative analytical efficacy of Critical Race Theory in analysis of racial equality. Critical Race Theory is critiqued and its limitations are explained, and as an alternative following Cole and Maisuria, 2007; Cole and Maisuria, 2009; and Cole, 2009, the Marxist concept of "racialisation" is proposed as a more theoretically comprehensive and sophisticated way of analysing injustice.

This chapter argues that without articulation and critique using the Marxist account of social class as a central component of the analysis to contextualise the capitalist mode of production, the analysis is superficial and incomplete. It is therefore the intention of section three to locate policies in the relations of production, which it is argued is best achieved through using the concept of *racialisation*.

Following this line of argument, the conclusion offers insights about the legacy of New Labour and future prospects for justice. In this final section, it is argued that the hegemonic project of New Labour is exposed only by the application of a Marxist analysis that is *not economically essentialist,* and one that is *intersectional.*

Section One: Widening Participation

The historic debate about whether Higher Education (HE) should be reserved for those who can financially afford it, or available to those who can show that they are academically suited, was settled for a while in 2003. As part of its social justice agenda, New Labour has driven widening participation policies in education, and within the 2003 White Paper "The Future of Higher Education," a target of getting 50 percent of 18- to 30-year-olds into HE was announced, and subsequently enshrined in the 2004 Higher Education Act (DfES, 2003). The aim was laudable—to remove the barriers to HE, coupled with raising aspirations of non-traditional students. However, the announcements were met with scepticism by right-wing traditionalists who predicted that educational standards would decline. It was claimed that opening access to education would mean that "too many" people would be admitted to HE, and the value of the bachelor's degree would deflate if half the population below 30 years of age had a HE qualification. Interestingly, those on the political left also attacked the government's agenda to increase the size of HE. Allen and Ainley (2007, and this volume) claimed that the government's push for a more expansive education system is complex and more consequential than simply a drop in standards, and that the agenda was not driven by a desire to educate the working classes, rather education was being used to train and up-skill the working class to function more efficiently in particular roles in society. Widening participation was therefore a facade disguising an instrumentalist capitalist vision, reducing education to a mechanism that instils the acquiring of narrow competency based abilities.

Recently, the widening participation initiative has attracted negative attention from liberal progressive's, who are in favour of widening particpation, because non-traditional students are concentrated at less prestigious universities, reinforcing social and cultural reproduction (Sutton Trust, 2004; Shepherd, 2009). Research has shown that widening access has been more strongly implemented in post-1992 institutions.[2] The result is that the majority of working-class students from Asian, Black, and other minority ethnic backgrounds[3] have been "segregated" (Curtis, 2006) at ex-polytechnic institutes and former Further Education colleges, whilst only a minority of working-class students and the majority of upper-class and middle-class students have been distributed across the higher echelons of a stratified system at traditional, well-endowed, richer, and more prestigious universities. Using statistics from the Higher Education Statistical Agency, Curtis (2006) articulates this stark divide by commenting that:

> Over 60% of London Metropolitan's students belong to ethnic minorities, plucked from local boroughs. In Bristol [part of the elite Russell Group of universities], less than 7% of students are from ethnic minority communities [in 2003–04].

This situation is widely expected to become more stark when the £3,000 per annum cap on undergraduate tuition fees is lifted, which will open the way for a significant hike; it is conceivable that some institutions in the Russell Group of universities will charge home students circa £15,000 to students. With this determinant, the correlation between the size of fees and the size of working-class Asian, Black, and other minority ethnic backgrounds students will become even more marked.

Variable tuition fees represented an interesting contradiction in New Labour's education policy. On the one hand, the widening participation agenda was designed to raise the aspiration of non-traditional pupils, while on the other hand, creating a significant hurdle to access to advanced education with the introduction of steep financial demands. Tomlinson (2008, p. 136) notes that the "contradictions of pursuing competitive market policies in education while affirming commitment to social justice quickly became obvious." These contradictions have not only had major impacts in segregating by social class, but also along ethnic lines. Tomlinson (2008, p. 139) notes that "[b]oth ethnic and social segregation was exacerbated by choice, as it became more apparent that this offered white parents even more legitimate ways of avoiding schools with high minority intakes." In other words, the articulation of the social justice and the choice agenda was rhetorical with wide-reaching consequences.

Choice and Stratification

Associated with paradoxes of the widening participation agenda, critics have highlighted that New Labour continued and accelerated marketisation in education (see Farnsworth, this volume). Some cultural analysts (for example, Hall, 2009), and other left-wing critics of the encroachment of market principles to education, believe that the private sector's raison d'être of profit making drives its modus operandi, which renders it incompatible with education that has the primary objective of providing an accessible public-sector service. This perception is substantiated by Hoxby (2000, 2003), who shows that school choice leads to inequalities between schools, because in many cases, the parent's choice of school is not genuine; it is actually the school, located in a stratified reputational system of merit, that chooses the most desirable parents and children. "Desirable" translates to parents who have the financial capital to "voluntarily" contribute monies to the school. In addition, these are also the parents who are able to fund extracurricular activities and private tuition for their children (Ball, 2008). The choice agenda aids the social stratification process, because the most desirable schools are oversubscribed, which in turn justifies selection through overt means. This is done, for example, by schools can deciding the desirability of children through interviewing parents (Crompton, 2008); but also through covert financial mechanisms, for example, establishing requirements for expensive school uniforms. This inevitably has resulted in children from working-class backgrounds, especially those who require a higher unit of resource such as English language tuition, being marginalised and thus less attractive to prosperous schools (Rueda & Vignoles, 2003).

Crucially, choice means polarisation, in that some educational institutions, such as the so-called "sink schools," have deteriorated, whilst at the same time, the more privileged schools have selected those students who are most likely to hit targets with the least investment in resources, thereby being more economically prudent and better for league table returns (Hill, Greaves Maisuria, 2009; Bousted, 2006). The summation of this situation is that privilege and deprivation is perpetuated and deepened by internal mechanisms, and stratification by class is normalised and systemic.

Attainment

The introduction of league tables has marked a new emphasis on the role of markets in education. New Labour has espoused the virtues of competition, pointing to statistics that show improvements in literacy and general attainment (Ball, 2008). However, critics have argued that the improved results are due to teachers' abandoning dialectical learning pedagogies to teach-to-the-test, ensuring that students are prepared directly for one-off exams, wherein successful results secure the reputation of the school in league tables (Ball, 2008). Anecdotal evidence suggests that some schools are sidelining all peripheral activities in the run-up to exams, especially the creative arts subjects— e.g., music and design—to focus on exam training by routinised and rote learning. The educational cost is that students are receiving short-term instrumentalist training rather than a rounded and holistic learning experience.

Perhaps the most significant impact of league tables is on teachers' professional autonomy. In England and Wales, children are tracked onto particular routes when they are entered for the General Certificate of Secondary Education (GCSE) at the age of 16. Teachers have to enter pupils for either the higher or foundation tier of GCSEs. The difference is that pupils who are entered for the higher tier can potentially achieve a grade from A* to D. The foundation tier has a grade boundary of between C to G. Closer analysis of this tiered approach to streaming, in combination with the pressure of league tables, exposes some grossly unfair practices. Gillborn (2005, p. 89) articulates these formulations: "[P]upils placed in the foundation tier know that the highest grades (A*, A, and B) are literally beyond them"; and similarly, those entered in the higher tier will fail if they do not reach a minimum grade of D. This has the inadvertent effect of teachers being coerced to be very selective about those whom they enter for the highest tier, in order to ensure a minimal failure rate (ibid.). The upshot is that before a child has even written an answer, they have been through a selection process to be a high or lower end achiever. These decisions have wide and lasting impacts, especially in the employment market in which employers are looking for the benchmark four GCSEs at grades As–Cs. In many ways, this situation is more discriminatory than the much maligned 11-plus tests of yesteryear (in which pupils were streamed into academic and vocational schools), because in the contemporary tiered system, children do not get a chance to sit an exam *before* being selected, whereas at least the 11-plus examinations made decisions based on the (albeit spurious) results of the tests. Furthermore, how teachers make decisions about which pupils are entered for which tier needs scrutiny, since the majority of Asian, Black, and other minority ethnic pupils have been entered for lower-tiered examinations (Gillborn, 2005, p. 90). Consequently, schooling is a restricting rather than enriching experience in which the sticky floor and glass ceiling limit aspirations and successes—another example of how New Labour's social justice agenda was tokenistic.

Underachievement by Asian, Black, and other minority ethnic pupils has been a live issue since the 1970s. Since then, despite criticism of the education system from antiracism campaigners, and the publications of the Swann Report (1985) and Rampton Report (1981), disproportional low attainment levels become the norm for some groups. By the time New Labour had come into power, the issue was largely seen as a crisis that would have generational social, cultural, and economic repercussions. The then newly elected government almost immediately commissioned OfSTED to assess the effectiveness of initiatives to raise the attainment of Asian, Black, and other minority ethnic pupils, especially those from Bangladeshi, Black Caribbean, Pakistani, and Gypsy Traveller backgrounds (Ofsted, 1999, p. 5). The report found that fostering a culture of high expectation, and not withstanding any particular group's failings, was a key factor to raising achievement (Ofsted, 1999, p. 7). The report focussed on teachers, suggesting that attainment was negatively affected by labelling students based on "impressions or hunches," especially at the primary school level. It is significant that in primary schools attainment was not monitored in an effective way (ibid.), and therefore trends of underachievement by class and "race" went unnoticed and resources were not targeted to those who needed them the most. In addition, the report said that equal opportunity policies, where they existed, had a negligible impact on raising the attainment of Asian, Black, and other minority ethnic pupils (ibid., pp. 7–8).

Since the Gillborn and Mirza (2000) report, global events have complicated the issue of underachievement. The London bombings and the consequent "War on Terror" have exacerbated racial tensions, which have percolated through to education. The "othering" of students actually or perceived to be from an Islamic background has created a discourse of Islamaphobia. Into New Labour's second term, Tomlinson noted "[b]lack boys were still the group most likely to be demonised as potential problems for school and society,—at least until Muslim youth vied for the demon label after 2005" (2008, p. 145). Allied with the institutional racism uncovered by the Macpherson report (1999), and coupled with the increase in Islamaphobia, the attainment levels of Islamic pupils was sidelined in favour of discussions about radicalisation and recruitment to extremist organisations.

Drawing on the empirical context and the themes outlined in section one, the next section will explore the efficacy of Critical Race Theory as an analytical tool to explain New Labour's education policy in relation to racial equality. Developing this analysis, section three will then critique the purchase that CRT has in analysing New Labour's "race" education policy.

Section Two: Whiteness and the Centralising of the Concept of "Race" in the Analysis of Inequality in New Labour's Britain

For a number of years, Critical Race Theory has been offering insight into struggles and conflicts of a racial nature in the United States, especially for those who reject the Marxist tradition of critiquing political economy and dismiss a class-based analysis of society. Despite the increasing popularity in the United Kingdom over recent years, the transfer of CRT from the United States context has not been embraced unanimously. This chapter is one of several recent works to critique the effectiveness of CRT as a tool of analysis for an education system that has, for more than ten years under New Labour, been gradually reformed in neoliberal terms, working largely for the benefit of already advantaged—for example, through the marketisation and choice agendas (Cole, 2008; Cole and Maisuria, 2007, 2009).

Earlier in this chapter I have noted the immanent contradictory effect that much of New Labour policy defeats the objective of social justice, because the reforms have disadvantaged the most needy in spite of their colour or ethnic background, for example, in the choice agenda (Ball, 2008). CRT proponents argue that class socioeconomic mechanisms are not the determinant factors accounting for the injustice to Asian, Black, and other minority ethnic people, and claim that an explanatory theory would need to focus on the concept of "race," either exclusively or predominantly, in relation to class differences and inequalities. As Darder and Torres (2004) put it, CRT is grounded in the "the uncompromising emphasis on 'race,'" and that CRT uses "'race' as the central unit of analysis" (p. 98). Gillborn is clear on the centrality of "race."

> CRT offers a challenge to educational studies more generally, and to the sociology of education in particular, to cease the ritualistic citation of "race" as just another point of departure on a list of exclusions to be mentioned and then bracketed away. CRT insists that racism be placed at the centre of analyses. (2006, p. 27)

Elsewhere, Gillborn has been even more forthright about the role of "race," unequivocally stating that "class is used to silence debates about 'race'" and "class is a smoke screen to promote racist action" (Gillborn, 2008).[4] Given this commitment to the fundamentality of "race," CRT theorists would contextualise poor access and attainment under New Labour in terms of an account of racial discrimination, and not couched in the discourse of *social* injustice, implicitly inferring a totalising of all forms of discrimination as *racial* injustice. Equally for CRT theorists, the vision for a more equitable education system would rest on an educational policy agenda having a substantive redistributive element to correct the inequality that Black (and presumably Asian and other minority ethnic) people have experienced, which has resulted in "black people having cumulative disadvantages" and "white people having cumulative advantages" (Mills and Pateman, 2007, p. 127), and for "reparations to be taken seriously" (Mills and Pateman, 2007, p. 107). Presumably, in practice this would involve, for example, giving preferential treatment to Asian, Black, and other minority ethnic people when it comes to admissions or even, perhaps, differential marking criteria. CRT seems to be endorsing policies of positive discrimination (which is currently illegal in Britain). The concern with this proposal is that it would be white people who would be disadvantaged at the expense of Asian, Black, and other minority ethnic people. Without straying into abstract idealism about a utopian society in which everyone is equal, the central concern with this proposition is that *power is simply in role reversal* (going from white empowerment to Black empowerment), which would no doubt do little to for social harmony and cohesion, and intensify "racial" divisions and antagonisms, which are currently being exploited by the white supremacist far-right British National Party.

CRT aims exclusively to address racial justice that is abstracted from, asserted, and prioritised over other forms of exclusion, such as class-based disadvantage. As exemplified earlier with school choice and widening participation, white people do not uniformly benefit from New Labour's education policies. However, even when there is no material evidence for white supremacy in the education system, the principle of positive discrimination will presumably apply to the oppressed white persons nonetheless. A genuine vision of emancipation would need to include *all* of those affected by social injustice.

CRT uses the concept of white supremacy to explain the differential in educational opportunity and outcome. It is difficult to pinpoint a succinct definition of white supremacy, or whiteness, because CRT theorists seem to use a variety of ways to explain it. However, using Gillborn (2007), Preston (2007), and McIntosh (1992), white supremacy can be understood as the invisible mechanism that acts as property, which allows access to forms of privilege. It is not exclusively something that operates on skin colour, although it can be linked to biological (mis)conceptions of "race." Contemporising Carmichael and Hamilton's (1967, p. 157) work, CRT has the "implicit...idea that the closer you get to whiteness, the better [off?] you are."

Evaluating New Labour's policy agenda, Gillborn concludes that *"education policy is an act of white supremacy"* (2005, p. 498, italics in original). However, CRT needs to distinguish how and why "white supremacy" as a conceptual and theoretical tool to explain manifestations of racism is distinct from, or even linked to, either institutional racism or structural forms of racism. Gillborn suggests that white supremacy is inherent in New Labour's policy making, and this is part of a wider project of creating a legacy of white power, stating that:

> [M]ainstream political parties, and the functioning of agencies like the education system itself, are actively implicated in maintaining and extending the grip that white people have on the major sources of power. (2005, p. 491)

The suggestion is that New Labour's education policy was used as a mechanism by which white supremacy is being perpetuated.

Furthermore, according to Gillborn, "New Labour's policy agenda is more narrowly focussed, more mean spirited and more obsessed with social control than at any time in the last half century" (2008, p. 71). Marxists would agree that the social control agenda is significant (see contributions to this volume), and this is perhaps most clearly seen and played out in education in the current New Labour "preventing terrorism" agenda, focussing on Muslims provoking an anti-Islamic sentiment. However, Marxists have specific problems with the conceptions of white supremacy and its application to policy and practice. These criticisms of CRT will form the basis of the following section, which provides the alternative, drawing upon the criticique of New Labour policy agenda that was outlined in section one, and explores the efficacy of deploying and centralising social-class analysis connecting to the mode of production, whilst acknowledging the importance of "race."

Section Three: The Intersectionality of "Race" and Social Class

CRT theorists and Marxists agree that New Labour's "race" education policy commitment to eradicating inequality has been tokenistic, and significant change, for a Party in power for more than ten years, has not been evident, given its supposed commitment to social justice. The difference between the two theoretical positions is that CRT frames this in the context of white supremacy,[5] and attempts to theorise the status quo by prioritising the explanatory significance of "race," as outlined in section two. I suggest that a more sophisticated analysis would require the dialectical centrality of social class (intersected with other identities), and articulated with an analysis of the mode of production. CRT's notion of "white supremacy" is purely descriptive. As Gillborn himself claims, "white supremacy is actually a wholly apt *descriptor* of the functioning and structure of contemporary education" (2005, p. 498) (my emphasis). As a "descriptor," it inadequately explains why racism is continually reproduced; in other words, *why* is racism important—*what* purpose does it serve and for *whom*? As I have argued, it is an inaccurate to suggest that being White bestows a superiority, as white people do not universally benefit from a neoliberal policy agenda, while *all* those from the bourgeoisie and petit-bourgeoisie generally do.

Indeed, CRT does offer some potentially useful conceptual tools that could contribute something to a Marxist critique (c.f. Cole, 2009); however, I follow Darder and Torres (2004, p. 100) in asking the crucial question:

> How do we launch a truly universal emancipatory political project anchored primarily upon a theory of "race"? Where is a critique of capitalism or an explicit anticapitalist vision in a critical theory of "race"?

In order to address these key questions, it is crucial to contextualise the initiatives of widening participation, the choice agenda, and patterns of differential achievement within an account of the New

Labour project of advancing neoliberalism, something that CRT does not do. As a capitalist collusive political party operating in a globalised world, New Labour was primarily concerned with creating the conditions for the reproduction and expansion of capital. The education system is where people are prepared "for the practical knowledge, acquired skills and learned abilities of an individual that make him or her potentially productive" (Johnson, 2000, p. 1); here, "productive" is used in the sense of creating the capacity to labour commodifiable as labour power. New Labour recognised that education was a key apparatus that could be used to maximise capital accumulation; in other words, education can be designed to perpetuate the logic of capitalism. This view is substantiated by Tomlinson (2001), who notes that:

> Governments of varying political persuasions around the world rediscovered human capital theory ... a theory which suggested that improving people's skills and capabilities makes them act in new productive ways, and assumed that investment in education will improve the quality of the workforce, which will in turn improve economic growth and productivity. By the 1990s government was firmly committed to the belief that only greater investment in human capital would enable the country to compete in the new global economy. (p. 4)

On this view, the widening participation agenda is very useful to upskill the workforce in order to contribute to the neoliberal global knowledge economy. Allen and Ainley's immanent critical analysis (2007, p. 92) of these reforms argues that they reduce education to a mechanical process of training and that: "For those who are not relegated to the vocational [education] route, widening participation to higher education is presented as the professionalization of the proletariat while masking an actual proletariatisation of the professions." In essence, education is needed by capitalism to produce the conditions for capital accumulation, an issue obfuscated in CRT analyses. Education, inter alia, is used to provide a workforce that is flexible, exploitable, and able to be economically active, contributing to the labour market (Hill, Greaves, Maisuria, 2009; Allen and Ainley, 2007).

In centralising "race," CRT does not recognise the seminal role that class plays in the formulation of neoliberal educational polices. For Marxists, New Labour's polices, such as widening participation, serve in class struggles on the side of capitalism. The dispute about the role of "race" and class is the main incompatibility between the

CRT and Marxism in analyses of inequality. The outcome is that CRT views New Labour as advancing a white supremacy ideology and legacy, whilst Marxism views its approach to education policy as a critique of a specifically capitalist neoliberal agenda.

A criticism levelled at the Marxist-inspired, class-based critique of racial inequality is that Marxists misrepresent formations and operations of whiteness. According to Preston (2007), Marxists misunderstand whiteness on the grounds that it is not exclusively based on one's skin colour. Rather, "white supremacy is a systemic and normalized system of oppression" that functions upon the property of whiteness as a commodity (2007, p. 122). Preston, a white and British (this is significant, given the empire of old and new [see Cole and Maisuria, 2007]) academic, explains this autobiographically: "what I naively thought to be a timeless property of my skin was a social construction that had acquired so much symbolic weight over time that it had become seemingly real: a racial formation and project" (ibid., p. 7). Therefore, for Preston, whiteness is not genetic nor simply a metaphysical abstraction, it is embodied in the lived experience meaning, conceptually, that whiteness is a material formation. I would argue that in New Labour's Britain, whiteness could have been confused with meritocratic aspirations of the working class. Take, for example, the television show *Goodness Gracious Me,* which was based on subverting British typologies. In one episode, called "The Competitive Mothers," two Indian mothers argued about the educational accomplishments of their respective sons. The protagonists displayed an ostentatious show of one-upmanship against each other, with every achievement gradually becoming more exaggerated. Whilst CRT would suggest that this exemplifies the two Indian mothers aspiring to display more whiteness through their son's merit, I would argue that the scene actually represents the aspiring Indian working class. By defining their son's as more successful, they were articulating the relationship between classes, whereby each mother is trying to outdo each other's middle-class credentials. Similarly, this can be seen in school choice, wherein many working-class parents are making drastic lifestyle changes in order to afford private education fees (Channel 4, 2007). This is a process that, in Marxist analysis, constitutes part of the ideological embourgeoisement of the working class, or the pressure for "upward mobility" (Marshall, 1990, p. 31). Embourgeoisement results, subjectively, if not objectively, in a blurring of the distinction between classes, which in turn undermines distinctiveness in class consciousness (Hill, Greaves, Maisuria, 2009). CRT is in essence a superficial cultural analysis that deploys an analysis of whiteness as an alternative to social-class analysis, and is bereft of the crucial implications of connection to the mode of production. Marxists do not suggest that culture is unimportant, quite the opposite; it is the recognition that social class can work through ambiguous and seemingly autonomous cultural forms. Following this line of argument, CRT is therefore in danger of being part of the problem of racism by not acknowledging the root causes of the discrimination, which is the capitalist system of exploitation. It is therefore New Labour's project for advancing neo-liberal capitalism, not white supremacy, that is the structural system of oppression.

On this view, it is understandable that racial inequality in education is a fixture, and since capitalism is a globalised historical project, the "picture that emerges is both shocking and revealing...[and in] key respects the contemporary situation is as bad, and in some cases worse, than anything that has gone before" (Gillborn, 2008 p. 86). In essence, the hegemonic project of New Labour[6] is revealed only by the application of a class-based analysis that is not economically essentialist, and one that is intersectional. For this reason, effective Marxist research and analysis is not colour blind, gender blind, or blind to critical identity subjectivities. Marxists recognise the dynamics of different identities and the particular discrimination they face in New Labours' Britain—this is a key strength of Marxist analysis compared to CRT, which totalises injustice to issues of 'race' in some instances, especially in north American scholarship.

One way in which Marxism intersects "race" and class in analyses of racial policy formulation is through the concept of *racialisation*. Robert Miles (1987) has defined racialisation as an ideological process whereby particular "races" at particular moments in history are differentiated by the capitalist class to increase the potential to exploit and accumulate capital.[7] It is not simply a fixed dichotomy of white (supreme) versus Black (subordinate), and at different times different "races" are demonised and assumed to be subordinate. There is no exact science as to how this process works or why a "race" is racialised, though it is a process that is "needed" by capitalism to survive and thrive. In the past, the Irish, the Jews, and the African-Caribbeans have been at the negative end of racialisation. The process of racialisation is ideological and, unlike the properties of whiteness in CRT, it has a substantive basis that is neither colour coded nor colour-blind. A prominent illustration of this was New Labour's policy of "choice," which can be seen to be creating hierarchies of schools differentiated by social class. These are the schools that have the most appeal and competition from middle-class parents who perceive a particular school as good because it is for the middle class (Ball, 2008). Of course, there are those parents who choose schools because of their racial majority, but primacy is on how the school fares in terms of class composition; in other words, for most parents, middle class equates to a high-performing status and access to positional competitive advantage.

The value of the concept of racialisation is where it connects to the mode of production. As Miles explains:

> [T]he process of racialisation cannot be adequately understood without a conception of, and explanation for the complex interplay of different modes of production and, in particular, of the social relations necessarily established in the course of material production (The process of racialisation is ideological and, unlike the properties of whiteness notion in CRT, it has a substantive basis which is neither colour-coded nor colour-blind rather it is framed by class which is crucially informed by, *inter alia*, "race").

Applied to analyses of "race" education policy, racialisation explains that the racially subjugated, whether they are the working-class Muslims or any other faction of the working class, have a functional value, in this case to the New Labour project for capitalism, because their (economic, cultural, financial, and social) vulnerable position renders them ripe to be uberexploited by the ruling elite interests. Marxists argue that education policy is part of a social organisational project that is designed to create a subordinated class through racialisation, supportive of those people who have the potential to accumulate the most surplus value.

The analytical framework of the "Authoritarian Personality" (Adorno et al., 1950) is useful to refer to here to further explicate the sophistication of the concept of racialisation, particularly where it works as an ideological mechanism to differentiate the "in-group" (superior) and "out-group" (inferior) to sustain class structures. At a micro level, Adorno et al. note, "A person can be identified with groups to which he [sic] does not formally belong" (ibid., p. 82). To return to the example of the competitive mothers, these Asians, who were historically the oppressed, are now, in New Labour's meritocratic Britain, aspiring to identify with (petit-)bourgeois, who were the agents of their oppression through labels such as *threatening* (taking our women) and/or *power seeking* (taking our jobs), well captured in the anachronism: "over-sexed, overpaid and over here," applied originally to North American servicemen during wartime and post-World War II Britain.

For CRT scholarship, the white working class is the much maligned group because they challenge the notion of white supremacy, especially in 2010, as they are amongst the lowest achievers in the education system. Furthermore, conflict and racism amongst working-class groups (white and nonwhite: i.e., Indian against Pakistanis or English against Irish) is an issue that CRT finds difficult to deal with.[8] The theoretical gain of a Marxist conception of racialisation lies in its analysis of class relations, which are often bound by "race," culture, gender, and other identities (see Cole and Maisuria, 2009).

Furthermore, to recognise the expansion of the increasing global movement of people, Sivanandan (2001), Cole (2008), and Cole and Maisuria (2007, 2009) have developed the concept of racialisation in order to include aspects of xenophobia. Xenoracialisation (a concept formulated by Cole, 2004) works in the same way as racialisation, except that it is xenophobic in form (i.e., the way it takes shape) and racist in substance (i.e., what it contains). Xeno-racism, as Sivanandan (2001) puts it, is:

> the "fear or hatred of strangers"...the defence and preservation of "our people", our way of life, our standard of living, our "race". If it is xenophobia, it is—in the way it denigrates and reifies people before segregating and/or expelling them—a xenophobia that bears all the marks of the old racism, except that it is not colour-coded. It is a racism that is not just directed at those with darker skins, from the former colonial countries, but at the newer categories of the displaced and dispossessed whites...—a racism that is meted out to impoverished strangers even if they are white. It is xeno-racism.

Xenoracialisation explains how racism does not have to be colour coded, and therefore accounts for the underachievement of the white working class. It is therefore too simplistic to suggest, as CRT does, that New Labour's education policy was based on notions of white supremacy (Cf. Gillborn, 2005, p. 498) —white people have also been the victims of neoliberalism. Thus, xeno-racism can explain racial injustice for those who are white skinned, as well as those who are not, something that is very difficult to adequately do with an ahistorical employment of a default *white* supremacy model. A comprehensive analysis of New Labour's "race" education policy needs to have a flexibility to account for all of those who are at the receiving end of injustice.

Conclusion

This chapter has provided a snapshot analysis of New Labour's education policy, focussing on racial inequality by contrasting Critical Race Theory and Marxists frameworks and their relative merits.

A central theme has been that, under the stewardship of New Labour, there has been a raft of changes to implement and accelerate neoliberal ideology. The first section examined three broad polices: widening participation, choice and stratification, and attainment. It has been argued that the New Labour rhetoric of social justice has done little in practice to alleviate class-based and "race"-based inequities in education.

The second section theorised the New Labour "race" education policy strategy. Using CRT, the concepts of white supremacy and the efficacy of centralising "race" were applied to the policy agenda outlined in section one. Evaluating and developing this analysis, the third section critiqued the CRT theorisation of racial discrimination from a Marxist perspective. It was argued that racism is more comprehensively explained by connecting analyses to the mode of production through the concepts of racialisation and xenoracialisation. The thrust of the argument was that, fundamentally, capitalism could not be maintained without a society divided by classes, but it could exist without the existence of racism. It was argued that, in principle, capitalist relations of production can be, and are, mostly colour blind, given the examples of the white Jewish and the white Irish experience.

This chapter has put forth an argument that any analysis of the New Labour "race" policy agenda has to firstly acknowledge the existence of social class, and secondly it must recognise the central importance of it in relation to "race." Thus, in line with the argument posited in this direction, the future of New Labour's education policy is likely to continue unabated, and the legacy will be that the New Labour policy agenda in education was framed by neoliberalism. All the mainstream political parties are committed to continuing the policies of choice with the expansion of semiprivatised education, further stratifying the working-class racialised pupils and their middle-class counterparts. The increasing role of the private sector in education will mean neoliberalisation will continue to be of primary importance. This assessment is supported by Callinicos (2006, p. 5), who states that:

> education is being very different from official proclamations about equality of opportunity and social justice....[Education is] in fact being driven by priorities shaped by the needs of big business.

At the time of writing just after the 2010 General Elections New Labour is scoring its lowest ever popularity polls. Furthermore, there is little optimism for real change in Britain. Monbiot (2008, p. 27) sums up the feeling of many by noting just before the election, that "[t]he prospect of a Tory in No 10 does worry me—but no more than another term for this [New Labour] cabinet." Despite this, it is crucial that resistance is not seen as futile, and teachers, university lecturers, and students need to work in solidarity for the goal of social justice in education. This quest for justice is inextricably linked to fighting the capitalist vision for education. Callinicos (2006, p. 7) sums up this sentiment.

> [o]pposing neo-liberalism in higher education should be part of the struggle for a society that really does give everyone an equal chance to realise themselves. Accordingly, my theoretical framework is provided by Marx's analysis of the capitalist economic system. What neo-liberalism ultimately represents is a particularly pure form of the logic of capital. Therefore, the struggle for better universities [and education] can't be separated from the movement against global capitalism itself.

Oliver Cox, writing in 1948 (p. 74), captured the essence of this chapter.

> There will be no more "crackers" or "niggers" after a socialist revolution because the social necessity for these types will have been removed. But the vision which capitalist theorists dread most is this: that there will be no more capitalists and capitalist exploitation. If we attempt to see race relations realistically, the meaning of capitalist function is inescapable.

It is for this reason that New Labour's education policy was not an act of whiteness (as property), rather it was part of the grander project of capitalism, and therefore representative of neoliberal practice.

Notes

1. I put "race" in inverted commas because the concept is a social construct rather than a biological fact. It has no substantive basis; this line of argument follows Darder and Torres (2004) who provide a succinct account of the use of the term "race."
2. By postcode analysis of 17,000 entries, those children from the richest 2 percent are more than four and a half times more likely to study at high-ranking universities. Indeed, this cohort is two times more likely

to attend university than the average child (Shepherd, 2009). This report substantiates previous research carried out by the Sutton Trust (2004) on the stratification of university students by social class.

3. Following (Cole and Maisuria, 2007) I will use the nomenclature "Asian, Black, and other minority ethnic" for four reasons: First, the term "Black," once popular as an all-encompassing nomenclature, had ceased to have that purchase from the late 1980s onwards: hence the need for the wider formulation. Second, with respect to this nomenclature, the omission of the word "other" between "and" and "ethnic minority" implies that only "ethnic minorities" (people of Cypriot and Irish origin, for example) are minority constituencies whereas Black people are not; this is, of course, not accurate. Third, the use of the term, "ethnic minority" has, in practice, meant that members of the dominant majority group are not referred to in terms of their ethnicity, with the implication that they do not have ethnicity (the sequencing of "minority" before "ethnic" does not carry this implication, since, the creation of a new formulation, together with the prioritising of the former over the latter, facilitates the conceptualisation of a majority ethnic group too). Fourth, "Black and ethnic minority" has the effect of excluding people of Asian and other origins who do not consider themselves "Black." The fact that people of Asian origin form the majority of "nonwhite" minority ethnic women and men is masked.

4. This comment could be interpreted in either of two ways: firstly, it could be perceived to be essentialist by suggesting that "race" is the exclusive feature in all discriminatory practice. Although, Gillborn has written about the need for CRT to be antiessentialist and inclusive of all struggles, for example Latino/a (Gillborn, 2008, p. 39), inexplicably he rules out a debate with Marxists upon the premise that "Marxists place class in a position that supersedes all other forms of exclusion" (ibid. p. 37). It is therefore ironic that the comment about class being used as a silencer was made at a major conference in London called "*Marxism* 2008" (my emphasis); another way to understand Gillborn's comments would be more palatable. I would agree that debates about class could be used by some to undermine ideological debates about "race"; this is certainly the case in some countries, such as Sweden. However, I would be confident in claiming that no Marxists would use class in this essentialist way because it simply does not make sense to exclude identities other than class in analyses about discrimination. In fact, I have made it perfectly clear (Cole and Maisuria, 2007, 2009) that a meaningful debate between Marxists and CRT theorists has to ensue in order to unite against discrimination in all its forms and parameters.

5. For a more detailed analysis of the explanatory limitations of "white supremacy," see Cole and Maisuria, 2007, 2009.

6. Although Stuart Hall (2009), and other cultural theorists, would agree that the New Labour policy agenda for racial equality has a stake

for ideological and political legacy, he is critical of a type of Marxist thinking that attempts to deduce a problem directly from macrotheory. Most Marxists would suggest that the policy agenda of New Labour is fully enmeshed in the neoliberal project; Hall (2009) is highly sceptical about whether neoliberal hegemony is an inevitability and argues for an analysis that does not have a linear trajectory and open to interruptions. Of course this is a proposition that may be analytically and strategically useful, since one of the interruptions may offer a socialist future, however, following Lenin, capitalism is some stages off imperialism, which would signal the fully formed state of capitalism. Furthermore, despite the debilitating global economic downturn, class consciousness is such that the working class still have faith in capitalism, and instead turn their frustrations on racialised members of the working class, for example the Poles, who are accused of taking jobs. Given this line of argument, the next interruption is more likely to be a new neoliberalism.

7. In adopting Miles's definition of racialisation, I should make it clear that there are a number of non-Marxist applications of the concept of racialisation. Indeed, the concept is a contested term that is widely used and differently interpreted (for an analysis, see Murji and Solomos [eds] 2005).

8. These crude categorisations are merely making a point and I am not suggesting the English are always white or that Indians are always nonwhite, and so forth.

References

Adorno, T. W. and Frenkel-Brunswick, E., Levinson, D. and Nevitt Sandford, R. (1950) The Authoritarian Personality, In Ellis Cashmore and James Jennings (eds) *Racism Essential Readings (2001)*, London: Sage.

Allen, M. and Ainley, A. (2007) *Education Make You Fick, Innit?: What's Gone Wrong with England's Schools, Colleges and Universities and How to Start Putting It Right*, London: Tufnell Press.

Ball, S. (2008) *The Education Debate*, London: Policy Press.

Blair, T. (1997) Speech to the 1997 Labour Party Conference Labour Party Conference. Brighton.

Bousted, M. (2006), ATL Warn Blair of 'Ghetto Schools' fear. [Online]. Available at: http://www.atl.org.uk/education-news/default.asp?article=%7BF5F78954-BCF6–4822–9322–8EBDCF6F025D%7D.

Callinicos, A. (2006) *Universities in a Neo-Liberal World*, London: Bookmarks Publication.

Carmichael, S. and Hamilton, C. (1967) 'Black Power: The Politics of Liberation in America '. In E. Cashmore and J. Jennings (eds), *Racism Essential Readings*, London: Sage.

Channel4. (2007) Admission Impossible. [Online]. Available at: http://www.channel4.com/health/microsites/A/admission_impossible/index.html.

Crompton, R. (2008) *Class & Stratification*, Cambridge: Polity.

Cole, M. (2004) ' "F*** You—Human Sewage: Contemporary Global Capitalism and the Xeno-Racialization of Asylum Seekers. *Contemporary Politics*, 10(2), pp. 159–165.

—— (2008) *Marxism and Educational Theory*, London: Routledge.

—— (2009) *Critical Race Theory and Education: A Marxist Response*, London: Routledge.

Cole, M. and Maisuria, A. (2007) 'The 'Shut the F*** Up', 'You Have No Rights Here': Critical Race Theory and Racialisation in post-7/7 Racist Britain, *Journal for Critical Education Policy Studies*, 5 (1).

—— (2009) Racism and Xenophobia in post-7/7 Britain: Critical Race Theory, (Xeno-) Racialization, Empire and Education: A Market Analysis, in Kelsh, D. Hill, D. and Macrine, S. (eds), *Teaching Class: Knowledge, Pedagogy, Subjectivity*, London: Routledge.

Cox, O. (1948), 'Racism Essential Readings', in E. Cashmore and J. Jennings (eds), *Racism Essential Readings*, London: Sage.

Curtis, P. (2006) 'Segregation, 2006 Style: Figures on the Ethnicity of Students in Higher Education Show a Disturbing Racial Divide among UNIVERSITIES'. *The Guardian*.

Darder, A. and Torres, R. D. (2004) *After Race: Racism after Multiculturalism*, New York and London: New York University Press.

Department for Education and Skills. (2003) The Future of Higher Education (White Paper). In Department for Education and Skills, London: The Stationery Office.

Gillborn, D. (2005) 'Education Policy as an Act of White Supremacy: Whiteness, Critical Race Theory And Education Reform'. *Journal of Education Policy*, 20 (4), 485–505.

—— (2006) 'Critical Race Theory and Education: Racism And Antiracism in Educational Theory and Praxis'. *Discourse: Studies in the Cultural Politics of Education*, 27 (1), 11–32.

—— (2007) 'It Takes a Nation of Millions (and a Particular Type of Education System) to Hold Us Back'. In B. Richardson (ed), *Tell It Like It Is: How Our Schools Fail Black Children*, London: Bookmarks Publications and Trentham Books.

—— (2008) *Race, Class & Exclusion, Marxism 2008—A Festival of Resistance*, London.

Gillborn, D. and Mirza, H. S. (2000) *Educational Inequality: Mapping Race, Class and Gender* in OFSTED (ed). London.

Hall, S. (2009) Cultural Studies and Its Theoretical Legacies. [Online]. Available at: http://cultstud.blogspot.com/2007/09/stuart-hall-cultural-studies-and-its.html.

Hill, D., Greaves, N. and Maisuria, A. (2009) 'Education, Inequality and Neoliberal Capitalism: a Classical Marxist Analysis'. In D. Hill and

R. Kumar (eds), *Global Neoliberalism and Education and Its Consequences*, New York: Routledge.

Hoxby, C. (2000) 'Does Competition Among Public Schools Benefit Students and Taxpayers?' *American Economic Review* (90), 1209–38.

———— (2003) 'School Choice and School Competition: Evidence from the United States'. *Swedish Economic Policy Review* (10), 9–66.

Johnson, P. (2000) *Human Capital: Glossary of Political Economy Terms, Department of Political Science*, Auburn University, Alabama, USA:

Labour Party. (1997) *New Labour. Because Britain Deserves Better.* In S. Office (ed). London: Election Manifesto (London, Labour Party).

Marshall, G. (1990) *In Praise of Sociology*, London: Unwin Hyman.

McIntosh, P. (1992) 'White Privilege and Male Privilege: A Personal Account of Coming to See Correspondences through Work in Women's Studies'. In R. Delgado and J. Stefancic (eds), *Critical White Studies: Looking Behind the Mirror* (pp. 291–299). Philadelphia: Temple University Press.

Macpherson, W. (1999) *The Stephen Lawrence Inquiry*, London: Home Department by Command of Her Majesty.

Miles, R. (1987) *Capitalism and Unfree Labour: Anomaly or Necessity?* London: Tavistock.

Mills, C. and Pateman, C. (2007) *Contract and Domination*, Malden: Polity Press.

Monbiot, G. (2008) 'This Government Has Been the Most Rightwing Since the Second World War'. *The Guardian*.

Murji, K. and Solomos, J. (eds) (2005) *Racialization: Studies in Theory and Practice*, Oxford: Oxford University Press.

Ofsted. (1999) *Raising the Attainment of Minority Ethnic Pupils: School and LEA Responses*, London.

Preston, J. (2007) *Whiteness and Class in Education*, Dordrecht: Springer.

Rampton, A. (1981) West Indian Children in Our Schools Interim report, London.

Swann, C. (1985) *Education for All in Committee of Enquiry into the Education of Children from Ethnic Minority Groups* (ed). London: Stationery Office.

Rueda, F. and Vignoles, A. (2003) *Class Ridden or Meritocratic? An Economic Analysis of Recent Changes in Britain*, London: London School of Economics and Political Science.

Shepherd, J. (2009) 'White, Middle-Class Families Dominate Top University Places'. *The Guardian*.

Sivanandan, A. (2001) 'Poverty Is the New Black'. *Race and Class* 2(42), 1–5.

Sutton Trust. (2004) The Missing 3000—State School Students Under-Represented at Leading Universities, London.

Tomlinson, S. (2001) *Education in a Post-Welfare Society*, Buckingham: Open University Press.

———— (2008) *Race and Education: Policy and Politics in Britain*, Maidenhead: McGrawHill Open University Press.

Walford, G. (2005) 'Introduction: Education and the Labour Government'. *Oxford Review of Education* 1, 31.

Chapter 9

Patterns of Conflict in Education: France, Italy, England

Ken Jones

The course of educational reform in England has been broader, deeper, and faster moving than that of any other country of Western Europe, cutting deeply into what remained, after Thatcherism, of the postwar policy settlement.[1] No sector or strand of education has been unaffected by a programme that ranges—as other chapters have demonstrated—from large-scale privatisation to microlevel classroom reform. Yet, despite a certain, persistent level of grievance, this is a programme that has not encountered forceful opposition. Teachers' unhappiness with an assessment regime based on high stakes testing has been well publicised, without being translated into a collective response. Discontent with the government's programme for "academy" schools—state-funded privately run institutions—has resulted in a number of local strikes, and in a lively national campaign, but not one conducted on a mass scale. School and university teachers have taken occasional, limited action over pay—the NUT's one-day strike in 2008 was the first national strike since 1987. University teachers have fought local campaigns against redundancies (for instance, London Metropolitan University 2004, Keele 2008), but have not effectively challenged a policy that aims to align Higher Education with business needs. Amongst university students, opposition to the imposition of tuition fees was initially strong, but has waned since, with the passing of the 2004 Higher Education Act, fees became law.

This pattern of continuing, but low-level and only sporadically organised discontent is increasingly at odds with the response to educational reform in other countries. Looking in 2008 at the map of Europe, west of the cold war frontier that ran between Trieste and

Stettin, one could imagine a giant "X" of protest, with its diagonals running from Ireland to Greece, and Germany to Portugal. In this year alone, there occurred:

- strikes and public protests against education cuts in Ireland;
- school students' strikes, supported by the GEW educational union, in Germany;
- teachers' strikes in Catalonia against a package of New Labour-style reforms, including against the further advantaging of the church-run but state-subsidised private sector;
- in Portugal, the largest demonstration ever organised by teachers' trade unions, which protested against a new system for the assessment of performance;
- in France, teacher strikes against job cuts, and school students mobilisation against changes to the curriculum of the lycées;
- most spectacularly, an autumn of protest in Italy and a hot Greek December, actions in which a range of forces—school and university students, unemployed or precariously employed categories, teachers, university researchers—were strongly engaged.

This chapter, in discussing such events, has both substantive and theoretical intentions. Substantively, it aims to trace contrasting patterns of educational conflict in Europe. It seeks to explore and explain the discrepancy between England and other countries of Europe—here, France and Italy—alike faced with a neoliberal policy orthodoxy, but responding to it in markedly discrepant ways. Thus, in one sense, that nation places itself in a long line of research and speculation about the "peculiarities of the English," or, occasionally, the British (Anderson 1964, Thompson 1965/1978, Johnson 1989, Gamble 1981)—about those historically embedded aspects of the English social formation that have offered neoliberal reform a place to make its home. The chapter's sharper focus, however, lies outside England. It aims to chart and explain the ways in which education has become increasingly central to social conflicts in Europe, as a site on which significant forces contest the place they are assigned in the reform programme championed by national governments and by transnational entities, including the European Union. This formulation suggests also something of the chapter's theoretical ambitions: it aims to integrate into the understanding of education policy an appreciation of the role of collective social actors, and to understand the impact of such actors, not just on government strategies but on the forms taken by the educational state.

The Centrality of Education (1)

As several writers have suggested (Hingel 2001, Laval and Weber 2002, Dion 2006), EU policy in the 1990s increasingly recognised the importance of education to economic policy. In 2000 the European Council (Heads of State) meeting in Lisbon took this recognition to a new level of emphasis. The Council declared that the EU, facing the challenges of a globalised knowledge economy, must transform itself by 2010 into "the most competitive and dynamic knowledge economy in the world" (European Parliament 2000). Education systems were placed at the centre of this transformation. They were now too significant to be left to the haphazard and variegated process of nationally determined change. "European policy in the field of education and training," the European Council declared, "must look beyond the incremental reform of existing systems. It must also take as its objectives the construction of a European educational space of lifelong education and training, and the emergence of a knowledge society." In this context, it would be advisable to adopt "a European framework that defines fundamental new educational competences." (European Commission 2001). Through the Lisbon discussions, and those of the Council meetings that followed, the governments of the member countries thus transferred to the European level the power to formulate and pursue large-scale questions relating to the orientation of education systems, regarded now as economically central. In Dale's formulation, the locus of policy making was, in some senses, "upscaled" from a national to a European level (Dale 2005).

The resulting policy framework has been concretised and monitored through the EU's programme for education and training, which allows for the coordination of member states' initiatives, and their checking against agreed benchmarks. The EU is complemented in this process of upscaling by the Organisation for Economic Co-operation and Development (OECD), which carries out thematic reviews of national policies in such areas as "equity" and "teacher effectiveness," publishes the influential annual volume of comparative data, "Education at a Glance," and runs the PISA programme for the comparative assessment of students' performance (Alexiadou 2005, OECD 2008). Such "global" policy influences have been further elaborated at the national level: governments have both adopted specific objectives, and more generally, cited the global "consensus" in an attempt to legitimate a national programme of reform (Laval 2004).

There has developed a rich repertoire from which projects of reform can draw. It centres on, firstly, an increased role for the private sector in the provision of public education, together with a rise in private influence on education policy more generally; this partial shift from public to private sometimes goes under the heading of "opening education to the wider world" (Ball and Youdell 2008). Secondly, it envisages higher levels of participation and attainment both in formal education, and in lifelong learning. At the same time, however, formal education is reshaped, with more emphasis on skills and competences, and less on what is regarded as outmoded disciplinary knowledge; differentiation amongst learners, though discouraged at primary and lower secondary levels, is being embedded at 14-plus or 16-plus, so that academic and vocational divisions are securely maintained. Lifelong learning, like Higher Education, involves cost sharing, with the "user's" contribution rising sharply. Thirdly, the educational workforce requires transformation, so that it is capable of addressing the need for skills and competences, and of working in a focussed and cost-effective way. Fourthly, educational governance must be reformed: local managements should be incentivised to promote change and local school systems responsive to parental choice; at the same time, the centralised evaluation of the work of schools and universities is developed to a new level of specification.

The Centrality of Education (2)

The changes promoted by governments and international agencies collide with the experiences and demands of other sections of the population.

The reform of schools and universities has become a focus of intense controversy and conflict across Europe, involving at least two major social actors—youth and those who work in public-sector education. In this section, I explore the basis of their discontents.

If education reform lacks popular legitimacy amongst college students, school students, and the youth population more generally, it is above all because it does not deliver on the promise of economic prosperity, which is central to its rhetoric of change. This is a problem that predates the recession of 2008. For more than 20 years, levels of youth unemployment in much of Europe have been exceptionally high—according to Eurostat figures, the 2006 figure reached more than 20 percent in France, Greece, and Italy, and nearly 20 percent in Spain (European Commission 2008: 75). René Bendit, in a survey of youth in Europe, concluded that the problem was structural rather than cyclical; a new social situation had come into being, that of precarity. Precarity cannot be captured solely by unemployment statistics—it embraces issues of pay, job security, and career and life course progression; it prevents individuals from managing their successive entrances into and exits from the labour market in a way that "conforms to their expectations" (Bendit 2006:59).

The mechanisms of precarity have two kinds of effect. For some—working-class and migrant youth, with low levels of qualification—they entail near-complete exclusion from secure employment. For others, those "of high educational background," precarity relates to a gap between levels of qualification and the types of employment that are available. Levels of educational attainment have risen, and expectations have been heightened, yet access to secure jobs, to housing, and to an "autonomous" adult life is harder to come by. The French researcher Frédéric Lebaron (2006) writes in this context about a "devalorisation" of educational qualifications, in which students become both intensely sceptical about the value of their studies, yet also watchful of policies that seem likely to create further status divisions in education, and to dislodge the hold of some groups on qualifications they regard as essential to the chance of individual career building. It was from this suspicious perspective that EU policy was read, and the dramatic onset of the 2008 recession, in the midst of protest against educational reform, could only strengthen the severity of such a reading.

Alongside youth, neoliberal reform has also sparked public-sector workers into opposition. Jobs are being lost by the tens of thousand; conditions, under tighter managerial control, worsened, and the meaning of professional work transformed in a way that lessens autonomy (Jones et al 2008: Chapter 9). But behind these important sectoral concerns lies another set of motivating factors. Peter Gowan has observed that:

> West European governments and business groups have used the EU since the 1950s to change the pattern of business exchanges both between the EU and the rest of the world and between the member states within the EU itself. But since the mid-1980s, the EU project has acquired an entirely new character...affecting relations between labour and capital not just in economics but in politics and social life more generally. (Gowan 2005)

In this context, educational change is seen as a strategy for changing the relationship between social classes to the advantage of dominant groups, threatening what are seen both as the historic achievements of working-class and progressive movements, and more broadly as constituent elements of national identity. Kees van der Pijl has argued that many European societies developed against the "classical liberalism" of Britain and the United States: in order to avoid defeat in military or economic competition, they attempted to establish developmental states, in which governments had a strong role in economic planning and social provision, and in which populations were mobilised in support of the national-social project (van der Pijl 2006). After the defeat of fascism, popular movements were able to push such development further, embedding commitments to equality in national constitutions, and inflecting the social order, at many levels, in democratic and socially inclusive directions (see also Canfora 2006, Chapter 13). It is this process—obviously uneven and incomplete, but capable nonetheless both of affecting the character of the state apparatus and of commanding a certain loyalty—which market-orientated policies put into reverse.

Educational struggles are, in this way, overdetermined by the terms of a wider conflict. They are seen as reactions to a process, both of disenfranchisement (van der Pijl 2006), through which key prerogatives of national parliaments have been displaced onto European structures, and of social dispossession and regression, in which historic commitments to equality are diluted, and goods once held in common are privatised, in a move typical of the accumulation strategy of neoliberalism (Harvey 2005). Thus, when educational workers mobilise against current policies, their protests often resonate with popular opinion, and their cause can become a symbol of the defence of a particular social model against the reform project advanced by transnational elites, and by a national political class that has accepted the global policy orthodoxy, but is not inclined to debate it. What might appear to be sectoral issues can, in this context, ignite wider conflagrations.

Such conflicts are triggered not only by issues of cutbacks or privatisation, but also by attempts to remake education at classroom level. As we have seen, for the EU, the world of learning is located at too great a distance from the "values of entrepreneurship and the world of the economy" (de Meeulemeester and Rochat 2001: 8). Establishing a new curriculum based on "problem-solving abilities, general cultivation and innovation abilities" (ibid.) entails uprooting the disciplinary traditions around which school and university knowledge has been organised, and with which parties of the left had strongly identified (Anderson 2009b). The imperatives of the EU here clash with the value systems of students, and the politics of knowledge becomes a new arena of conflict. The modularisation of Higher Education curricula, for instance, uncontroversial in Britain, is seen in other parts of Europe as something strongly to be resisted—opposition to the "Bologna Process," which promoted a credit-based modular system, and a three-year undergraduate degree, has been integral to militant campaigns against university reform in Spain, France, and Greece. For its critics, modularisation strips knowledge of its complexity, reducing it to a series of bite-sized entities to be consumed by a student body taught to pursue certification rather than learning, acculturated to accept the measurement, in reductive form, of knowledge. Thus, while for the EU the linking of education to economic imperatives is central to its modernisation, for many students, such a connexion involves a process of degradation.

As in the case of popular mobilisation in support of educational institutions, which remain, in many respects, inegalitarian, there is something of the imaginary in this defence of traditions that have historically been linked to elitism and educational stratification, and are now presented as bastions of critical humanism. It is only in the context of precarity that the protests can be fully understood, in both their material dimensions and their historicist allegiances. Students argue that it is the mass university that will be most affected by modularisation and the demands of "work": the *grandes écoles* and the "Serie A" universities, which students think the Italian state wishes to create, will be relatively immune: knowledge, therefore, will be stratified: the value of the degree is related not necessarily to quality of knowledge but to the position of the university in the hierarchy of the educational market" (Do and Roggero 2009). For similar reasons, school students have been wary of reforms that seem to weaken disciplinary tradition—the opposition of French lycéen(e)s to changes in the baccalauréat, expressed in the student strikes of 2005 and 2008, illustrate such fears.

France

Van der Pijl's analysis provides two insights into current patterns of mobilisation. The first is that they are driven by political as well as by economic factors: the deteriorating position of youth—and of workers more generally—in the labour market has an obvious impact on levels of protest; but so, too, does a population's notion of the meaning of its education system in relation to what are seen as key elements of national identity. The second is that the forms taken by such movements need to be understood in terms of the location—historical, as well as contemporary—of a particular national state within a world system. As Theda Skocpol argued, "international relations" intersect with "pre-existing class and political structures to promote and shape divergent as well as similar changes in various countries" (1979: 19). Van der Pijl's formulation gives this insight a dialectical twist: "the ability of different societies to submit to capitalist discipline varies, and the very pressure to do so tends paradoxically to reactivate the specific heritage of each separate society in new combinations" (2006:31).

It is from the vantage point provided by such insights that the following sections trace recent episodes of policy contestation in France and Italy, and go on to compare them with developments in England. In France since 2003, there has been a succession of mobilisations against government-driven change, involving, at their centre, both teachers and young people—school students, university students, and the unemployed.

The largest of these was the spring 2006 campaign against the *Contrat Première Embauche* (CPE).[2] The trigger for the movement was the legislative response of the de Villepin government to youth uprisings in the suburbs of major cities in late 2005, whose fires— almost literally—illuminated a racialised condition of near-permanent social exclusion. The government interpreted the unrest as evidence that France required, in both its labour market and its education system, a dose of modernisation. Its response included an educational dimension, labelled "equal opportunity," which strengthened academic/vocational tracking at 14, and an element of employment law that aimed to increase the chances of employment by flexibilising the youth labour market—that is, by making it easier for companies to take on and lay off young workers.

Proposed in January, the CPE had within two months given rise to an immense opposition. Tuesday 7th March 2006 saw demonstrations in 160 towns and cities, involving a million people, most of them Higher Education students and school students. From the 7th onwards, most French universities were occupied. By the 18th March, a movement of students and workers had been created, with a million and a half people on the streets; and in the demonstrations of Tuesday 4th April, this number doubled again. In Paris, 750,000 took to the streets, and 250, 000 in Marseilles; there was a mass strike by workers in the public sector. As protests took more dramatic forms, with roads blocked and railway stations occupied, the government gave in and on 10th April announced the withdrawal of the law.

The movement against the CPE showed that the extension of neoliberalism to the public sector, and to particular sectors of the labour market, remained a controversial and uncertain project, and

that opposition to such change retained an impressive social resonance, built around a sense of solidarity that was an end as well as
a means. The sociologist Bertrand Geay had noted the significance
of the organisations created by an earlier wave of protest, in 2003:
the strike-generated *assemblées générales* (general assemblies) of
schoolworkers and citizens were lived by their participants as a kind
of "retour à l'essentiel"—in which the founding principles of public education were reactivated, and knowledge and the conditions of
its diffusion became matters for public appropriation (Geay 2003).
Something similar happened in 2006. The frequent mass mobilisations became "weekly rendez-vous" where "the employed, the unemployed, parents and grand-parents" joined with students from schools
and universities. One basis for such mobilisation, contra accounts
which suggested their definitive weakening (Rayou and van Zanten
2005), was the continuing resonance of "old" commitments—to
equality, to democracy, and to professional self-definition, which provided a perspective from which to understand and react to present
miseries.

These traditions of social republicanism have been accompanied
by, if not completely linked to, newer interests: the precarity of youth
is at the heart of the French social crisis, and the movement against
the CPE demonstrated this in the strongest of ways. But the movement's course and outcome also suggested something of the uncertainties of opposition, at several levels. The first problem, here, was
constituted by internal divisions that related not just to differences
in political opinion but to gulfs in social experience. Sociologists
have written about the parallel lives of "deux jeunesses"—the youth
of the *cités* (estates, social housing) and the "scholarised youth" of
the lycées and the universities. Mauger (2006) emphasises that these
categories, while both internally heterogenous, and partially over-
lapping, reflect a real divergence of experience and prospects. The
social segregation of life on the estates is a world away from that of
many lycéen(e)s, and the risk of long periods of unemployment much
higher, and these differences were reflected in the protest movement.
But by underlining the insecurity of those who might have thought
that their qualifications would keep them from the life of precarity
that lay ahead of those with fewer educational resources, the anti-
CPE movement brought together sections of the population which
had previously lived segregated lives, in both social and spatial terms.
It created, at least temporarily, an "improbable" alliance of social categories (Mauger 2006)—an alliance whose tensions were, nonetheless, considerable.

Movements for change in the postwar period saw themselves as modernising forces, and gave modernisation what was, in broad terms, an egalitarian content. The past was seen in terms of obscurantism, classroom authoritarianism, and privilege. For those in the twenty-first century who continue to work in this tradition, the terms of the counterposition have changed. The "past" signifies a period of partial democratisation and social reform, a resource to be defended. Yet, for many of those marginalised youth who have hurled their energies into protest, the attachment of social movements to an imagined "good time," when structural reforms brought about improvements in the condition of the masses, is itself part of the problem. In the words of one participant:

> We (the students) are struggling against the system because to us it seems unequal; they (the youth of the *banlieues*) are fighting because the system excludes them *a priori*...And they also consider us to be part of the system (which is true), and therefore they direct their hatred towards everybody, including us. For them, even the rebellious part of the system still belongs within it....For me the violence (of some of the banlieue youth) is not part of our action, but it poses the problem of how to renew the dialogue with these people, so that their struggle lends weight to ours.[3]

The second problem relates to the movement's political scope and continuity. The concessions that ended the mobilisation were the least the government could have offered, and amounted to much less than what many protestors wanted. A national assembly of students in Dijon called for the cancellation of the government's entire recent legislation on "equal opportunities," for an amnesty for those arrested during the riots in the *banlieues*, and changes in new laws on immigration (Visco 2006). Teachers, students, and parents traced a direct line between government intentions for the labour market and its school policy, which aimed to strengthen tracking; in the words of one lycéen, "we're mobilising not only against the new employment law, but against the new legislation on 'equal opportunities'"; and in those of a Sorbonne student, "the withdrawal of the CPE is an important demand, but it is not the principal grievance of those who have launched this movement."[4] A major difficulty in securing these demands, which addressed the whole range of educational, labour market, and civil liberties issues facing youth, was one of representation. The movement was a vast and turbulent social force, but relied for its negotiating capacity on organisations—the main trade union federations that had more limited aims. Linked to this was a problem of political expression and continuity: for all its momentary impact, the movement was not easily translated onto the political plane; the 2007 Presidential elections were contested, in the main, by candidates who favoured a neoliberal transformation of the social model, and were won by the most right-wing of these figures, Nicolas Sarkozy. As one protestor commented, governments refuse ever to consider closed the question of the social model's future; after enormous efforts of mobilisation have achieved concessions, the French government would, after a brief pause, want to play "extra time" to achieve a result in its favour. This, essentially, is Sarkozy's project.

It is not, however, a project that has become consensual, and if the political problems of opposition have not been resolved, then nor have those of government. In van der Pijl's terms, the ability of French society to respond to calls for neoliberal discipline remains limited. Two years after the CPE protests, in the context of widening social protest against rising unemployment, the same combination of forces continued to mobilise against reform, with the memory of 2005/2006 shaping the actions of both protestors and politicians. In November 2008, teachers struck against a cluster of policies. Their protests—the third round of action that year— centred on job losses, but were linked also to a cluster of policies seen as devaluing the "professionalism" of teachers and discriminating against working-class students: the abolition of schooling for the under-threes and the network of specialised help for ESN pupils, a cut in the number of hours in baccalauréat classes in the lycées, phasing out university departments for teacher training, surveillance of what teachers wrote in the blogosphere, and constant administrative pressure. According to the FSU, some 200,000 people joined in the 20th November demonstrations. The Minister of Education, Xavier Darcos, dismissed the protests, claiming that they belonged to an old and disappearing tradition. More alarming for the government was the mobilisation of lycéen(e)s and the reemergence of protest in the *banlieues*—anxious headteachers reported that hooded youth from the estates were appearing outside their gates. Having earlier declared that "hesitation" formed no part of his vocabulary, Darcos announced that he was postponing for a year the lycée reform. His reasons, *Le Monde* inferred, had everything to do with the balance of forces between reform and its opponents, in which economic crisis and youth revolt threatened to reignite the fires of 2005/2006 and expose France to the Greek experience of youth revolt.

Italy

The leftist writer Rossana Rossanda has pointed out that the precarity that provided the focus for French protest had become institutionalised in Italy without significant opposition: it was the norm in all but the biggest organisations in the services sector, and was a fact of life in education and involved 2.5 million workers across the country. Unions and centre-left parties tended to confine themselves to denunciations of the phenomenon, while, in effect, they encouraged a process of *arrangiarsi*—of personal accommodation to circumstances perceived as unalterable (Rossanda 2006).

But, at least in relation to education, Rossanda is overstating the case. Precarity may be a fact of educational life, but it is also a source of persistent grievance, which feeds into a wider opposition to reform. The campaigns against the "Moratti laws," drawn up by the 2001–2006 Berlusconi government, mobilised hundreds of thousands of students and teachers. Launched by smaller "autonomous" unions such as Cobas-Scuola, the campaign was joined in 2004 by the larger education confederations. The movement saw Moratti's reforms as harbingers of privatisation and austerity, and of an institutional and a cultural transformation of the Italian school, by means of which national knowledge traditions would be replaced by competences, and lateral lines of communication between teachers involved in a common educational project would be redrawn to emphasise the vertical transmission of government initiatives. The demands of the action were couched in defensive terms. Citing the constitution of 1948, into which they read a guarantee of teacher autonomy and collegiality and a commitment to equal opportunity, the unions opposed measures of regionalised decentralisation—seen as a vehicle for uneven development and increased managerialism—and the shortening of the primary school day. Sections of the movement sought to go further and to organise around the defence of education a wider-reaching campaign. The occupations in which university students were involved in the autumn of 2005 attempted to express such an alternative, criticising the exclusionary policies of Moratti, and insisting on the introduction of a national law demanding the right to study and free access to knowledge (Yeaw, 2005).

With the return to office of Berlusconi in 2008, these contests were renewed with increased vigour. According to Anderson (2009a: 6), the scale of his victory tempted Berlusconi to pursue a "tougher socio-economic agenda," especially at those points in which achieving the desiderata of global policy orthodoxy could be linked to an attack on "opposition constituencies"—in particular the *ceti medi riflessivi*—civic-minded professionals and public employees whom some writers have identified as a core progressive force (Ginsborg 2002). Thus, while tackling tax evasion was not on the agenda, the reform of education certainly was. In the summer of 2008, the government announced legislation that affected both schools and universities; it combined cultural conservatism with economic neo-liberalism, and linked educational restructuring to financial cutbacks. At the school level, the reforms (the "Gelmini Laws") included:

- in primary schools, a single-class teacher ("maestro unico") to replace the current system of three teachers rotating between two classes;
- in lower and upper-secondary schools, the reintroduction of the "good conduct grade," with a low mark meaning that students have failed their end-of-year examinations;
- a grading system in primary and secondary schools, with students who do not achieve a pass grade made to repeat the year;
- in primary and lower-secondary schools, separate "inclusion classes" for those (foreign) students judged to have poor Italian.

In addition to these measures, the draft law presented to Parliament by the Berlusconian deputy Valentina Aprea in July 2008—and approvingly noted by the OECD—sought to bring about a more systematic and longer-term reform, involving school autonomy, the competitive recruitment of teachers, and the closer management of their work (OECD 2008: 106).

In Higher Education, the government planned large-scale cuts and a reduction in the recruitment of staff: one new lecturer for every five retirees. The law also "envisaged the possibility that universities (might) convert themselves into private foundations" (Muratore 2008).

The response that these measures called into being was diverse and passionate. By early October, students occupying the Università L'Orientale in Naples acclaimed a wave of student strikes and faculty occupations that extended from "Turin to Palermo," mobilising undergraduates, doctoral students, and researchers—a category whose precariousness could only be increased by the reductions in recruitment (Rete 2008). On 17th October, a strike called by the autonomous unions mobilised hundreds of thousands of protestors. By the end of October, there had been another national strike, across education sectors, this time called by the larger, recognised unions—Flc-Cgil, UiL, and Cisl-Scuola—and *La Repubblica* was reporting that the movement had the backing of 50 percent of the Italian population (Diamanti 2008). The day of 14th November saw demonstrations across Italy, with perhaps a million people mobilising in Rome; and there was a further national strike, called by the autonomous unions, on 12th December. As in France, educational protest was the precursor of wider action: in February 2009, the metalworking and public-sector unions called a one-day strike against the whole range of Berlusconi's social and labour policies.

As van der Pijl suggests, we need to distinguish between the different components of this uprising, to establish some sense of a diversity of motivation and objectives, and some sense, too, of points of convergence and unity. The most spectacular element of the protests was the movement calling itself *L'Onda*, the wave. Based in the universities, but involving also students from the *licei* and the *scuole medie*, as well as many from the precarious sectors, the wave surged through the centre of many Italian cities, blocking the streets and reclaiming public space—for instance, some of the bridges in Venice, from which protest had been banned. In its political articulation, the wave tended to reprise some of the classic themes of Italian autonomous politics: it was a sector of the movement that was "not political in the strict sense of the term, but rather a defence of [protestors'] own concrete needs and conditions" (Anon 2008a). It refused to be "represented and instrumentalised by anyone" (Anon 2008: 3), and presented itself as a:

> radical refusal of the imposition of an economic model (starting within the national education sector), of cultural forms (racism) and of repressive actions (police). The movement calls itself the "anomalous Wave", referring to the fact that it does not rely on traditional forms of representation, that it is transversal and not predictable. The Wave is more emotional than organizational, more improvised than structured. In relation to its anomalous nature, the recognition of "being precarious" as a common identity is central, as the different subjects that participate in the movement recognize themselves in this condition. (Anon 2008: 4)

The political logic of this section of the movement pointed towards "autoriform" and "autoformazione"—the self-organisation of all the precarious, and all knowledge workers, *outside* of the established structures—an exodus articulated in the slogans "free knowledge" and "free university," which imagined a university outside the state. These were objectives at odds with the emphases of the mainstream (centre-left) trade union movement, which wanted to rally support around what one of its leaders called the "defence of the public school system" against a government whose "only logic" was one of "cutting funds and jobs" (Muratore 2008). While many in the movement did not accept that the issues were as limited as this, the notion of "defending the public school" had considerable resonance. As in France, the principle of free access to all levels of an integrated education system was seen as an historic social conquest, embedded in the postwar constitution. It was recognised, of course, that the system was riddled with clientilism, inferior in size and attainment to that of other European countries, and weakened by years of neo-liberal management; but for reasons both symbolic and material, it was still worth defending, and to defend it was, for some, to vindicate the social movements of an earlier period.[5] That the university was organised on a class basis was beyond doubt, wrote Benedetto Vecchi, in *Il Manifesto*, but the movement of 1968 had introduced a factor that was a "living contradiction" of this principle: the concept of access to knowledge as a universal social right (Vecchi 2008). Likewise, the political scientist Nadia Urbinati could speak simultaneously both of the corruption of the Italian state, including the university, and of that same university as a collective good "built with the collective funding of the Italian people."[6] From this latter point of view, Berlusconi's project was plain—the "transformation of the social identity of the country," so that private values triumphed over public ones (Pullano 2008).[7]

It was this wider, historical view of the stakes of the conflict that animated many protestors—but the movement was not only built on backward glances. For many, the protests "had placed at the centre of the debate the great question of the *future*" (Anon 2008a). Here, two issues were linked. The first was that of the "governing class," seen as incompetent and amoral, and bent upon the pillaging of the public sector by means of privatisation (Mattei 2008). The second was generational: the people whose interests the political class had particularly damaged were the young, for whom the years ahead would be an ordeal of precarity: "they have wasted the past and now they are asking us to give up our future. They think that because they have passed a law, we will come to a stop. They don't understand that we are going forward, that we have nothing to lose"[8] (Maltese 2008). From this self-perception of youth, as a generation at risk, came the slogan that served to unify the early states of the movement: "non pagheremo noi la vostra crisi"—we won't pay for your crisis.

It would be a mistake, however, to think that the only responses to the Gelmini debacle were those of the wave and the unions. Van der Pijl's point that global pressures activate national responses *in new combinations* has an application that runs wider than an analysis of the components of resistance. It applies also to the dominant policy, and the terms in which it is debated. For some, the reforms were an Italian instance of a global trend (Vecchi 2008); the form it took was nationally specific, but not exceptional. If the situation in the universities was "feudal" then this was "the peculiarly Italian interpretation" of the tendency for the university to turn itself into a commercial entity so as to compete in the "education and knowledge market" (Do and Roggero 2009). A different position, well represented amongst journalists and academic commentators, was that the crisis offered an opportunity for the kinds of reform that might make Italy a "normal" country, like all the others of the West. In this sense, the protests were interpreted as a kind of lens turned less upon the crisis of neoliberalism than upon the structural defects, especially at a higher level, of Italy's education system; and the protest movement was potentially the vehicle for modernising change, a movement of "reformism from below," a project for another kind of university (Maltese 2008). Singled out, here, was the need to break down the power of the professoriat, the "barons." The Italian university, according to Rossi, has been deformed by the workings of a "historically hierarchical" mode of functioning, "which empowers primarily full professors in recruitment procedures and in all university administrative matters while keeping the other parts of the teaching and research staff in a rigidly subaltern condition in terms of career autonomy and decision-making power" (Rossi 2006: 278–9). Out of this baronial power grows a web of clientilism.

It is difficult to overestimate the disgust and despair with which the protest movement regarded this aspect of the university system, which presented not just a sectoral problem but a window to the totality of Italian life. For Vecchi, the *baroni* were "a caste like many others in Italy," for Urbinati, a reminder that "we're amongst the most corrupt states in the world" (Vecchi 2008, Pullano 2008), while other critiques denounced Italy even more comprehensively, as a "land where nothing changes; where all attempts at change are blocked...with no space for imagination, creativity, innovation" (Veltri 2008). The art historian Salvatore Settis drew from his experiences of global academia to compare the Italian university—"we are outside Europe, we have been third-worldised"—and those of the Anglo-Saxon world, where competition for jobs was regulated by transparent procedures, and research funding was merit based (Miliani 2008). Maltese, like-wise, praised the course taken by university reform in France, which had concluded with a decision that "funds should be allocated on a rigorously meritocratic basis" (Maltese 2008). Urbinati, too, made comparisons overseas: England had "developed a means of evaluat-ing research that distributes resources on the basis of merit" (Pullano 2008).

The passion of this critique is striking, but so are its ambivalences: its terms supply popular understanding, but they are also the chosen ideological instruments of elites. "Baronialism" is a target both of the movement's anger and of the polemic of neoliberalism, which has long been eager to counterpose the evils of "producer control" to the disciplines of the market (*Economist* 2008). That the university is "rigged" is the bitter contention of unemployed researchers, but also of those who want to remodel it on business lines (Vecchi 2008, Perotti 2008). The particular figure in which reform is linked to a market-inflected notion of fairness is "merit." As Rosalind Innes has pointed out, "merit" provides the framework in which a great num-ber of reforms, whose effects are likely to contribute to processes of marketisation, can be legitimised: fair and open competition for uni-versity places, effective evaluation of the work of schools, and a more equitable system of research funding, again based on competition and audit (Innes 2008). For reformers of this disposition, the Gelmini laws were not a serious project. The cuts they proposed were not linked to any discernible educational purpose. They failed to address the biggest problem, which was the incapacity of the state to control key processes of governance: it could plan neither the distribution of teachers across the national territory nor the creation of academic posts, and it had no means of preventing the "cancellation" of its poli-cies by local and regional authorities who refused to put them into practice on the ground. From this point of view, modernisation had failed again (Bordignon and Checchi 2008)—but the problems thus highlighted stemmed less from a neoliberal world order, not from an historic, national predicament. In the attempt to realise in local circumstances what it took to be a global orthodoxy, the Italian state had only revealed its familiar weaknesses.

By December 2008, the movement had arrived at a pause—perhaps a halt—with many ambiguities intact. Berlusconi, explained *La Repubblica*, had no intention of "setting the piazza alight," espe-cially when it seemed that educational protests were linking up with wider concerns about the economic crisis. Change to the teaching hours in the *liceo* and the technical college would be delayed; other changes would be diluted—only if parents wanted it would the *maestro unico* idea be introduced in a school. More money would be found for the university (*La Repubblica* 2008, Martini 2008). These concessions, of course, left the stakes of the conflict unclaimed. The movement had demonstrated its capacity to temporarily block reform, to mobilise in great numbers, and to create a counterculture of opposition that seethed with critique, discontent, and the desire for alternatives. For autonomists, this was the main point: whether or not the Gelmini reforms succeeded, the vital thing remained the struggle to develop and embody a counterpower, able to construct a different kind of knowledge, a different kind of university. Strengthened by *L'Onda,* that struggle would go on. For others, it was problems of the movement that were most pressing. As in France, it had scorched the snake, not killed it; the blows it could inflict were not decisive. It lacked a credible political alternative to the government, and, more widely, to a governing class that was in agreement with the need for reform, albeit divided on the means of attaining it: "no cuts and let's talk" was the offer that Berlusconi received from Walter Veltroni, leader of the centre-left PD (*La Repubblica* 2008a). The offer suggested that the Gelmini reforms, suitably repackaged, might, in some ways, live on.

Some Reflections

In "The Education Debate" (2008), Stephen Ball summarises "the outcome of the debate [amongst researchers] about globalization" and education policy. Following Lingard and Rizvi (2000), he concludes that globalisation "does not impinge on all nation states and at all times in exactly the same way." Some states are "more able and more likely to deflect or mediate global policy trends, while others...are required to accept and respond to external reform imperatives" (2008: 29). National policies need, therefore, to be understood as "the product of a nexus of influences and interdependencies," the intermingling of global and local logics.

It is certainly possible to understand in these terms the recent, halting course of policy making in France and Italy. But the experiences reviewed in this chapter suggest that we can usefully reformulate Ball's argument, so as to arrive at a different object of analysis. To focus on "policy" as the object of study seems overly to privilege the actions and projects of government and of organisations that contribute supportively to its programmes—and, thus, a priori to decentre other social actors. (In most current work, even where "resistance and countermovements" are acknowledged, there is, in practice, a tendency to note their influence rather than fully to explore their terms, strategies, and effects.)

Yet, the impact of globalisation, of which Lingard and Rizvi write, reaches the educational space of France and Italy as much through the responses of social movements as through the policies of government. And for this reason, if we wish fully to understand this space, we need to work with a broader concept than that of "policy" or "policy making." A better alternative might be "educational contestation," a concept that would enable analysts to focus on a range of social actors and to explore fully the intellectual and political resources with which they work. The concept might also lead to a stronger understanding of the *politics* of policy making, that is, of the ways in which key decisions, strategies, projects, and achievements bear the marks of contestation, and express an orientation—perhaps accommodating, perhaps uncompromising—towards other actors and projects. In this context, much work in the Marxist tradition of writing about the state remains illuminating, especially, it seems to me, that of theorists such as Gramsci and Poulantzas, who have attempted to understand processes through which states, always in unstable conditions of class contestation, and of changes in the relations of production, attempt to adapt both their forms and their strategies.

Gramsci's contributions here are well known (Gramsci 1934/1971: 59, 105). Analysing the dynamics of Italian state formation under fascism, he wrote of passive revolution, or "revolution-restoration," as a process in which the ruling social groups, through state intervention rather than popular mobilisation, sought to promote sweeping institutional change and national renewal; and in which reform was linked not to the extension of democracy, but to the preservation of existing power structures in the face of a radical challenge, which had been defeated but not eradicated (Jones 2004). As Johnson and Steinberg put it, with a particularly insightful stress on what state power does in such periods, "passive revolution is the demobilization or disorganization of forms of popular agency" (2004: 12).

Poulantzas's work, notably *State, Power, Socialism* (1978), addresses a different conjuncture, one in which the state was attempting both to contain the social energies unleashed in the 1960s and 1970s, and to manage the transition from the long boom of the period 1945–1975 to the restructured capitalism that followed the slump of the mid-1970s. This complex experience sensitised Poulantzas to the relationship between state forms and social conflicts. If state power was always provisional, fragile, and limited, this was because both class and nonclass struggles, to some extent, escaped state control, with the state's effectiveness "always being shaped by capacities and forces that lie beyond it" (Jessop 2008: 126). The extent of this shaping varied between different sectors of the state, some being more heavily "screened" from the influence of the "popular masses" than others.

The stress on the "masses" is a distinctive feature of Poulantzas's state theory, but it is counterbalanced by other emphases. Currents of influence do not move only in one direction, from the masses to the state; they also flow the other way. Poulantzas shares Gramsci's fascination with the innovative capacities of the state, its ability to devise new forms in which hegemony can be secured, populations controlled, and antagonists disorganised. He was one of the first to theorise, prophetically, the emergence of an "authoritarian statism" that involved intensified control over "every sphere of socio-economic life, combined with the radical decline of the institutions of political democracy" (1978: 204). This insight, into the reciprocal relationship between a resurgent state power and a crisis of popular politics, provided a basis for concrete analyses. Thus, for instance, Poulantzas was able to identify the significance, in terms of class contestation, of developments that were later described as the "network state"—policy communities that "cement dominant interests outside the state apparatus with forces inside, at the expense of popular forces" (Jessop 2008: 132).

England

The work of Gramsci and Poulantzas illuminates the recent course of education policy in England, enabling us to understand the "modernisation" programme of Blair's government as an instance of passive revolution, in which the relationship between social forces has been reconfigured in new institutional arrangements. This was not solely a Blairite achievement. Much of the underlabouring for New Labour's programme of the New Labour government had already been completed by Conservative administrations. Thatcher's victories in the 1980s had weakened labour movement traditions of equal opportunity, reduced the influence of elected local authorities, and defeated teachers, both in trade union terms and in relation to their ability to shape classroom processes. The level of contestation that Blair faced in 1997 was therefore unusually low. New Labour was able to populate an "emptied" space of education with new institutions and social actors—a shift that I have elsewhere called "re-agenting"(Jones 2004). In re-agenting, the development of policy through an explicitly political process of encounter between different social interests becomes less important than its elaboration through networks of agencies, local and national (for instance, OfSTED, the Teaching Development Agency, the Specialist Schools Trust), whose origins and points of reference lie in the priorities of national government (Jones 2004: 43–4). The complex of networks, organisations, and auditing regimes established under Blair has constituted a new state apparatus of education, concerned not only with the administration of an established system, but with an ongoing and unending effort to create, motivate, resource, support, and guide the forces that can make policy happen. It has enabled the organisation of the world of education around the project of raising levels of performance, measured in terms of examination success. The other side of this process is, as Johnson and Steinberg noted, the demobilisation of oppositional agency. New Labour has worked consistently to ensure that the conditions in which contestation might be revived cannot be re-created: its much-noted micromanagement of targets and procedures leaves no space for any agency that might seek to modify or contradict its programme.

The limits of these achievements need delineating. They have not resolved historic weaknesses of English education. Levels of educational inequality remain high, and levels of educational performance uneven (Brook 2008). Recession will bring further problems. In the period of financial boom, New Labour did not face the discontents of a volatile, precarious sector of unemployed youth. That may change, especially as the relatively high levels of state spending that the boom enabled will not be maintained. Nevertheless, politically and institutionally, Blair's (and Thatcher's) legacy marks out England as distinct from France and Italy.

In *States and Social Revolutions* Skocpol takes issue with a Marxism that she finds indifferent to national circumstance. Its assumption has been, she writes, that:

> every nation, perhaps stimulated by the example or influence of earlier-developing countries, would sooner or later undergo a more or less compressed version of the same fundamental kind of transformation apparently experienced by England. As Marx put it in 1867, "the country that is more developed industrially only shows to the less developed the image of its own future."

Skocpol's particular concern is that this formulation lacks any attention to national state forms, which have a crucial role in advancing or holding back social transformations. One might apply the argument to the field of education. Neo-liberalism has provided a model for change, but this has not, of course, been implemented uniformly. In France and in Italy, a new educational state, based on a qualitatively different relationship of social forces, has not yet been created. One might say that, in contrast to England, where reform essentially began with a Conservative victory in a decisive war of manoeuvre, successive Italian and French governments have fought a long war of position against their opponents—an attritional process stretching from the 1990s to the present day. This process has not yet reached a decisive outcome. New norms reflecting global policy orthodoxy have not credibly been established. Nor have these governments been able to weaken opposition to the point at which the state can yet enforce new policies, institutions, and social relations. Valentina Aprea, introducing her proposed reforms of the school, praised the shift accomplished by Blair from a producer to a commissioner state, and sought to emulate that change in Italy (De Anna 2009). Likewise, in France: in the matter of education, "on veut faire tout comme vous," Sarkozy told Gordon Brown, on his presidential visit to London in 2008.[9]

Such ambitions may not be realised; the conditions that gave rise to the English version of education reform—a decisive political victory of the right, a brief window of economic opportunity—are unlikely to be repeated. Indeed, the attempt to achieve an "English" system, in conditions where opposition remains mobilised, may give rise to new forms of educational contestation. England, therefore, may represent not so much the terminus of a route along which all European societies must travel, as a specific and limited phenomenon. "We want to do everything like you"—but that isn't possible—not now, and, perhaps, not ever.

Notes

1. Thanks to Richard Hatcher for his comments on an earlier draft of this chapter.
2. The following paragraphs are an expanded and updated version of the account of the anti-CPE campaign given in Jones et al (2008).
3. "Cécile" interviewed in Visco (2006).
4. "André" lycéen from Pau, interviewed in "Paroles des lycéens" *L'Ecole Emancipée* 90 (7) April 2006, p. 13; 'Cécile',in Visco (2006).
5. In Anderson's summary: "Spending on education, falling in the budget since 1990, accounts for a mere 4.6% of GDP (Denmark 8.4%). Only half of the population has any kind of post-compulsory schooling, nearly 20 points below the European average. No more than a fifth of 20-year-olds enter higher education, and three-fifths of those drop out" (Anderson 2009: 8).

6. Urbinati, interviewed in Pullano (2008).
7. Domenico Pantaleo, General Secretary of the Flc-Cgil, quoted in Muratore (2008).
8. "A student from Bologna" demonstrating in the Piazza Navona, Rome. Quoted in Maltese (2008).
9. Sarkozy's words, quoted by Michel Monsauret, French cultural attaché in Lukes (2008).

References

Alexiadou, N. (2005) 'Europeanisation and Education Policy' in D. Coulby, C. Jones and E. Zambeta *World Yearbook of Education 2005: Globalisation and Nationalism in Education,* London, Kogan Page.
Anderson, P. (1964) 'Origins of the Present Crisis', *New Left Review* 23, January/February, 26–54.
——— (2009a) 'An Entire Order Converted into What It Was Intended to End', *London Review of Books* 31 (4) 3–8.
——— (2009b) 'An Invertebrate Left,' *London Review of Books,* 31: 5, 12–18.
Anon. (2008) 'The Anomalous Wave So Far: The Education Rebellion in Italy October–November 2008' E-Pamphlet Circulated by Eddo-Factory www.edu-factory.org, accessed November 29.
——— (2008a) L'onda che ci travolge' April online 15th November http://www.aprileonline.info/, accessed 19th January 2009.
Antunes, F. (2006) 'Globalisation and Europification of Education Policies: Routes, Processes and Metamorphoses', *European Educational Research Journal,* 5: 1, 38–56.
Ball, S. J. (1990) Politics *and Policy-making in Education: Explorations in Policy Sociology,* London: Routledge.
——— (2008) *The Education Debate,* Bristol: Policy Press.
Ball, S. J. and Youdell, D. (2008) *Hidden Privatisation in Public Education* Brussels: Education International.
Bendit, R. (2006) 'Youth Sociology and Comparative Analysis in the European Union Member States', *Revista de Sociologia,* 79, 49–76.
Bordignon, M. and Checchi, D. (2008) 'La Scuola degli Tagli senza un Progetto', in *La Voce* http://www.lavoce.info/articoli/pagina1000656.html, accessed 27th February 2009.
Brook, A-M. (2008) *Raising Education Achievement and Breaking the Cycle of Inequality in the United Kingdom,* Economics Department Working Papers No. 633, Paris: OECD.
Canfora, L. (2006) translated S. Jones *Democracy in Europe: A History of an Ideology,* Oxford: Blackwell.
Dale, R. (2005) 'Globalisation, Knowledge Economy and Comparative Education', *Comparative Education,* 41: 2, 117–149.
De Anna, F. (2009) Lo Stato secondo Valentina. *Scuola Oggi,* 5th March, accessed at *http://www.flcgil.it/content/view/full/63701.*

Demeeulemeester, J-L and Rochat, D. (2001) *The European Policy Regarding Education and Training: A Critical Assessment* Skope Research Paper No.21 Autumn 2001, Centre on Skills, Knowledge and Organisational Performance Oxford and Warwick Universities.

Diamanti, I. (2008) *Genitori, professori, studenti. Ma non solo: un italiano su due condivide la protesta anti-Gelmini, La Repubblica* 27th October.

Dion, D-P. (2006) The Lisbon Process: A European Odyssey, *European Journal of Education,* 40: 3, 295–313.

Do, P. and Roggero, G. (2009) *We Won't Pay for Your Crisis: Italian Struggles against Education Reform, in Mute: Culture and Politics after the Net* (submitted 22nd January, accessed 26th January) www.metamute.org.

Drevon, J.-M. (2006) Y en a ras le bol de ces guignols! *Ecole Emancipée,* 90: 7, *avril, pp.* 4–5.

Economist. (2008) *Higher Education in Italy: A Case for Change,* 13th November.

European Commission. (2001) *The Concrete Future Objectives of Education Systems,* Brussels: European Commission http://europa.eu/scadplus/leg/en/cha/c11049.htm.

——— (2008) *Key Figures on Europe* 2007/8, Luxemburg: European Commission.

European Parliament. (2000) Lisbon European Council 23–24 March 2000, Presidency Conclusions (2000), Lisbon http://www.europarl.europa.eu/summits/lis1_en.htm.

Gamble, A. (1981) *Britain in Decline; Economic Policy, Political Strategy and the British State,* Basingstoke: Macmillan.

Geay, B. (2003) Un processus de réattachement à l'institution, *Le Monde de l'Education,* No. 317, September, p. 12.

Ginsborg, P. (2002) *Italy and Its Discontents: 1980–2000.* Harmondsworth: Penguin.

Gowan, P. (2005) A Salutary Shock for bien-pensant Europe, *Radical Philosophy,*133, September/October.

Gramsci, A. (1934/1971) *Selections from the Prison Notebooks,* edited and translated Q. Hoare and G. Nowell-Smith, London: Lawrence and Wishart.

Harvey, D. (2005) *The New Imperialism,* Oxford: Oxford University Press.

Hingel, A. (2001) *Education Policies and European Governance: Contribution to the Interservice Groups on European Governance,* Brussels: European Commission, http://ec.europa.eu/governance/areas/group12/contribution_education_en.pdf, accessed 27th February 2009.

Innes, R. (2008) Merit, Ideology and the Ongoing Disarticulation of Public Education in Italy, www.educationineurope.org.uk, accessed 19th January 2009.

Jessop, B. (2008) *State Power: A Strategic-Relational Approach,* Cambridge: Polity.

Johnson, R. (1989) Thatcherism and English Education: Breaking the Mould or Confirming the Pattern? *History of Education,* 18: 2, 91–121.

Johnson, R. and Steinberg, D. (2004) Distinctiveness and Difference within New Labour, in R. Johnson and D. Steinberg (eds) *Blairism and the War of Persuasion: Labour's Passive Revolution*, London: Lawrence and Wishart.

Jones, K. (2004) An Old Future, a New Past: Labour Remakes the English School, in R. Johnson and D. Steinberg (eds) *Blairism and the War of Persuasion: Labour's Passive Revolution*, London: Lawrence and Wishart.

Jones, K., Cunchillos, C., Hatcher, R., Hirtt, N., Innes, R., Johsua, S. and Klausenitzer, J. (2008) *Schooling in Western Europe: The New Order and Its Adversaries*, Basingstoke: Palgrave Macmillan.

Laval, C. (2004) *L'Europe libérale aux commandes de l'école: a propos du rapport Thélot et du projet de « loi d'orientation pour l'avenir de l'école*, Website of the Institut du Recherches de la FSU http://institut.fsu.fr/chantiers/education/laval_thelot.htm, accessed 27th February 2009.

Laval, C. Weber, L. et al (2002) *Le nouvel ordre éducatif mondial*, Paris: Nouveaux Regards/Syllepse Paris.

Lebaron, F. (2006) *Avenir probable et construction du possible. Un mouvement porteur d'avenir, Nouveaux Regards, Revue de l'Institut de recherches ee la FSU No. 34*, juillet-septembre pp. 4–7.

Lingard, B. and Rizvi, F. (2000) Globalisation and the Fear of Homogenization in Education, in S. J. Ball, *Sociology of Education: Major Themes, Volume IV: Politics and Policies*, London: Routledge-Falmer.

Lukes, J. (2008) Effervescent Impressions of French and English Education, *Education and Politics* (Socialist Education Association Newsletter), 94, August, 10–14.

Maltese, C. (2008) L'Onda diventa grande: 'Né tagli né baroni', *La Repubblica*, 15th November.

Martini, E. (2008) Scuola, la retromarcia, *Il Manifesto*, 12th December.

Mattei, U. (2008) Del Saccheggio nel Segno della Continuità, *Il Manifesto*, 1st November.

Mauger, G. (2006) De l'émeute de novembre aux manifestations anti-CPE: une alliance improbable? *Nouveaux Regards, Revue de l'Institut de recherches de la FSU No. 34* juillet-septembre 8–13.

Miliani, S. (2008) Intervista a Salvatore Settis, *L'Unità*, 16th October.

Muratore, L. (2008) Trade Unions Organise Strike against Government School Reforms, *European Industrial Relations Observatory* www.eurofound.europa.eu/eiro/2008/10/articles/it0810059i.htm, accessed 19th January 2009.

OECD. (2008) *Education at a Glance 2008: OECD Indicators*, Paris: OECD.

Perotti, R. (2008) *L'Universita Truccata*, Turin: Einaudi.

Poulantzas, N. (1978) *State, Power, Socialism*, London: Verso.

Pullano, T. (2008) Il modello USA? Non in Italia, *Il Manifesto*, 31st October.

Rayou, P. and van Zanten, A. (2005) *Enquête sur les nouveaux enseignants*, Paris, Bayard.

La Repubblica. (2008) *Università, rinviata la riforma,* 2nd November.
——— (2008a) Veltroni a governo: no ai tagli et dialoghiamo, 10th November.
Rete (Network) of Doctoral Students and Researchers. (2008) *Communiqué: la réforme Tremonti-Gelmini doit être bloquée,* Naples: Università di Napoli L'Orientale, October 2008, circulated on the mail list of the European Social Forum, accessed 19th October.
Rossanda, R. (2006) Pourquoi la révolte française n'a pas gagné en Italie, *Le Monde Diplomatique,* May, pp. 4–5.
Rossi, U. (2006) The Struggles of Precarious Researchers and Demands for Social Change in (post-) Berlusconian Italy, *ACME—An International E-journal for Critical Geographies,* 4: 2, 277–286.
Skocpol, T. (1979) *States and Social Revolutions: A Comparative Analysis of France, Russia and China* Cambridge: Cambridge University Press.
Thompson, E. P. (1965/1978) The Peculiarities of the English in *The Poverty of Theory and Other Essays,* London: Merlin, pp. 35–91.
Van der Pijl, K. (2006) A Lockean *Europe, New Left Review,* 37 Jan/Feb 9: 38.
Vecchi, B. (2008) L'Università Dismessa—al libero mercato dei centri di eccellenza, *Il Manifesto* 16th October.
Veltri, G. (2008) Il Paese di Gomma, *L'Unità* 16th October.
Visco, G. (2006) *Il movimento anti-CPE tra autonomia studentesca e sindacati,* Paper to the Italian Political Studies Association Bologna.
Yeaw, K. (2005) Scuola per tutti, libero sapere per tutti: The Student Struggle in Italy, *Counterpunch,* 14th October 2005, www.counterpunch.org.

Afterword

New Labour's Legacy...the Con-Dems and Zombie Blairism

Anthony Green

New Labour finally left office at the 2010 General Election making way for the first coalition government in Britain since the Second World War, led by a pairing of elite former public school-boys David Cameron (Eton College), the Tory party leader and Prime Minister, and Nick Clegg (Westminster School) the Liberal Democrat as Deputy Prime Minister, the first UK two-party coalition government since the 1930s. This government quickly acquired the ambiguous popular label the Con-Dems. The primary objectives and political context for the new administration has been to continue the processes of shifting power to the private sector, thus displacing public service and economic provision and more immediately to move relatively swiftly to reduce the national budget deficit bequeathed by Gordon Brown's outgoing Labour government. New Labour under Blair and Brown (the latter first as Chancellor of the Exchequer and subsequently, Prime Minister from June 2007) had participated in fuelling the illusion of prosperity by stoking the financial bubble, encouraging debt as well as unregulated innovation and ever more complexity (derivatives) rather than distinctly supporting growth in sustainable "real" production. In their final period in power, Labour under Brown were then forced to deal with the emergent financial crisis in the UK by printing money through quantitative easing (QE), and stemming the threatened banking collapse through their re-financialisation and partial nationalisation of banks as confidence began to disperse setting off the most recent recession, probably the deepest and most critical for the social, political, and economic status quo since the 1930s in the United States, UK, and beyond.

The endemic structural instability and weaknesses of national and global capitalism are evident in the gross failure to manage risk as the hubris of finance capitalism's most recent boom gave way to disillusion and bust. The recession and attendant credit crunch show few clear signs of swiftly dissipating, indeed (at the time of writing in August, early September, 2010) continues threatening to re-double into long term stagnation, as is recognised by the US Treasury authorities, currently seriously contemplating a new round of quantitative easing (QE2) and public sector investment, though less so in the UK where Con-Dem economic policy is determinedly deflationary (headlined by proposed 40 percent cuts in government departmental budgets!). Thus, the UK policy is to be one of austere budgetary measures with deep reductions in public spending, shrinking the state while broadly maintaining levels and regressive distributional patterns of taxation, including raising Value Added Tax, and reducing Corporation Tax which together proportionately impact hardest on lower income groups and the least secure. All these are designed to free capital to support the private finance sectors and confidence in "the markets." The basic function of the UK capitalist state remains then to maintain the morale of the better off (the wealthiest top 10%) and the banks who cannot be allowed to stumble let alone fail. While the city of London remains the single largest source of tax revenue and foreign earnings structural reform is unlikely, despite setting up a Future of Banking Commission doing no more materially than demonstrating the appearance of concern, in order to save the blushes of the Liberal Democrat side of the coalition government.

Moreover, neither in the United States nor the UK, despite much discussion of increasing "regulation" of the finance sector, can it be assumed that neo-liberalism is dead and neo-Keynesian modes to be reinstated, let alone democratic and productive re-structuration for an equitable system of social and economic relations of production. Returning to neo-liberal TINA of business as usual once the worst is over underpins the broad approach to managing the crisis. In the meantime unemployment is rising and particularly bleak in the regions traditionally adversely affected (the north of England, plus Wales) and amongst young people, especially for newly qualified university graduates as well as those contemplating rising university tuition fees. These young people are increasingly looking like an emergent reserve army of overqualified human capital, many of whom may well be joining the ranks of *precarity* (Jones, this volume) and redundant labour power.

So far as Blair's contribution and legacy in all this is concerned, the current Con-Dems in many respects model themselves as New Labour more or less in disguise. Just as New Labour retained much of the framework of the previous Tory administration, the Con-Dems maintain much that was New Labour. Below the presentational surfaces (which are important in their own right, see below), both New Labour and the Con-Dems as a government are broadly neo-liberal in practical policy terms, pragmatic and social conviction free on social equity while ever mindful of social order and cohesion, centrally concerned to let the markets determine policy contexts. In reality policy operates to support elite, capitalist class interests and their movers and shakers in order to maintain the confidence of parliamentary political middle England. Thus, the Con-Dems policy profile is Blairite while maintaining a distinctly Thatcher "lite" undertow of elite paranoia and Tory class hatred, despite presenting a glossing smile and jaunty style of camaraderie and can-do, with assertions of commitments to equity and fairness. All these are familiar as Blair's style during the early phases of his premiership.

Blair's abiding influence is to have set the cosmetic political tone for the Con-Dems in much of its presentational and rhetorical forms. Reminiscent of, though if anything less plausible than early Blair, nevertheless blaring the equivalents of New Labour's theme of *inclusion* ("fairness" in the Con-Dems chosen vocabulary) and local initiative free of central control, not unlike New Labour and their projection of the need for community based enhanced social capital building, while blurring the realities of power and the political economy of its mechanisms and social effects of meagre "trickle down," at best. This is especially clear in positions currently taken by George Osborne, the new Chancellor of the Exchequer on the social ramifications of the incoming government's emergency budget. It drew sharp criticism from the Institute for Fiscal Studies of the government's claiming, again not unlike New Labour, to have a progressive bias and support for economic equity while in fact most likely to be hitting the poorest hardest and leaving the richest least affected (Browne and Levell, 2010). Plus, Michael Gove, the new Secretary of State for Education, is effectively reinforcing social differentiation while deploying the vocabulary of choice and diversity (originating in the Thatcher period) and expanding opportunities for social capitalisation by and for the better placed through entrenching the academies programme initiated by New Labour. With the Con-Dems the academies policy has acquired an even more distinctly "good schools" label and a comfortable association with promoting professional cooperation with

academies supporting neighbouring schools in difficulties, by forming "partnerships." This complements policy initiatives for drawing on
parental and community energy and involvement for "free schools."
The latter are to be parent, philanthropic and interest group run (often
strongly religious), much like academies, free from local authority control, free to set curricula, staff conditions of service and pupil entrance
procedures as well as freeing teachers' hands in dealing with disruptive
students. These renewals, revamping and extensions of the academies
programme continue to reinforce the deconstruction of remaining ves-
tiges of systemic comprehensive educational aspirations while doing little to generate progressive social and educational dialogue and energy
Woods envisages as a possibility (this volume). Simultaneously, Gove,
in mature New Labour style, is maintaining target setting and league
tables of school performance, drawing powers to himself at the centre and further undermining democratic accountability by weakening
local education authority powers. These undemocratic political moves
are obfuscated under the rhetoric of Gove's claiming enthusiasm for
releasing social energy in diversity and choice citing, for instance, neoliberal implications of the contemporary Swedish model. The latter
has been admirably critiqued by Suzanne Wiborg, drawing attention
to the emergent socially regressive aspects of contemporary Swedish
education's market oriented shift (Wiborg, 2010).

Furthermore, Gove's claiming credit for endorsing a "pupil premium" policy that will be progressive for educational equity, in effect
continues endorsement of the previous weakly redistributive Labour
policy themes. However, the policy will not see funds being targeted
to specific needy pupils in schools or to developing services such as
additional after school and summer schools for pupils who will benefit from more educational provision. These funds are more likely to
be absorbed into the hard pressed regular school budgets and educational label "academy" is reinforced as the badge of aspiration for
schools determined not to be left behind in the jostling for status
and distinction and a fillip for selective education. The overall framework remains that oversubscribed and therefore "good" schools will
continue to be choosing parents/pupils because the necessary surplus of places to allow a "market" to operate does not exist. More
fundamentally, nor will this combat structural features of social capitalism with the favourably placed social, cultural and economically
capitalised parents continuing to be more likely to secure the school
places of "choices." Many "sink" schools will continue to flounder.
All these mechanisms fuel social differentiation and class consolidation in the social sphere articulating structurally with that in the

economic sphere. In turn, such processes are promoted through the vacuous talk of the new government's aspirations for a Big Society underpinning the ideological work of disguising its further exposing public education to commercial, corporate, and sectional interests. The prospects are that economic and financial policy, along with education policy are most likely in interaction with each other, to prove to be effectively elitist, divisive, regressively shifting the burden of risk socially downwards (Marris, 1996). The effect is further consolidating class divisions, reinforcing, probably strengthening the material effects of the thirteen years of New Labour governments, which had presided over a period of continued social polarisation so far as education and opening of society are concerned (Blanden and Machin, 2007).

New Labour's superficial appeal to the "social" and "active communities" (for instance in the broad theme of social inclusion and more specifically in Education Action Zones policy) has thus morphed into Cameron's Big Society, whose ideological effect is obfuscation of social polarisation and class consolidation by appearing to democratise through devolving to the local, voluntary, active and can do. The Big Society format is most likely to turn out to be a rather un-clever public relations exercise rather than a convincing democratic political theme, though sitting nicely with many Liberal Democrat junior partners' consciences. Though thinly disguised as ideological devices, cynical and vacuous as they are, these policies, like all such phenomena do provide sites for conscientisation, materials for challenging the hegemonic appeals, not least by taking them seriously and demanding in progressive social and democratic terms that they be realised on all the levels of economic and social empowerment (as Woods suggests this volume). Immanent critique will demonstrate the impossibilities of doing so without a more radical approach to social change. More broadly, the struggle is, of course, longstanding and can be put in the context of ongoing assault on socialised production in the lifetime of many older working and non-working retired people, especially so since there is some historical awareness (and much more to be developed) of the social and economic meanings of changes since the 1970s, constituting re-alignment of forces in political economy and capital restructuring to claw back the gains of productive labour since the 1940s (see Farnsworth, this volume). This period of class struggle has seen capitalisation by enclosure and appropriation (Harvey, 2003; and Bellamy, this volume) in the face of falling profit rates. Now, in its present crisis of maintaining expansive economic vigour, capital is ever more blatantly assisted by the state, the elite powers shifting once more from capitalisation by stealth to direct means of privatising public wealth.

Finally, the most high profile and immediate aspect of Blair's legacy is in spectacularly contributing to the iconography of excess, hypocrisy, and self promotional capitalisation for his and his family's personal enrichment, presented as philanthropy, good fortune, piety and the reward for talent and contributions to public service. The fanfare and hype for the publication of Blair's political memoir (Blair, 2010) conjures up an image which is a far cry from the sentiments he expressed at the onset of his Parliamentary career reported at the opening of this volume. We now see explicit commodifying and capitalising for personal gain on the social problematics of equity/fairness with attendant deepening cynicism and acquiescence. In turn, the New Labour resource of liberal conscience dissipates into the realism of possessive individualism prioritising property, hanging onto what you've got, especially as it looks like possibly contracting, or at least, growing somewhat more slowly in the short-term future. The piety of donating the profits of this book to the most prominent military charity (The Royal British Legion) to support injured service personnel, contributes to a culture of cynicism and eagerness to capitalise commercially on insider knowledge, experience and fame.

Blairism constitutes the current UK parliamentary political system's spectre and default, the zombie living dead that now haunts and re-energises both the political and the educational trajectories of the Con-Dems in office and sections of the Labour Party now in turmoil, currently attempting to adopt a new image, political trajectory, and leadership. Blair has set the bar in each context for deliberately or inadvertently consolidating the power of the dominant elites and their corporate allies while massaging the "radical centre," as Anthony Giddens had characterised New Labour as a political formation while academically formulating the Third Way (Giddens: 1998). In this political comfort zone, the capitalist mode of production, draws in, beguiles, and makes hypocrites of all but the most resolute of resisters and conscientious opponents who struggle in and against its enveloping relations of production and corrosive modes of sociality. Blair's career and legacy, as well as what is now in prospect for the socially least well placed, are instructive in this respect, and liberal guilt alone for those who have taken their opportunities within, rather than working to build collectively against the dominant structures, will provide little critical purchase on the complex structural issues involved in the confident grip of emergent deepening of neo-liberalism and global financial capitalism.

In the meantime, the toxic ecological context of humanising nature moves on a pace through climate. The prospects for urgent coordinated action on a global scale to address these problems has shifted further to the margins of realistic possibility in the face of defending national and global corporate unsustainable capitalist interests. The issues in Marxist class struggle analysis terms, the *What is to be done?* question, concerns how to dialogue about, strategise, and democratically mobilise to resist and build a movement to transform these structures. How to turn the increasingly less subtle but effective class aggression from above into pedagogic action for class formation and mobilisation from below? After all, the cuts in the public sector undermine the growing ranks of those already insecure hitting the less well off hardest. The origins of the crises clearly stem from the policies, practices and inactions of the most powerful, the financial sector and the dominant corporate elites, who can well afford the meagre austerity measures current policies require of them, much more so than the poorer sections of society. Whatever happens, the crisis of capitalism currently in flow will be educative in the fullest, broadest, and deepest terms, the context for creation of critical understanding for immanent and ideological critique informing action in each context. There continue to be myriad educative opportunities for socially radical work. While there are few signs of systemic and extensive progressive national, regional and coordinated global mobilisation, the "middle" continues to hold in the UK. Opportunities clearly abound to realise without irony something of Tony Blair's original statement of ideals, aims and objectives for viable socialist and sustainable democratic social order and Marxism continues to have the task of articulating a politics capable of offering an anticapitalist alternative to the disastrous prospects embedded in these long-term processes of ecological and social degradation.

References

Blair, T. (2010) *A Journey,* London: Random House.

Blanden, J. and Machin, S. (2007) *Recent Changes in Intergenerational Mobility in Britain,* Sutton Trust Report, available at: http://www.suttontrust.com/reports/mainreport.pdf/.

Browne, J. and Levell, P. (2010) The Distributional Effects of Tax and Benefit Reforms to Be Introduced Between June 2010 and April 2014: A Revised Assessment, IFS Briefing Note BN108, available at: http://www.ifs.org.uk/bns/bn108.pdf/.

Giddens, A. (1998) *The Third Way: The Renewal of Social Democracy,* Cambridge: Polity Press.

Harvey, D. (2003) *The New Imperialism,* Oxford: Oxford University Press.

Marris, P. (1996) *Politics of Uncertainty,* London: Routledge.

Wiborg, S. (2010) *The Swedish Free Schools. Do they work?* Llakes Research Report.

Contributors

PATRICK AINLEY. Ainley is Professor of Training and Education at the University of Greenwich School of Education and Training, and has been writing and researching on schools, colleges, and universities since the UK Youth Training Schemes of the 1980s. His latest book with Martin Allen is *Lost Generation? New Strategies for Youth and Education*, Continuum: March 2010.

MARTIN ALLEN. Allen is a writer researcher and a part-time teacher at a comprehensive school in West London. He is an active member of the National Union of Teachers.

MOLLY BELLAMY. Bellamy works at the Institute of Work Based Learning at Middlesex University as the Director of Postgraduate and Undergraduate Programmes. She is interested in "Cultural Political Economy" (Norman Fairclough.) Her Doctoral Thesis (Institute of Education) is about the role of academic literacies as a vehicle for structural change in the knowledge-based economy. Recent publications include Bellamy, M. and Hawkes J. (2002). *An Inter-textual Approach to Work Based Learning, in Knowledge, Learning and Work* Hollifield D. (Ed), University of Wales Press.

KEVIN FARNSWORTH (UNIVERSITY OF SHEFFIELD). Farnsworth's interests centre primarily on business power and the various ways business is able to influence the shape of social and public policy—for instance, at the level of intergovernmental organisations and within different forms of capitalist states to frame the power, views, interests, and needs of business and "rival" interests. Recent publications include *Corporate Power and Social Policy in a Global Economy*: Bristol: Policy Press (2004).

DENIS GLEESON (UNIVERSITY OF WARWICK). Gleeson is a sociologist and Professor of Education at the University of Warwick. He has published widely on the relationship between the state, education policy, and employment. He is particularly interested in the class-based nature of vocational education and training and its impact on the distribution of power, pedagogy, and practice in society—particularly among learners, professionals, and leaders. His recent work focuses on governance and accountability in the remaking of professional cultures in a postmarket environment. Recent publications include (with Knights, D.) "Challenging Dualism: Professionalism in 'Troubled Times'" *Sociology* 40 (2), 277–295 (2006).

ANTHONY GREEN. Green lectures in Sociology of Education at the Institute of Education, University of London, co-convenes Marxism and Education Renewing Dialogues (MERD), and is Series Editor for Marxism and Education.

KEN JONES. Jones is Professor of Education at Goldsmiths, University of London. His research focuses on two areas: the first is policy and its contestation ("Schooling in Western Europe: The New Order and its Adversaries" 2008); the second is the (re)emergence and development of "creativity" as a theme in educational and cultural policy. Recent work includes "Culture and Creative Learning" (Arts Council England, 2009).

ALPESH MAISURIA. Maisuria is a Senior Lecturer, is a Fellow of the Higher Education Academy, and is affiliated to the Institute of Education University of London, UK, and Uppsala University, Sweden. He publishes on aspects of social justice and education, particularly the intersection of social class with "race." His most recent work has examined the efficacy of Critical Race Theory and the concept of racialisation in a UK, U.S., and Swedish context. He co-convenes the Marxism and Education Renewing Dialogues (MERD) seminar series.

PHILIP A. WOODS is the Chair in Educational Leadership and Policy at University of Gloucestershire.

TERRY WRIGLEY (UNIVERSITY OF EDINBURGH). Wrigley's research interests include school development (especially schools in challenging circumstances), democratic schools, school self-evaluation methodologies. and active learning for active citizenship. Recent publications include *Another School is Possible* London: Bookmarks/ Trentham (2006).

Name Index

Subject Index